"Our world is filled with storms. Turbulent problems assail the lives of many. In the midst of these storms, you need an anchor that can give you stability. Jesus is that anchor. He empowers and emboldens all who trust in Him. In *Anchored in Jesus*, veteran pastor Johnny Hunt shows us how to find firm footing in any instable environment. I highly recommend this book."

Steve Gaines, PhD
Pastor, Bellevue Baptist Church, Memphis, TN

"My dear friend Johnny Hunt has written a book on Jesus from his heart, not his head. In these days filled with storm and strife, waves and wind, we all need an anchor that will hold. This book will not only anchor you to Jesus but the *real* Jesus—not the Jesus of Hollywood but heaven; not the cultural Jesus but the biblical Jesus; not the Jesus many want Him to be but the Jesus we all need Him to be. Whether you are in a storm, going into a storm, or coming out of a storm, you need to read this book!"

James Merritt
Pastor, Cross Pointe Church, Duluth, GA
Author, *52 Weeks with Jesus*

"Johnny Hunt is a walking illustration of the transforming life of Jesus Christ. The very title of this book, *Anchored in Jesus*, personifies his life story and the living legacy of his testimony. To this day, through his writing, speaking, and leading, Johnny motivates thousands upon thousands of people to win with Jesus daily. Get this book, read it, and share another copy with a friend!"

Dr. Ronnie Floyd
President/CEO, Southern Baptist Convention Executive Committee

"It is fitting that Johnny Hunt would write a book entitled *Anchored in Jesus* because that is exactly where he has been through the decades I have known and loved him. These words are not just some type of theoretical treatise but have been practically beaten out on the anvil of his personal experience."

O.S. Hawkins
President/CEO
GuideStone Financial Resources

"I am always blessed and encouraged by the teaching ministry of my dear friend Johnny Hunt. This book does that once again. *Anchored in Jesus* teaches us just how all-sufficient and wonderful our Savior is. This book will stir your heart and inspire a greater passion for King Jesus."

Danny Akin
President, Southeastern Baptist Theological Seminary
Wake Forest, NC

"Pastor Johnny Hunt has always been about Jesus! I am thankful for his latest book, *Anchored in Jesus*, which reminds us that Christ is enough and He still is the same yesterday, today and tomorrow. May this book ignite our hearts like the disciples who walked the road with Jesus, saying, "Did not our heart burn within us while He talked with us on the road...?" (Luke 24:32). You can hear His voice as you read this book: 'You are anchored in *Me*!'"

Jeff Crook
Pastor, Christ Place Church, Flowery Branch, GA

"In this topsy-turvy world, everyone needs an anchor as the winds and waves of life howl about us. My friend and beloved brother in Christ shares why an anchor is critical, but even more critical, why that anchor must be Jesus. Johnny eloquently describes how 'the peace that surpasses understanding' can only be found moored to the anchor secured by none other than the Creator of those winds and waves."

Sonny Perdue
United States Secretary of Agriculture

"Pastor Johnny has mentored thousands of pastors, including me, in what it means to serve Jesus as a faithful shepherd. You won't find a man in our generation more committed to God's Word, God's people, and God's Great Commission."

J.D. Greear, PhD
Pastor, The Summit Church, Raleigh-Durham, NC
President, Southern Baptist Convention

"While I have never served on active duty in the military, I have pastored in a Navy town for 29 years. The Navy anchor symbolizes no drifting while in wind or waves. Johnny Hunt will help you stand firm against the drifting current of our culture in his book *Anchored in Jesus*."

Ted Traylor
Senior Pastor, Olive Baptist Church, Pensacola, FL

ANCHORED IN JESUS

Johnny Hunt

HARVEST HOUSE PUBLISHERS
EUGENE, OREGON

Cover design by BEMA Creative

Original Cover Art by Chris Moore / Bema Creative

Anchored in Jesus
Copyright © 2019 by Johnny Hunt
Published by Harvest House Publishers
Eugene, Oregon 97408
www.harvesthousepublishers.com

ISBN 978-0-7369-7835-4 (pbk)
ISBN 978-0-7369-7836-1 (eBook)

Library of Congress Cataloging-in-Publication Data is on file at the Library of Congress, Washington, DC.

Printed in the United States of America
19 20 21 22 23 24 25 26 27 / BP-GL / 10 9 8 7 6 5 4 3 2 1

CONTENTS

THE POWER OF LIVING DAILY IN JESUS

The careers of both architects and mariners rise and fall on anchors. An architect uses the term to refer to the strong foundation in bedrock required for any large structure. A mariner uses it to refer to a physical anchor that keeps a ship in place so that it doesn't drift into harm's way. I believe we can learn something crucial from both of them.

If we hope to live successfully as followers of Jesus, we need a solid foundation that anchors us to bedrock. If we hope to finish well, we need a strong anchor to keep us from drifting into trouble.

For the Christian, that anchor is Jesus Himself.

Getting anchored in Jesus keeps us from getting "tossed to and fro and carried about with every wind of doctrine, by the trickery of men, in the cunning craftiness of deceitful plotting." Getting anchored in Jesus enables us to speak the truth in love so that we "may grow up in all things into Him who is the head—Christ" (Ephesians 4:14-15).

Getting anchored in Jesus will enable you and me to produce healthy fruit that yields a life of positive influence and godly character. Don't let anyone deceive you: what happens in private inevitably becomes public. All of us are constantly engaged in an internal battle that sooner or later goes external: "For the flesh lusts against the Spirit, and the Spirit against the flesh; and these are contrary to one another, so that you do not do the things that you wish" (Galatians 5:17).

Do you know of any man who feels frustrated that he's not doing the things that he longs to do? I'm sure you do; maybe you're even that man. How, then, can you become the man that Jesus calls you to be? Is it even possible, given this fierce battle between flesh and Spirit? I know it's possible—but only as you and I yield more and more to the staggering power of Christ.

Paul describes our situation like this: "Walk in the Spirit, and you shall not fulfill the lust of the flesh" (Galatians 5:16). In other words, as we invite God's Holy Spirit to fill us—as we make it a daily habit to walk in Jesus and to be controlled by Him—our lives start changing in amazing ways.

Sounds simple enough, doesn't it? But we all know it's no easy struggle! If we want to "walk in the Spirit," it will mean the battle of our lives. More than one godly person has told me, "The Christian life is not just difficult, it's impossible." Only a consistent experience of "Christ in us" will enable us to enjoy the hope of glory.

My whole world changed as a young man when I discovered that Jesus made available to me everything I need to access the divine power it takes to live in Him. "Encouragement fuels enthusiasm," it's said, and I feel thrilled to know that the same Lord who has called me to a life of obedience has also furnished me with the grace and power I need to live out that calling. All of this makes me wildly enthusiastic about the future.

And it can do the same for you.

In my early years after coming to faith in Jesus, I started learning dozens of key principles about my newfound relationship with God. Before Christ, my life consisted mostly of gambling, drinking, cursing, fighting, and the like. There wasn't much else. Charles H. Spurgeon, a famous English preacher from the 1800s, once said that when God saved him, he lost 80 percent of his vocabulary. For me, the percentage was probably more like 90 percent. At the beginning, that meant my testimony for Christ focused primarily on what I had to quit.

In time, however, godly men challenged me to think less about what I had to give up and more about what I had received. They asked me what had I started doing *right*, through Christ's power? I can't begin to explain what a difference that simple change in perspective has made.

To this day, it amazes me that when Christ came to live in me, the old started dying and the new sprang to life. I can personally testify that Jesus quite literally changes our desires. We start *wanting* to do what pleases Him. It's as though new sap starts coursing through our veins. God prunes off the old leaves and makes room for fresh growth.

Today my life is all about what I am becoming in Christ—the internal godliness, the external righteousness, the fruit of His Spirit—none of which I can produce on my own. It is no longer mostly about what I give up, but vastly more about what I have gained and about what I pursue.

Oh, how I want to become like Jesus! That's my goal, the endgame. Beyond question, the ultimate challenge of a life anchored in Jesus is becoming more like Christ.

Years ago, Eddie Carswell of Newsong wrote a chorus that I think captures it wonderfully:

> Jesus, be Jesus in me,
> No longer me, but thee,
> Resurrection power, fill me this hour,
> Jesus, be Jesus in me.[1]

Do you want that? I know I long to become more like Jesus, to increasingly reflect Christ in my day-to-day life. What other life is worth pursuing for any man who claims to follow Jesus? In fact, it's the *only* life worth seeking.

May God help you and me to pursue Jesus, to allow Him to transform us, and to fight the good fight in His power. And may His Spirit remind us daily that *everything* begins when we make sure we're anchored in Jesus.

1

ANCHORING IN THE REAL JESUS

At the end of the day, nothing is more important than knowing Jesus and being known by Him.

That's especially important today, because we live in an era of multiplying counterfeits. Counterfeit money, counterfeit designer brands, counterfeit identities, even counterfeit extra virgin olive oil (no, really). It's estimated these counterfeits cost the world economy hundreds of billions of dollars each year. None of these counterfeits, however, comes even close to the havoc created by counterfeit faith.

Never in history have we seen as many counterfeit versions of Jesus as we see today. If a church preaches a biblical truth that offends some people, they simply leave and look for a place that makes them feel more comfortable. Often that involves a counterfeit Jesus.

Does a holy, sin-hating Jesus offend you? Then seek a Jesus who never does anything to offend anyone. Is a fire-and-brimstone Jesus more your style? Lucky for you, it's not hard to find a group that fixates on divine judgment. Want a Jesus who promises you wealth and comfort? You can find that kind of counterfeit Christ nearly anywhere.

Of course, in order to embrace these counterfeits, we have to lay aside our Bibles. We have to exchange the real Jesus of Scripture for a counterfeit who will allow us to adopt a skewed belief to match our ungodly behavior.

Never before have I seen such a smorgasbord of "Jesus options" as I see today. And never in history have we more desperately needed to anchor ourselves in the real Jesus and His unchanging character as described in His eternal Word. Jesus is *the* greatest revelation of God, while the Bible is the second greatest revelation of God (next only to Jesus Himself). If you want to get anchored in Jesus, make sure you steer clear of some common counterfeits.

The "No Offense" Jesus

Many churches today invite you to come to their worship services, where you'll never have to worry about feeling offended or being made to feel bad. They champion the counterfeit Jesus who will never tell you anything you don't want to hear. These churches encourage you to define the truth as you see it and to apply that truth in a way that never requires you to change anything you do.

These groups have forgotten the word *repentance*—yet the real Jesus said, "Unless you repent you will all likewise perish" (Luke 13:3). Preachers of this counterfeit Christ must remain vigilant, because to maintain the lie they must skip or jump over countless obvious truths in Scripture. The mantra for these organizations when challenged on their teaching is, "Well, that's your interpretation."

Keep in mind, though, that the Bible was written in the language of the common man so that *everyone* could understand God's simple truths. Author Randy Alcorn often says, "A moment after we die we will know exactly how we should have lived." A proper perspective of death has a way of giving great clarity to how a man should live!

Clear, convicting biblical messages have often pointed out some sin in my own life. At these times, I begin to feel a sense of shame, guilt, and fear. Yet I'm so grateful that as I humble myself and repent of my sin, I receive God's unconditional forgiveness, mercy, and compassion. While many today look for a Jesus who will never make them feel guilty, I know that if I lack the capacity to sense any guilt, I will never experience divine conviction that leads me to seek God's grace. In His mercy, God loves me as I am; but He loves me too much to leave me as I am. God-prompted guilt can cause me to say, "Lord, please forgive me. I am wrong." I then move toward the person I sinned against and seek his or her forgiveness.

God used Holy Spirit-induced guilt to inspire the psalmist to write:

> Search me, O God, and know my heart;
> Try me, and know my anxieties;
> And see if there is any wicked way in me,
> And lead me in the way everlasting.
> (Psalm 139:23-24)

Thank God that the Holy Spirit convicts me of my guilt and offers me the grace of God. In the very first Sunday night service I ever attended, the Spirit convicted me of my sin, I was converted to Jesus, and became a follower of Christ.

The "Forget the Old Testament" Jesus

The morning after I came to faith, my wife purchased for me my first Bible. From day one, I fell in love with God's Word. It was all new to me, so revealing and refreshing. I soon read, in what many consider the greatest book of doctrine and theology in the entire Bible, something Paul wrote about the power and authority of Scripture:

> Now we know that whatever the law says, it says to those
> who are under the law, that every mouth may be stopped,
> and all the world may become guilty before God. There-
> fore by the deeds of the law no flesh will be justified in His
> sight, for by the law is the knowledge of sin.
>
> But now the righteousness of God apart from the law
> is revealed, being witnessed by the Law and the Proph-
> ets, even the righteousness of God, through faith in Jesus
> Christ, to all and on all who believe. For there is no differ-
> ence; for all have sinned and fall short of the glory of God
> (Romans 3:19-23).

By studying passages like these as a newborn Christian, I began
to grow in and through the Word. I am so grateful to God for the
Bible. I remember writing in the flyleaf of my first Bible, "The Bible
will keep you from sin and sin will keep you from the Bible." The
B-I-B-L-E, yes, that's the book for me!

I learned that Jesus is concealed in the Old Testament and
revealed in the New Testament. So many Old Testament passages,
beginning with Genesis 3, speak of God's provision for my sin
through the coming of the Messiah, Jesus Christ our Lord. I began
to memorize many great Old Testament passages, such as Psalm 22
and Isaiah 53. In texts like these, our faithful God reminded His
ancient people that from *their* race Messiah would come to redeem
anyone who placed his or her faith in Him. Every Christmas, my
spiritual walk received deep encouragement as we read Old Testament prophecies, given hundreds of years before the birth of Jesus,
that found their fulfillment in Christ. The New Testament then
reached back to the Old Testament to name the individuals through
whom Messiah had come.

Who does not feel blessed to hear the great, ancient stories of
God's victories as He fought for His people? Paul even tells us that

the Rock that followed the Israelites in the wilderness was Christ
Himself (1 Corinthians 10:4). Bottom line, I thank God for my
Bible, both the Old and the New Testaments.

Yet here we are in the twenty-first century, with increasing numbers of contemporary "churches" attacking the Old Testament, sow-
ing doubt and confusion among God's people. Never forget that
the Jesus we worship as our Savior and Messiah repeatedly gave His
full, unequivocal approval to *all* of the Old Testament. How blessed
we are to know that Jesus frequently pulled from the Old Testament, even using the story of Jonah to picture His own resurrection.
Scripture—which in Christ's day included only the Old Testament,
since the New Testament had yet to be written—"cannot be broken,"
Jesus insisted (John 10:35). He made it clear that what the Old Testament declares, God declares (see Matthew 22:30-32). The Bible
knows *nothing* of a Jesus who rejected the Old Testament. Instead,
He often says things like this:

> "Do not think that I came to destroy the Law or the Proph-
> ets. I did not come to destroy but to fulfill. For assuredly, I
> say to you, till heaven and earth pass away, one jot or one
> tittle will by no means pass from the law till all is fulfilled"
> (Matthew 5:17-18).

So then, if Jesus publicly declared such a wholehearted commitment to the entire Bible, how can we do otherwise? We can't, if we
want to be fully anchored in Him.

Does this mean I understand everything God did in the Old Testament? Hardly. Nevertheless, I have no problem believing that the
God of the Old Testament is the God of the New Testament. Jesus
referred to His Father as the God of Abraham, Isaac, and Jacob, and
the apostles did the same, even after Pentecost (Luke 20:37; Acts

3:13)—and of course, the God of Abraham, Isaac, and Jacob is the God of the Old Testament.

While we may see more examples of judgment in the Old Testament, over and over again that same God of judgment displays incredible acts of mercy and forgiveness. We see our heavenly Father extending His power against His own people in severe acts of discipline, and then as they repent, He uses that same hand of power to judge the pagan nations that abused them.

The "Spirit Trumps the Word" Jesus

I have come to see that God the Holy Spirit and the sacred Scriptures never disagree. They speak with one voice, the voice of Almighty God.

Have you ever heard someone say that the Holy Spirit told them to do something totally contrary to Scripture? I have—and rest assured, the Holy Spirit said no such thing. He never speaks in opposition to the very Word He inspired. Why would He? When we believe the Lord is leading us, and we think we have heard His small, still voice, the guidance we believe we have received can always be confirmed with Scripture.

To be controlled by the Spirit is to walk according to the Word. To be filled with the Spirit is to obey God's Word. While the Word of God without the Spirit of God is powerless, the Spirit of God without the Word of God is directionless. To be filled with the Spirit and to be filled with the Word is to find yourself anchored in Jesus.

The "Doctrine Doesn't Matter" Jesus

In our day, many professing Christians have very little commitment to Bible doctrine. Such a lack of commitment causes many of them to drift into the dangerous waters of confusion and counterfeit teaching. Consider that the Bible teaches the *doctrine* that Jesus is "full of grace and truth" (John 1:14). Now, is He full of both grace and truth all the time, or is He full of grace sometimes and full of truth at other times?

The Bible makes it clear that Jesus is *always* full of *both* grace and truth. That is why the Scripture teaches us to speak "the truth in love" (Ephesians 4:15). We must never separate these two. God's imperative to us always includes both.

Remember when Jesus predicted Peter's denial, even when the big fisherman brashly declared his undying commitment? In that prophecy, Jesus spoke the truth in grace. He spoke grace in forewarning Peter of his denial, and truth in His insistence that everything would turn out just as He said (even though His words stung).

But let's make the question even more dramatic. Was Jesus *still* full of grace when He told His best friend, "Get behind Me, Satan!" (Matthew 16:23)? Doesn't that sound awfully harsh? Yes, it does—but being gracious does not necessarily mean being nice. The Bible reminds us, "Faithful are the wounds of a friend, but the kisses of an enemy are deceitful" (Proverbs 27:6). It also says, "Rebuke a wise man, and he will love you" (Proverbs 9:8b).

When Scripture teaches us that Jesus is "full of grace," it means that He will *always* do for us whatever we need to bring us closer to His likeness. Whether we need encouragement, rebuke, hope, or conviction, the grace of Jesus will supply it. Jesus is an absolutely faithful friend. For that reason:

- Jesus loves us, but He refuses to flatter us.
- Jesus loves us like we are, but He loves us too much to leave us as we are.
- Jesus tells us the truth, even when it hurts, in order to help us.

Everyone needs a faithful friend—and you and I can have no

closer friend than Jesus. *That's* grace. He was (and is) always full of grace, but that doesn't mean He always seems nice while He's blessing us with that grace (see Romans 11:22). Getting anchored in Jesus means getting anchored in sound doctrine (see 1 Timothy 1:8-11; 6:3-5; Titus 1:7-9; 2:1-5).

The "I Don't Care How You Act" Jesus

As we become anchored in Jesus, the Lord is faithful to convict us of wrong and to expose our sin in order to get His grace and truth into us. As this truth gets assimilated into our lives, it becomes part of our DNA. And when that begins to happen, our behavior starts to resemble our beliefs.

As you journey along with me in *Anchored in Jesus*, we will see how each chapter deals with subjects that came straight from the heart and mouth of Jesus. Many times, the Holy Spirit later inspired Christ's followers to further develop the truths they heard that had so transformed them. The real Jesus, in whom we need to get anchored, issued both warnings and encouragements so we would know how to cooperate with His Spirit to see our lives transformed.

When I first became a Christian, I spent most of my early years thinking about the changes that had come into my life and all the vile things that I no longer did. As I began to grow, however, my attention shifted. I began to focus more on the good, new things Jesus had brought into my life.

I discovered that His grace gave me the power to obey and even the power to change my desires. I now *wanted* to do those things that please Him. Soon I began displaying the fruit of a new life in Christ. Jesus helps us to become godly.

No wonder Paul encouraged new converts to follow him *as he followed Christ.* He told them, "Imitate me, just as I also imitate Christ" (1 Corinthians 11:1). A Christian anchored in Jesus starts to become increasingly like Christ. Paul named Christlikeness as his most prized goal (see Philippians 3). To become godly is to have the fruit of Christ's life habitually displayed in your life. Oh, how I desire to be a godly man!

Let's Get Oriented

Allow me to give you a quick overview of what you'll find in *Anchored in Jesus.* I find that it helps me to grasp an idea or set of concepts when I can picture what's coming, and I hope what follows will help you to get oriented in our journey together.

In Part 1, we will focus on Jesus Himself. Enough of the counterfeits! What does the real Jesus look like, and how does He instruct us to live in this world for our benefit and His Father's glory? We'll spend some time appreciating four beautiful portraits of our Lord as painted in the New Testament: Messiah, Lord, Savior, and High Priest. To wrap up the section, we will hear from Jesus Himself on how to "abide" in Him—an indispensable key for any man who wants to grow in Christ and live out his purpose in life.

In Part 2, our focus will turn to developing the kind of "fruit" that Jesus wants all of His followers to produce. That process begins *internally* and then shifts to the *external* qualities and actions through which others can see the glory of God in us. The fruit of the Spirit in our lives makes this possible—and only Jesus can produce that fruit.

As we yield our lives to Christ's control, He manifests His life in us and through us. It's important to remember that spiritual fruit does not grow for our benefit, but for those to whom we minister. It's *Christ's* life, reproduced in *us*, for *His* glory. Others see our good works (our fruit) and glorify our Father in heaven (see Matthew 5:16).

As we live in a day of counterfeits, it should not surprise us that plastic fruit seems to be everywhere. The counterfeit is easy to produce and in some ways resembles real spiritual fruit. Genuine spiritual fruit, however, lasts even in difficult times, while counterfeit fruit dries up and blows away. The fruit of the Spirit takes time and discipline to grow and make our life greener. Jesus ministers to others through the fruit He develops in us.

I would guess that three of the most used words in the Christian faith are *love*, *joy*, and *peace*. When the *love* of John 3:16 becomes a reality to us, we experience the *joy* of John 15—a joy that remains. The Bible tells us we can enjoy "peace with God" through faith in Jesus Christ, leading to the "peace of God" (see Romans 5:1-5). *Peace* is an inner serenity that controls us, regardless of our outward circumstances. God demonstrated His *love* toward us while we were yet sinners, sending His Son to earth to provide a way for us to enter His presence. At the cross, the war ended and God's *peace* came. As a result of Jesus' work on Calvary, and through faith, we can experience God's *joy* deep within. More hymns and songs have been written about these three words—*love*, *joy*, and *peace*—than any others found in Scripture.

Since these gifts are all anchored in Jesus, when we get anchored in Him, He gives us the ability to live differently with others. As His love increasingly takes root in us, related traits blossom in us, such as patience, kindness, goodness, faithfulness, gentleness, and self-control. Just as Christ showed patience with us, so we can now show patience with others. We, too, can pass over someone's mistreatment of us and show them kindness instead. In fact, when we get anchored in Jesus, we can actually do good deeds for them. The question *What would Jesus do?* takes on more significance as we seek to treat others as Jesus has treated us. We, too, can show mercy even when mercy is not extended to us. How is this possible? Jesus makes it happen.

I call the trait of "self-control" the Biggy, because I desperately need it, especially whenever the wheels come off. My temper, attitude, and desires all require self-control. Again, I cannot make myself the man Jesus calls me to be. Only as His fruit grows in me can I become who He desires me to be. The word *temperate* in 1 Corinthians 9:25 describes the key attribute that puts self-control on display: "And everyone who competes for the prize is temperate in all things. Now they do it to obtain a perishable crown, but we for an imperishable crown. Therefore I run thus: not with uncertainty. Thus I fight: not as one who beats the air. But I discipline my body and bring it into subjection, lest, when I have preached to others, I myself should become disqualified" (1 Corinthians 9:25-27). By getting a handle on self-control, we prepare ourselves to become powerhouse men of God.

In the third and final section of *Anchored in Jesus*, I want to encourage all of us to fight the good fight of faith. Pursue with energy and diligence whatever path God has called you to follow! The Lord wants you and me to play to win, and so to close this book, I attempt to spur us on to the high calling Jesus has in mind for each of us.

Position over Location

To the Christian, location is not nearly as important as position. The apostle Paul often would introduce his writings with words like this: "To all the saints in Christ Jesus who are in Philippi." Note "in Christ Jesus" (position) and "in Philippi" (location). The *real* comes when we are in Christ Jesus. Nothing trumps being in Jesus and anchored in Him.

I have always loved the book of James, written by the Lord's halfbrother. Many scholars refer to James as the "practical theologian" of the New Testament. He challenges us to be "doers of the word" (James 1:22) and insists that each believing man must be a doer who acts (James 1:25). I have tried hard to follow James's counsel in my own life and ministry, but I know I still often find it easier to focus on what I do more than on who I am and to whom I belong.

When we anchor ourselves in the real Jesus of Scripture, however, the "doing" tends to follow a lot more naturally from the "being." When we get anchored in Jesus, our character becomes more consistent, changing us forever. As a result, Galatians 2:20 gets increasingly fleshed out in our lives:

> I have been crucified with Christ; it is no longer I who live, but Christ lives in me; and the life which I now live in the flesh I live by faith in the Son of God, who loved me and gave Himself for me.

The lives we live now, anchored in Jesus, grow out of the faithfulness of God. His attributes increasingly become our attributes. What an amazing thought! As a Christian man, don't you want that? I long for Paul's words to be true of me so that I will "walk worthy of the Lord, fully pleasing Him, being fruitful in every good work and increasing in the knowledge of God" (Colossians 1:10).

Anchoring ourselves in Jesus is the *only* way to make that happen. And the best approach I know of to firmly set that anchor in place is to secure it in the powerful, unchanging, sovereign character of the Lord Jesus Christ Himself. Let's begin the initial part of our journey, therefore, by lingering over the Bible's wonderful portrait of Jesus as the Messiah, the Son of God.

Part 1

JESUS, THE ONLY TRUE ANCHOR

2

A MESSIAH
WHO CHANGES
EVERYTHING

In late 2017, Netflix announced it would create a ten-episode television series called *Messiah*. The streaming service said the show would chronicle "the modern world's reaction to a man who first appears in the Middle East, creating a groundswell of followers around him and claiming he is the Messiah. Is he sent from God or is he a dangerous fraud bent on dismantling the world's geopolitical order?"[2]

What comes to mind when you hear the word *Messiah*? The word itself means "anointed one" and originally referred to someone anointed with oil and set apart for some special task. Over time, it came to refer to a unique servant of God, sent by the Lord Himself to set the world aright. The Old Testament has scores of prophecies about this Messiah, whom Christians believe appeared on earth in the first century in the person of Jesus Christ (the word *Christ* is the Greek form of the Hebrew title *Messiah*).

The producers of the series *Messiah* asked, "What if someone showed up in 2018 amid strange occurrences and was thought to be the Messiah? What would society do? How would the media cover him? Would millions simply quit work? Could governments collapse? It's a series that could change everything."[3]

The series hadn't yet aired by the time I wrote this book, so I don't know if it could really "change everything." But I do know that the real Messiah did indeed change everything—and He's still changing everything today.

The Glory of the Heavenly Messiah

Jesus was no ordinary Messiah. In fact, Scripture claims that Jesus came to earth from heaven at the command of His heavenly Father. For that reason, the New Testament often identifies Jesus as "the [Messiah], the Son of God" (e.g., Matthew 16:16; 26:63; Mark 1:1; John 11:27). John even says he wrote his Gospel "so that you may believe that Jesus is the Christ [Messiah], the Son of God, and that by believing you may have life in his name" (John 20:31 ESV). For good reason, therefore, the apostle Paul could call Jesus "the Christ, who is God over all, blessed forever" (Romans 9:5 ESV).

One of Jesus' favorite titles for Himself was "the Son of Man," and He left little doubt about His place of origin: "No one has ascended to heaven but He who came down from heaven, that is, the Son of Man." A little later He declared, "He who comes from above is above all" (John 3:13,31). And in case anyone misunderstood, He would say even more explicitly, "I have come down from heaven, not to do My own will, but the will of Him who sent Me" (John 6:38). When some religious leaders grumbled about His claim, He declared, "As the living Father sent Me, and I live because of the Father, so he who feeds on Me will live because of Me. This is the bread which came down from heaven...He who eats this bread will live forever" (John 6:57-58).

While Jesus often used metaphorical language, He made this point crystal clear: Jesus is the Messiah, the "Mighty God" of Isaiah 9:6. I wonder if the apostle Paul had Isaiah's text in mind when he described Jesus as "being in the form of God" (Philippians 2:6). The word *being* stresses the essence of a person's nature, his continual state or condition. In fact, Jesus has *always* been God; at no time was Jesus *not* God. He is God today and at no moment in the future will He ever cease to be God. Jesus is eternally God.

See Jesus, See God

The apostle John tells us, "No one has seen God at any time. The only begotten Son, who is in the bosom of the Father, He has declared Him" (John 1:18). Jesus came in the flesh to explain, declare, and make known who God is. If you want to know what God is like, then look at Jesus. If you want to know what God says to humanity, then listen to Jesus. If you want to know how God represents Himself to the world, then observe the life of Christ.

One day, Jesus and a disciple named Philip had a short conversation about this very issue.

> Philip said to Him, "Lord, show us the Father, and it is sufficient for us."
>
> Jesus said to him, "Have I been with you so long, and yet you have not known Me, Philip? He who has seen Me has seen the Father; so how can you say, 'Show us the Father'? Do you not believe that I am in the Father, and the Father in Me? The words that I speak to you I do not speak on My own authority; but the Father who dwells in Me does the works" (John 14:8-10).

To know Jesus is to know God. No wonder that when Jesus spoke to the Pharisees, He could say, "Most assuredly, I say to you, before Abraham was, I AM" (John 8:58). Jesus used the special covenant name of God to refer to Himself, translated "I AM" (*eimi* in Greek, *YHWH* in Hebrew). Grammatically, it makes no more sense in English than in Greek to say, "Before Abraham was, I AM." It would make much more sense to say, "Before Abraham was, I existed," but Jesus cared much more about theological truth than about grammatical accuracy. He fully intended to declare, "I am God Almighty, the *Yahweh* you know from the Old Testament" (John 8:57-59). Jesus is the eternal Son of God, the "Mighty God" of Isaiah 6:9.

When you look at Jesus, you're looking into the face of God. Paul called Jesus "the image of the invisible God, the firstborn over all creation" (Colossians 1:15). The Greek word translated "image" is the term from which we get our English word *icon*, which refers to a copy or a likeness.

Ancient people used the word *image* to describe an engraving on wood, an etching in metal, the brand of an animal hide, an impression in clay, or an image stamped on some other medium. When Jesus arrived in this world, the planet had "God" stamped all over it.

Do you know that God's image is stamped on *your* soul? You'll never find real meaning in life until you understand that you were not merely made *by* God; you were made *for* God. He wants you to represent Him to this world! *You* are God's icon to reach a planet estranged from Him.

The Hope of the Promised Messiah

We live in a world that desperately needs hope. On our diseased rock, death reigns, evil often triumphs, and hope too often seems absent. Since God knows our desperate condition better than we do, almost from the very beginning He has laced His Word with shining markers of hope. And the brightest, most dazzling of all those markers were His repeated promises of a coming Messiah.

God delivered the very first such marker immediately after Adam and Eve sinned. After the Lord pronounced their sentence, He also gave the guilty couple a bright beacon of hope. He told the serpent who had deceived them,

> "I will put enmity between you and the woman,
>   and between your offspring and her offspring;
> he shall bruise your head,
>   and you shall bruise his heel."
> (Genesis 3:15 ESV)

Bible scholars often call this verse "the first mention of the gospel," because in veiled form it prophesies both the defeat of Satan and the triumph of the Messiah through the cross.

Over the centuries, the Lord added promise after promise and detail after detail regarding this coming Messiah, always pointing to the day when He would provide salvation for His people and redemption for His creation. By the time of Jesus, the Jewish people had a heightened expectation for Messiah's arrival, even wondering whether John the Baptist might be the predicted one (see John 7:40-43).

Soon after Jesus began His public ministry, the crowds who heard His words, observed His behavior, and gasped at His miracles began to wonder, *Could this be the Messiah?* Some said yes, some said no, and most didn't dare to commit themselves one way or another. The Gospel of John offers some good snapshots of the situation:

- "Andrew…found his own brother Simon, and said to him, 'We have found the Messiah'" (John 1:40-41).
- "Do the rulers know indeed that this is truly the Christ [Messiah]?" (John 7:26).
- "When the Christ comes, will He do more signs than these which this Man has done?" (John 7:31).

- "Still others asked, 'How can the Messiah come from Galilee? Does not Scripture say that the Messiah will come from David's descendants and from Bethlehem, the town where David lived?' Thus the people were divided because of Jesus" (John 7:41-43 NIV).

In fact, both the law and the prophets had for centuries witnessed to the coming Messiah. Although neither the common people nor their scholars had a clear picture of the Messiah, their Bibles contained all the information required to identify Him. The problem was that the Old Testament presents what *seems* like two contrasting pictures of the Anointed One. While some texts depict Him as a conquering king, others portray Him as more of a suffering savior. How could both be right?

More than a Historical Curiosity

I've visited Israel many times, and on one trip I wanted to go up to the Temple Mount. I arrived on a Friday, during the Muslim observance of Ramadan. From noon to 2:00 p.m., about 300,000 Muslims took over the sacred space for their call to prayer. For centuries, Muslims have controlled Temple Mount, building on it both the Dome of the Rock and the al Aqsa mosque. Archaeologists don't know exactly where Herod's temple used to stand, but they know it was on Temple Mount. During feasts like Ramadan, however, Jews can't pray up there, lest they spark a riot.

So, where do observant Jews go to pray? They head to the Wailing Wall, one level down. So that's where we went too. I visited Wailing Wall and prayed Bible promises.

What's so special about the Wailing Wall? When the Romans destroyed Jerusalem in AD 70, they left only the Wailing Wall standing. It's a retaining wall that helps keep Temple Mount in place. The

Romans left it standing simply to say, "Take a look, and don't ever forget who we are and what we can do to you."

Many Jewish people today look back to the time of Nehemiah and believe that the restorer of Jerusalem's walls will one day build another wall and another temple. Praying at the Wailing Wall gives them hope that Messiah is coming. As Christians, of course, we believe that Messiah already has come, and that one day He will come again.

I mention the Temple Mount because I see it as much more than a historical curiosity. Did you know that the cross of Jesus stood just north of the temple altar? And did you know that Temple Mount and Mt. Moriah are closely connected? Further, did you know that when Abraham tried to offer Isaac as a sacrifice, as recounted in Genesis 22, he did so on Mt. Moriah?

Abraham provides an amazing picture of the God who would sacrifice His only Son to satisfy the demands of His holy nature—except that in Abraham's case, God intervened and provided another sacrifice, a ram caught in a thicket. Abraham therefore called the place "The LORD Will Provide," and the text in Genesis adds, "And to this day it is said, 'On the mountain of the LORD it will be provided'" (Genesis 22:14 NIV).

More than two thousand years ago, through a virgin birth, God the Son clothed Himself in human flesh and came into this world to become our sacrifice. Unlike with Isaac, however, God did not spare Jesus, but allowed Him to fully taste death for all of us.

Don't make the common mistake that it was God the Father who tipped His wrath on His hapless Son. Jesus, as the second Person of the Trinity, controlled the lever that tipped that awful divine wrath on Himself. No one took Jesus' life; He laid it down freely, of His own accord. No wonder the prophet Isaiah, writing six hundred years before the birth of Jesus, said of Him, "He was wounded for our transgressions…by His stripes we are healed" (Isaiah 53:5). We are healed by the stripes of Jesus, the Messiah—the One Isaiah would also call "Everlasting Father" (Isaiah 9:6).

After Jesus rose from the dead, the apostles and their associates looked back to these ancient Hebrew prophecies to prove that Messiah *had* come in the Person of Jesus. Luke tells us that an educated believer named Apollos "vigorously refuted his Jewish opponents in public debate, proving from the Scriptures that Jesus was the Messiah" (Acts 18:28 NIV). Peter went even further, pointing to the Second Coming of Christ when he told the crowds, "Repent, then, and turn to God, so that your sins may be wiped out, that times of refreshing may come from the Lord, and that he may send the Messiah, who has been appointed for you—even Jesus. Heaven must receive him until the time comes for God to restore everything, as he promised long ago through his holy prophets" (Acts 3:19-21 NIV). Peter's hope remains our own hope to this very day.

The Grace of the Suffering Messiah

The New Testament's classic passage on Jesus the Messiah is found in Philippians 2:5-11. In those cherished verses, and in unforgettable language, the apostle Paul lays out for us the staggering lengths and agonizing depths that Jesus went to in order to be our Messiah. He writes that Christ Jesus:

> Who, being in very nature God,
>   did not consider equality with God something to be used to his own advantage;
> rather, he made himself nothing
>   by taking the very nature of a servant,
>   being made in human likeness.
> And being found in appearance as a man,

> he humbled himself
> by becoming obedient to death—
>   even death on a cross!
> (Philippians 2:5-9 NIV)

Theologians refer to these verses as the *kenosis* passage, a Greek term referring to the "self-emptying" of our Lord in the incarnation. Jesus "emptied" Himself of many of His divine prerogatives in order to serve and minister to others on earth as the Messiah. The eternal God, Jesus, willingly chose to clothe Himself in human flesh, thus becoming Immanuel, "God with us." Jesus lived among us as the God-man.

Paul tells us that even though Jesus was God, He did not consider equality with God something to use for His own advantage. Jesus didn't clench His hands around His divine prerogatives and refuse to give them up. Though Christ had all the rights, privileges, and honor of deity, He refused to cling to those rights. Instead, for our sake, He willingly gave up many of them for a season.

Let's be clear: Jesus did *not* empty Himself of deity, nor did He exchange His deity for humanity. He emptied Himself of many outward, invisible manifestations of the Godhead, but not of His divine nature or attributes. Instead, Jesus willingly set aside many of His divine privileges. Let me suggest just five examples of this "emptying."

First, of His own free will Jesus left the throne room of heaven, where for ages upon ages multitudes of angels had cried out to Him, "Holy, holy, holy is the LORD God Almighty." He took up residence in a virgin's womb, clothed Himself in human flesh, and was born into a world that despised Him and ultimately killed Him. Now, think about that.

Jesus grew tired, just like us—yet He remained fully God.

He grew hungry, just like us—yet He remained fully God.

He grew thirsty, just like us—yet He remained wholly God. Amazing!

Second, Jesus willingly submitted Himself to the sovereign will of His Father. He told the crowds, "The Son can do nothing of Himself, but what He sees the Father do; for whatever He does, the Son also does in like manner" (John 5:19).

Third, Jesus at times divested Himself of important information that God the Father clearly possessed. In speaking about the time of His Second Coming, for example, He declared, "But of that day and hour no one knows, not even the angels of heaven, but My Father only" (Matthew 24:36).

Fourth, Jesus sacrificed for a time His eternal riches. Although He was rich, He became poor so that you and I might be rich (see 2 Corinthians 8:9).

Fifth, as the only human who never sinned, Jesus took our place on the cross, placing on Himself the penalty for our sins. At the moment of that terrible exchange, the Father turned His face away from His Son, because at that instant His Son bore the sins of the whole world. Jesus fully experienced the abandonment and despair that inevitably results from the outpouring of God's wrath against sin. "[God] made Him who knew no sin to be sin for us, that we might become the righteousness of God in Him" (2 Corinthians 5:21).

We will never be able to fully grasp how much Jesus gave up when He took on human flesh. At the same time, however, He didn't give up everything. This is why Jesus could still walk on water, because only God can walk on water. This is why Jesus could say to a terrible storm, "Be muzzled" (the original Greek term), and the sea would instantly grow calm. This is why He could say to a deceased little girl, "Arise," and she would immediately come back to life. He was human *and* God at the same time. And so on the Mount of Transfiguration, the very essence of Jesus began to shine forth, His face dazzling as the sun. Why? Because He's the God-man!

God took the deficit in my spiritual account and transferred it to Jesus' account, and then He took the assets in Christ's account and put them in my account. From me, Jesus got only sin; from Jesus, I got only riches. Think of that the next time you remember the moment you came to faith in Jesus.

I once told a well-to-do man, "I would love for you to come and visit with us at our church." I'll never forget his shocking response. In all my years of ministry—and I've been at this for more than forty years—I'd never heard anyone say anything like it.

"I bet you would," he replied. "A lot of people would like to have me and my money in their church."

I honestly couldn't care less what any man has in the way of worldly wealth. When a man comes to God, he has absolutely *nothing* to bring, except for his sin. No man can ever truthfully say, "When I came to Jesus, I gave up an awful lot."

No, he didn't.

But by God's grace, *Jesus* did.

The Peace of the Reigning Messiah

While the *kenosis* passage describes the self-emptying of Jesus, it doesn't leave Him there. Thank God! To the contrary, it exalts Him as the One whom God anointed as King of kings and Lord of lords. The passage continues:

> Therefore God exalted him to the highest place
> and gave him the name that is above every name,
> that at the name of Jesus every knee should bow,
> in heaven and on earth and under the earth,
> and every tongue acknowledge that Jesus Christ is Lord,
> to the glory of God the Father.
> (Philippians 2:9-11 NIV)

In this remarkable passage, Paul tells us that God exalted Jesus to the highest place—but the apostle's statement jars me. How do you exalt *God*? How can you lift up the Highest even higher? How can you raise up someone who already occupies the summit?

At Christmastime, I've heard people ask, "What kind of gift do you give someone who already has everything?" We usually ask the question with tongue in cheek, but in this case, I'm not asking a tongue-in-cheek question. How does God exalt *God*?

I'm not sure I know the answer to my question, but I do know God's exaltation of Jesus did not involve Christ's nature or His eternal place within the Trinity. It's not as though when Jesus came to earth, He left a vacant seat that someone else could fill!

Just before His arrest and crucifixion, Jesus prayed what we call His "high priestly prayer." In it He said, "And now, O Father, glorify Me together with Yourself, with the glory which I had with You before the world was" (John 17:5). While such a request staggers me, Jesus' return to the same glory He shared with the Father before His incarnation did not require a further exaltation but a restoration.

So again, how does God exalt God?

I think the answer involves Christ's status as the God-man. It appears that God gave Jesus privileges after His ascension that He did not have prior to the incarnation. Let me suggest three examples.

First, if Jesus had not lived among us as a man, He could not have fully identified with those He came to save. The book of Hebrews tells us that Jesus, the God-man, can fully "sympathize with our weaknesses" (Hebrews 4:15). If you've ever wondered, *Can God really understand what's going on in my life?* the answer is yes! Jesus, who became one of us, can perfectly sympathize with our weaknesses.

Second, as a man, Jesus overcame every temptation thrown at

Him. In the desert, Satan told Jesus, "Listen, you've not eaten in forty days. Why not turn these stones into bread? You're hungry, aren't you?" When that temptation failed, the devil tried again: "If you're really God, then jump from the pinnacle of the temple. Hey, the angels of God wouldn't let God dash His foot against a stone, would they?" That approach failed too. Finally, the devil tried the biggest temptation of them all. "Bow down and worship me," he said. "Do you see all these vast lands? They're all under my control. If you will bow down and worship me, I will give you all of them." Jesus resisted that temptation and every other one He ever faced.

This is why we can never say to God, "Lord, you just don't know how strong a temptation this is!" Yes, He does. He endured *far* stronger temptations than any of us ever will, and yet He never once gave in to a single one. For that reason, God has highly exalted His Son and given Him a name He shares with no one, anywhere.

Third, do you know one of the greatest things Jesus accomplished as a man? He came to earth, where Satan ruled, and defeated hell. John tells us that Jesus came to "destroy the works of the devil" (1 John 3:8). Through His work on the cross, Jesus defeated death and the grave. I've lost count how many times I've visited the cemetery, and barring a miracle, I'll be back many times more. But when Jesus went to the cemetery, He kicked the end out of the grave and made a tunnel out of it.

Jesus alone conquered sin. And because of that ultimate triumph, God has exalted Him to the highest place. At the name of Jesus, every knee will bow and every tongue confess that Jesus Christ is Lord, to the glory of God the Father.

One day, Hitler will bow at the feet of Jesus and say, "Jesus Christ is Lord."

One day, Antichrist will bow at Jesus' feet and say, "Jesus Christ is Lord."

One day, every atheist who ever lived will bow at the Messiah's feet and say, "Jesus Christ is Lord." No, this is no "God delusion"; it's God who became man.

The entire intelligent universe is destined one day to worship Jesus Christ as Lord, from angels in heaven to demons in hell, from men in coal mines to astronauts in orbit, from obedient believers on the earth to lost men and women in hades. *Everything* that has breath will one day acknowledge Jesus Christ is Lord, to the glory of God. *How* they acknowledge Him, however, will differ radically.

Some will confess Him as Lord with overflowing, grateful hearts. His peace will rule their cleansed souls as they delight in His reign as Prince of Peace, of whom it is said, "Of the increase of His government and peace there will be no end" (Isaiah 9:7). Others will confess Him as Lord while overcome with abject terror and soul-crushing regret. But however they do it, everyone, everywhere, one day *will* confess that Jesus Christ is Lord.

I sat with a lady one night who, I learned, was just a few months older than I am. "Pray for me," she said. "All I want to do is to go to be with Jesus. I am ready to close my eyes for good." She said it with as much of a smile as someone in great pain can manage.

What gives a woman such confidence and peace, knowing that even as she closes her eyes in death, she'll wake up and see *Him*? That woman knew Jesus is alive. She knew Him as her Messiah. And she willingly, eagerly, and joyfully counted Him as the King of kings and Lord of lords—*her* King and *her* Lord.

Does that kind of peace reign in your own heart?

The only person worthy of ultimate exaltation chose a life of utter humility. The Lord Jesus Christ abandoned His golden throne in favor of a dirty sheep pen. He took His majesty and placed it in the midst of madness. In Jesus, glorious deity entered the world on the floor of a filthy stall.

And now He calls us to follow His example.

A Call to Servanthood

No greater example of a servant exists than the Lord Jesus Christ. If it ever becomes your sincere desire to say, "I want to be as much like Jesus as I possibly can," you will become a *great* servant.

God never calls any Christian to a life of self-centeredness. The Christian life is not about what you can get but about what you give. It's a life of self-surrender to the will of God, to the needs of your fellow man, and to the example of Jesus Christ.

John 13 may give us the best illustration of a genuine servant. It describes Jesus washing the feet of His disciples, a dirty job typically reserved for lowly servants.

Foot washing was a normal practice in the ancient Middle East. When a guest came in off the dusty roads, custom dictated that someone waiting at the door should wash the visitor's feet. Jesus broke from custom, however, when He chose to do the work Himself. His action staggered His disciples because they considered the job too menial for anyone but a servant. And yet the Lord Jesus, God in the flesh, demonstrated that *no* service to a fellow human is too low.

After He finished His unsettling object lesson, Jesus told His men,

> "You call me 'Teacher' and 'Lord,' and rightly so, for that is what I am. Now that I, your Lord and Teacher, have washed your feet, you also should wash one another's feet. I have set you an example that you should do as I have done for you. Very truly I tell you, no servant is greater than his master, nor is a messenger greater than the one who sent

him. Now that you know these things, you will be blessed
if you do them" (John 13:13-17 NIV).

Did you catch that last phrase? "*If* you do them." God blesses us
when we serve others, not merely when we talk about serving them,
study serving them, or encourage others to serve them.

Somehow, in the twenty-first century, we talk about theology far
more than we do something practical with it. We lack what I'd call
"theological pragmatism."

I not only want people to know the gospel, but I long for them to
embrace the Christ and undergo a radical personal transformation.
More than anything, I want that radical personal transformation to
begin with me.

The Only Way to Know God's Will

"Let this mind be in you," Paul tells us, "which was also in Christ
Jesus" (Philippians 2:5). Elsewhere the apostle declares, "We have
the mind of Christ" (1 Corinthians 2:16).

And what is "the mind of Christ"? In essence, it's a submissive
attitude. God has given us the mind of the Messiah so that we can
submit ourselves to live the way He would have us to live. To have
the mind of Christ is to display in your life the attitude that Christ
exhibited while He walked this earth.

The life of Jesus teaches us that the only way we will *ever* know
the will of God for our lives is to realize that when we became Christians, we surrendered our rights. The only right we have now is to
live out God's perfect will for us. His will trumps ours. Jesus habitually chose to submit His will to that of His Father, for our benefit.
So, if He was willing to do that for us, then how could we refuse to
do the same for Him?

Remember that Jesus laid aside His privileges to benefit others.

Our Messiah did not consider any treasure too great to be surrendered. He laid aside His glory, His comfort, His reputation, and the infinite honor due His name in order to win our salvation. In doing so, He did not think of Himself but of others. This is the mind of Christ.

Let this mind be in you.

3

A LORD WHO DESERVES DEVOTION

When I fly, I often pray, "Lord, please put me beside someone who needs to know about the love of Christ." That prayer has brought me lots of divine appointments! When I feel drained after a long trip, however, sometimes I say, "Lord, please put me in a seat with nobody around me. I'm tired and I want to rest."

Several years ago, right before Mother's Day, I felt exhausted after spending some extended ministry time in Colorado Springs. I'd had a short night, my flight was late, and I didn't get to bed until 1:40 a.m. I had a board meeting scheduled for 7:00 a.m. the next day—and you know why they call them "board," don't you?

As I sat at the window, completely spent, I thought, *I'm going to doze a little and then I'll be able to enjoy my family when I arrive home tomorrow evening.*

When the flight attendant came by to serve beverages, she looked at me and said, "You mean to tell me that we're not going to get to hear you preach a Mother's Day message on Sunday morning?"

Although I didn't recognize her, she clearly recognized me, and so she continued: "My daughters enjoy hearing you preach, and they've never really enjoyed preachers. You keep their attention."

The young woman sitting in the seat next to me overheard our exchange and immediately chipped in, "It's no coincidence that the Lord has put me beside a preacher!"

I thought, *This is gonna be interesting.*

It turned out that my seatmate had moved from Detroit to Colorado Springs. As a young girl, she'd dreamed of working for James Dobson—but clearly, her life didn't match the type of witness his ministry deserved.

For the next hour, I described how Jesus Christ can make a difference in a person's life. Toward the end of our conversation, I told her, "Before you get off this plane, you need to get right with God. You need to ask Christ to forgive you for where you've drifted." I recommended a wonderful church in Colorado Springs, and then I added, "Go back and finish your education. I encourage you to follow the dream that God placed in your heart. I hope that one day I'll see an article from Focus on the Family that you helped write."

Do you know why I still remember this encounter from all those years ago? I remember it because it illustrates for me a single potent truth that plays out in two very different ways.

The Devotion of a Heart Submitted to Christ

How we respond to the lordship of Jesus Christ puts us in one of two seats, seats that move us toward two very different destinations. Peter says it like this: "But in your hearts revere Christ as Lord. Always be prepared to give an answer to everyone who asks you to give the reason for the hope that you have" (1 Peter 3:15 NIV).

Christian men need a holy, humble heart for Christ as Lord. The apostle here gives us a picture of a heart over which Christ rules. The verse reminds me of Matthew 6:33, where Jesus said, "But seek first the kingdom of God and His righteousness, and all these things shall be added to you." When Christ is Lord, He's King in your life. And when He's King, you don't have to worry about what you'll eat or what you'll wear; when you put Him first, He'll take care of it all.

Somehow, though, we tend to get this all turned around, just as that young lady did on the plane so many years ago. We think that if we submit to the lordship of Jesus Christ, He'll make us do the very thing we detest the most. So we refuse to surrender.

But in this passage, Peter gives us a biblical snapshot of the joy-filled, surrendered servant. He pictures for us the devotion of a life in which Christ rules as Lord. Did you know that to revere Christ as Lord takes personal devotion on your part? This passage helps to explain how the contemporary American church got to where it is. Sadly, we really don't understand lordship.

Peter insists that every Christian man is to give Jesus a special place in his heart. The word translated "revere" means to turn *everything* over to Christ. Suppose someone were to ask you, "Is Jesus Lord of your life?" To answer yes would mean that you have allowed Christ to rule in your heart, that you have given Him free access to every area of your life. You have turned everything over to Him and you live only to please and glorify Him. It means that if anything in your life conflicts with who Jesus is and what He stands for, then God will reveal that to you, you will repent of it, and you will say with passion, "I want to please God more than anything." To call Christ "Lord" means to fear displeasing Jesus infinitely more than you fear what men might do to you.

In some older translations, the word translated "revere" is rendered "sanctified." The underlying Greek term was used in pagan religions to refer to the act of setting apart a building as a temple, thus designating it as religious in character, to be used for worship. In a similar way, we are to set aside our hearts to Christ. We designate our lives as temples to be used for the Lord's purposes. We are to live for the Lord's pleasure, according to His design.

My, You Look Different

When you submit yourself to Christ's lordship, your life will look distinctly different from men who don't belong to Christ. To "revere" or "sanctify" Jesus in your heart means that you live to honor Him, to acknowledge Christ as the Holy One in your life. You give first place to Him, willingly choosing to obey Him in everything.

"Lord" is the English translation of the Greek term *kyrios*, which in this passage refers to Jesus as Yahweh of the Old Testament. Peter was exhorting his fellow Christians to set apart the Lord Jesus as Yahweh. They were to consider Jesus as very God, giving first place to Him in their hearts, obeying Him before anything or anybody else.

Have you set aside Christ as the Lord of your life? Have you committed yourself to live in obedience to Jesus Christ?

This is crucial because the Christian faith makes no sense unless we first set apart Jesus Christ as Lord of our lives—nor will the Christian lifestyle *ever* work. Most church attenders today feel miserable because they have never sanctified Jesus as King over everything in their lives. They have divided loyalties, as though one foot stood on dry pavement and the other on ice. Any foot disconnected from Christ as Lord skates on a banana peel. Life is slippery, and Peter is telling us that men need to set apart Jesus as Lord in a distinct, definite act of the will.

My life purpose is to follow Jesus Christ as the very Lord of *everything* in my life, for His eternal purposes. Everything I am, everything I have, must be surrendered to Him. It bears repeating: the Christian life makes sense in no other way, nor does it work.

Jesus Himself highlighted this issue through a pointed question He asked His disciples. "Why do you call me 'Lord, Lord,'" He wondered aloud, "and not do the things which I say?" (Luke 6:46).

If we call a person "Lord," our obedience is expected. If you were to call me "Lord," not only would I own you, but I would own everything you have. I'd be the owner, the master. Giving lip service to Christ's lordship is totally insufficient…and yet I fear that the average church attender today does exactly that. Genuine faith, however, *always* produces obedience. It cannot do otherwise.

How do you know if Jesus is Lord of a man's life? You can see that the man obeys Christ. It really is that simple.

Good Tree, Bad Tree

How can we tell a good tree from a bad tree? Jesus told us, "Every good tree bears good fruit, but a bad tree bears bad fruit" (Matthew 7:17 NIV). Jesus gave us this saying to describe the difference between a genuine disciple and a phony one. In speaking this way, He had less interest in agriculture than in salvation-culture.

Every now and then, a woman will say to me, "I don't know if my husband's saved or not. But he's a bad dude." Well, Jesus told us that bad trees bear bad fruit. He went even further when He said, "A good tree cannot bear bad fruit, and a bad tree cannot bear good fruit. Every tree that does not bear good fruit is cut down and thrown into the fire. Thus, by their fruit you will recognize them" (Matthew 7:18-20 NIV).

If someone were to show me a piece of tree bark and ask if I could identify the type of tree it came from, I'm pretty sure I'd fail. If somebody were to bring me a leaf and ask me to identify the tree from the leaf, I doubt I'd do much better. But bring me an apple, and I'll tell you it came from an apple tree. Bring me a lemon, and I'll tell you it came from a lemon tree. Bring me a peach, and I'll tell you it came from a peach tree. Jesus did not tell us we will know men by their bark or by their leaves but by their *fruit*. Jesus is telling us, "Who really belongs to Me? Look at the fruit the man's life produces. An apple tree produces apples. It's just like that."

If it's an olive tree, it will produce olives.

If it's a Christian, it will produce obedience to Jesus as Lord.

So let me ask: Is Jesus *your* Lord? Do *you* obey Him? What kind of fruit are you producing?

One of the evidences that Jesus Christ became Lord of my life is that He began to develop me—not all at once, but over time. I hope that I have the proper bark and the right leaves, but I pray in the name of Jesus that my life increasingly bears the fruit of the lordship of Jesus Christ.

Further and Further

Jesus went even a step further. He made a statement that I guarantee made His disciples a little nervous. He told them, "Not everyone who says to me, 'Lord, Lord,' will enter the kingdom of heaven, but only the one who does the will of my Father who is in heaven" (Matthew 7:21 NIV).

Merely saying "Jesus is my Lord" doesn't make it so. Jesus insisted that not everyone who speaks the words has really submitted to Jesus as Lord. It's not the people who *call* Jesus "Lord" who enter the kingdom of heaven, but only the people who *do* the will of God.

Are *you* doing the will of God?

Look around and you'll see countless people *not* doing the will of God, who nevertheless claim to know Jesus as Lord. But how can He be their Lord of everything if they never give Him any of their finances? How can He be their Lord when they never give Him any of their time? How can He be their Lord and yet they keep all their talents for themselves? Show me who you serve with your talents, and I'll show you the Lord of your life. Everybody worships someone or something, but not everybody worships at the same throne.

As if all this weren't enough, Jesus went even further. He told His startled men, "Many will say to me on that day, 'Lord, Lord, did we not prophesy in your name and in your name drive out demons and in your name perform many miracles?' Then I will tell them plainly, 'I never knew you. Away from me, you evildoers!'" (Matthew 7:22-23 NIV).

On the day of judgment, Jesus will tell these men—religious guys who called Him "Lord" but who didn't bother to obey Him—"I never knew you. Depart from me, you lawbreakers!"

The barrenness of this sort of "faith" demonstrates its true character. The faith that *says* but does not *do* is really unbelief...which means that, according to God's Word, our churches overflow with unbelieving men. These guys acknowledge with their lips that Jesus Christ is Lord, but their lives prove their barrenness. Their actions deny the God who died to save them. Christ is to be preferred above all else!

Peter calls baptism a sign of a good conscience toward the lordship of Christ (see 1 Peter 3:21). So if that's true, then how under heaven can somebody say, "Jesus Christ is Lord," and then say, "Nope" when Jesus calls him to be baptized?

Paul instructs us to set aside a proportional amount of our income to give to God's work on the first day of the week (see 1 Corinthians 16:2). How, then, can someone say, "Jesus is Lord," but "Nope" to supporting the ministry of the church?

"We could use your help here to serve the Lord," a church elder says to a man one day.

"Sorry, ain't got time."

"Do you see that man over there?" whispers the Spirit. "I'd like you to ask him how he's doing."

Uh, no. Evangelism isn't my gift.

The Bible says that when Jesus is Lord, He's preferred. He's Lord of our life, and if we have anything left over, we might serve somewhere else; but our service starts with Him. He should never get our leftovers. Life is full of decisions, and the question is often, Who are you going to serve?

If you have a choice between a tee time at 9:00 a.m. on Sunday morning or going to worship the Lord with His people, what do you choose?

If you have a choice between going to the beach and honoring Christ by serving with God's people, what do you prefer?

You can't call Jesus "Lord" and take a vacation from Him.

Enthrone Jesus

I love how the hymn "At the Name of Jesus" puts it: "In your hearts, enthrone [Jesus]; there let Him subdue all that is not holy, all that is not true." The heart is the central part of a man's existence, which is why God's Word says, "Above all else, guard your heart, for everything you do flows from it" (Proverbs 4:23 NIV). A heart controlled by Christ pursues all that is holy and true.

Can you sing with a clear conscience and a full heart the words of this famous hymn?

> All hail the power of Jesus' name, let angels prostrate fall.
> Bring forth the royal diadem and crown Him Lord of all.
> O that with yonder sacred throng we at His feet may fall.
> We'll join the everlasting song and crown Him Lord of all.

Jesus *is* Lord. But is He *your* Lord? And does the fruit of your life show it? The night I came forward at church to get saved, I said, "I want to give my heart and life to Jesus Christ." I'll never forget that night. I didn't know it, but I was sanctifying the Lord God in my heart. I was setting aside Jesus as Lord of my life.

I didn't come forward thinking, *Man, I am on my way to hell* (even though I was). I didn't walk to the front thinking, *I am scared! Let's get this contracted, secure my membership, get me in that tank before I go to hell.* None of those thoughts swam in my head. I had been told that Jesus Christ was in the life-changing business, and I thought that if He could change my life and change my want-to's and desires, then I was a candidate. And He made good on His word! He changed my life.

Did I miss hell? Oh, yes! Did Jesus forgive my sins? Oh, yes! Did He cleanse me? Oh, yes! But bottom line, He brought me into a relationship of obedience to God. When I devoted myself to Him, He did some things in my life in a single week that some men still haven't done fifteen years after they got saved. The question is, how devoted are we to Christ as Lord? He can do a lot in a very short time if the devotion is real.

An Artificial Distinction

The issue of Christ's lordship is a major problem in the church today. Somehow we've created an artificial distinction between trusting Christ as Savior and confessing Him as Lord. We've made two experiences out of just one.

The result? We have a host of men in our churches who have "accepted Christ" in order to miss hell and gain heaven, but who seem completely unconcerned about obeying the Lord.

Listen, salvation is not a cafeteria line where we can take the Saviorhood of Jesus Christ and pass on His lordship. We're not free to take what we want and leave the rest. We cannot get saved on the installment plan, with fingers crossed and inner reservations, as though one could take Christ on layaway. We have only one option: We receive Jesus as Lord or we reject Him.

My favorite verse in the whole Bible is Romans 10:13, which says, "For 'whoever calls on the name of the LORD shall be saved.'" When I put my faith in Christ many years ago, I did not understand lordship, but I received Him as Lord nonetheless. I didn't know the Bible, since I'd never owned one, but I believed all of it. How is that possible? Well, I don't understand electricity, but I believe in light switches. I don't understand automobiles, but I drive one.

Once we receive Jesus as Lord, our options end. We're no longer our own; He's bought us at the price of His own shed blood (see 1 Corinthians 6:20).

On January 7, 1973, I devoted my life to Jesus Christ as Lord. On that day, He saved me and I became part of the family of God. My salvation had nothing to do with my later call to preach. On the day of my salvation, Jesus made me into a Christian, not a preacher. Preachers can go to hell; Christians don't. On the day I received Jesus as Lord, my options ended. I'd been bought at a price.

I belong to Him, and that makes all the difference.

The Development of a Disciple's Heart

One little saying has made a lot of people uncomfortable: "If He's not Lord of all, He's not Lord at all." While I agree wholeheartedly that Jesus is Lord of all, I will also insist that He prepares us, over time, to understand what lordship entails.

Jesus knows we can't "get it" all at once. That's why He once told His men, "I have much more to say to you, more than you can now bear" (John 16:12 NIV). Jesus didn't tell them everything they needed to know in one big download. Did they need to know those things?

Absolutely. But He prepared them to receive it all. They had to be *developed* as disciples.

The night I came to Jesus Christ, I didn't know my Bible. I didn't understand lordship. Despite that, the Bible was still true and lordship was a reality. So how did the reality come to be true in my experience?

From that night on, God began to develop me. He started to take me from Point A to Point B and beyond. Peter gets at this truth when he writes, "Always be prepared to give an answer to everyone who asks you to give the reason for the hope that you have" (1 Peter 3:15 NIV). God instructs us to be "prepared" to speak to others about the difference it makes to have Christ as Lord. And how do we get prepared? I think it's crucial to understand that while *lordship is positional, preparedness is progressive.*

There's only one way to accept Jesus, and that's as Lord. You can't receive Him for what He is not! He *is* Lord, and that's how I received Him. How could I ask Him to become less so that I could become more? That's just crazy.

My development as a believer looks a lot like my development as a human. I was born into this world as a child, but I didn't remain a child. Just so, while I didn't understand anything about "lordship" when I became a Christian, today I'm still wearing the same skin in which God birthed me. It's stretched a lot, though! God is developing me.

This is why I study my Bible diligently. This is why I gather with God's people for worship every Sunday. This is why I take advantage of training opportunities. I want to progress. I want God to develop me. I want Him to take me from Point F to Point G to Point H and beyond.

Be Prepared to Give an Answer

For what purpose is God developing me? Peter says the Lord wants to prepare me, in part, so that I can give an answer to anyone who wants to know what makes my life so different.

The Greek word translated "answer" means to provide a credible explanation of some personal conviction. The Christian discipline of apologetics refers to the marshaling of evidence from all possible sources to declare the validity of claims to Christian truth.

We have a reliable Bible, an inerrant, good, perfect Word from Almighty God Himself. Our faith is defensible, so that we can speak with both integrity and authority. Regardless of who wants answers, we can speak God's Word to them with confidence.

When the Bible says, "Always be prepared to give an answer," it's picturing something similar to a defense presented in court. The phrase is used to describe an attorney who talks his client out of a charge brought against him. It means to answer back, to give a defense. The underlying Greek word more literally could be translated "talk off from." OK, Peter, talk off from what? Talk off from the lordship of Christ.

Ever since Jesus became my Savior, I've been "talking off from" His lordship. When the young lady on the plane realized she was sitting beside a preacher, I began to "talk off from" the lordship of Jesus Christ. I began to give a defense of the Christian's need for Christ to be Lord.

The word *defense* (*apologia*) doesn't mean to apologize. I never apologize for being a Christian! The word means "to defend." If you're going to give a credible answer, you must understand what you believe and why you are a Christian. You also must be able to articulate your belief. The Bible instructs us to do this humbly, thoughtfully, reasonably, and biblically.

When I first became a Christian, I thought I was supposed to tell everybody about Jesus. I'd go to work and say, "Mr. Solomon, I got saved and Jesus Christ changed my life." He would respond, "Well, Johnny, I'm a Jew." I didn't even know what a Jew was. So I would say, "It doesn't matter. He'll save anybody." I knew it made no difference who you were or what you'd done. I shared the gospel with everyone I knew, because I didn't know any better.

Afterwards, I'd often go to a friend, Alfred Joyner, for advice. He discipled me before people saw discipleship as cool. Alfred was a truck driver, not a pastor. I would come to Alfred and say, "I talked to Mr. Solomon today, and here's what he said." Alfred would then take his Bible, turn to a particular passage, and read verses like Romans 10:10-13 to explain to me that Jesus came to save Jew and Gentile alike. Before too long, I had a good answer to give. I could "talk off" from the Bible about the lordship of Jesus Christ to anybody God might put in my life.

A year and a half after I became a Christian, do you know what people started calling me? "Preacher." They gave me that title before I was one. In fact, although I wasn't yet a preacher, I was a witness. I had learned some things about developing my walk with Jesus.

God also sent me another discipler named Mitchell Bennett. I can still remember the color of shirt he wore when I asked him specific questions. He would say, "Johnny, the Bible speaks to that." I didn't know it, but God was taking me from Point A to Point B and beyond. He was developing me.

The moment I put my faith in Christ, Jesus became my Lord positionally. I've never had more of Jesus than the night I received Him. We don't receive Him on installment plans; we get all of Him, all at once. When Jesus Christ is Lord, that's the top rung of the ladder. No one gets more or higher or better than that. Positionally, you have it all from the beginning. But developmentally, you can grow over time.

And God *expects* you and me to grow.

A Suffering World Needs Hope

It helps me to recall that *suffering* provides the context for Peter's first letter. As we Christians suffer in a fallen world, the apostle expects that observers will note the remarkable optimism and hope we have. And so he writes, "In your hearts revere Christ as Lord. Always be prepared to give an answer to everyone who asks you to give the reason for the hope that you have" (1 Peter 3:15 NIV).

We need to be ready always to give a defense. A defense to whom? To everyone. That's inclusive, relating to all life circumstances. We are witnesses, not prosecuting attorneys. That's why it's so important to shore up our witness with a life that backs up our defense. In a loving and respectful manner, we're to present an account of what we believe and why we believe it.

Several years ago, the community where I used to live asked if my wife and I would host an open house in order to raise money to help needy children. We considered it a wonderful cause and so said yes. A lot of people came through our home.

Visitors went upstairs, around the house, and then exited from our basement, where I had a pool table. On the pool table I had placed stacks of my life story, *From the Poolroom to the Pulpit*, with a sign next to them that said, "Take one. Free gift." People took hundreds of copies.

Those in charge of the event later told me, "Mr. Hunt, the most common statement we heard about your home was, 'It was amazing what we did not see: liquor cabinets. And it was amazing what we did see: pictures of Christ, a lot about the family, and needlepoints that referred to eternity.'"

In this suffering world, people *will* ask about the reason for our hope. How do they know we have a hope? They know it because those with hope act differently than those without it. They respond differently to pain and hardship. Believers might be dying, too, but they have joy, real joy, wonderful joy. And why do they have that joy? They have it because they put the Lord Jesus on the throne of their heart.

When people observe you, do they see a difference? Do they see something they want but don't yet have? The absence of hope in the lives of unbelievers causes them to inquire about the reason for the hope they see in believers. The victorious life of a disciple of Jesus prompts sincere questions from those who don't yet know the Savior.

When a man asks you why you have hope, be ready to give him a reason for what you believe. Be prepared to explain how the hope you have in Christ enables you to live as you do.

What Was That Book?

I boarded a plane one day for a one-hour flight home. I happened to be sitting at the bulkhead, so I had to stow my stuff overhead. I grabbed my Bible and a copy of Oswald Chambers's *My Utmost for His Highest*, sat down, and started to read. Those two items often prompt conversation.

On any flight, many men will be seated near you. Many of them flip through their *Playboy* magazines and other pornography, completely unashamed of it. They won't even try to hide the covers. (At the same time, a lot of us Christians feel intimidated even to open our Bibles.)

When I got off the plane, a man sitting nearby asked me, "What were you reading? What was that book you had with the Bible?"

"A few devotional thoughts from a fellow who encouraged preachers all his life," I replied.

"Please give me the name of it," he said, and wrote down the title. I had no more conversation with the man and I don't know his name; he was there and then gone. I do know, though, that when people see a difference in your life, they'll ask questions. They'll ask because you seem to have hope in a world that they trudge through as hopeless.

When you find yourself in such a situation, don't back up. Don't back away. Don't back down. Humbly and honorably step to the front of the line and be able to give a reason for the hope in you. Prepare yourself to tell others of your hope in Christ. Be able to speak from the Bible about your relationship with the Lord.

"But no one *ever* asks me those questions," you say.

I wonder—could that be because you have no fruit in your life? Do you say, "Lord, Lord," but don't do what He says? If so, you can change all that, starting right now.

Your Final Destination

I walked up to an airline counter the other day. A woman looked at my ticket and asked me, "Mr. Hunt, is Atlanta your final destination?"

"Ma'am," I said, "I sure hope not. I don't want to stay here forever."

But if we don't feel comfortable down here on earth responding to Jesus as Lord, then what makes us think we'll feel any more comfortable responding to Jesus as Lord in heaven? What makes us think heaven will even be our final destination?

Eddie Carswell, an original member of NewSong, called me one day after his stepfather died. He was getting ready to visit the cemetery and he couldn't find the verse, "to be absent from the body and to be present with the Lord." Every now and then, I also forget the location of some verse. I told him the text he wanted is found in

2 Corinthians 5:8. He answered, "Brother Johnny, I started studying it in my mind before I located it in the Bible, and God gave me a new song: 'It's not far from here.'"

I'm going to spend eternity with the Lord, and I want to remind you that it's not far from here. How far is it? Just a heartbeat away. Do me a favor and make sure that the Lord you'll greet up there is the Lord you've made a habit of obeying down here.

4

A SAVIOR LIKE
NO OTHER

One of my favorite places to visit in Israel is the city of Capernaum. Its ancient ruins sit on the northern shore of the Sea of Galilee, where the city served as the headquarters for Jesus' earthly ministry. I cannot speak about Capernaum without seeing myself walking through its crumbling gates.

One of the things I love about Capernaum is that it had only one synagogue, and the Gospel of Mark says that Jesus preached there. To stand where I know Jesus once spoke just thrills me.

Jesus once healed a paralytic in Capernaum after the man's friends tore the roof off the "house" (maybe the synagogue?) where Jesus was speaking in order to get him in front of the Savior. When they had lowered him into the room, Jesus said to the lame man, "Son, your sins are forgiven you" (Mark 2:5). Some religious leaders sitting nearby immediately took exception, thinking, "Why does this Man speak blasphemies like this? Who can forgive sins but God alone?" (v. 7).

Now, these men had a front-row seat; they saw and heard everything. In Jesus' day, Sadducees and Pharisees always received the most prominent seats, right down front. Something like that still happens today in many places around the world. When I visited Vietnam some years ago, we arrived after the building already had filled up. Dozens of people stood outside, unable to get in. But when we Americans got there, the event organizers met us and took us to our front-row seats.

These religious leaders in Capernaum saw the man's friends taking apart the roof, they witnessed the man getting lowered to the floor with ropes, and they heard Jesus tell the man his sins had been forgiven. Jesus sensed their indignant response and Mark tells us He asked them, "Which is easier, to say to the paralytic, 'Your sins are forgiven you,' or to say, 'Arise, take up your bed and walk'?" (v. 9). Of course, physically it's just as easy to say one sentence as it is the other; but the two statements have vastly different implications. Jesus then continued, "'But that you may know that the Son of Man has power on earth to forgive sins'—He said to the paralytic, 'I say to you, arise, take up your bed, and go to your house'" (vv. 10-11).

Instantly, the man's paralysis disappeared. He jumped up, picked up his pallet, and walked out of the room. Everyone there should have shouted, "Jesus is God! He can forgive sins!" But that's not what happened. While everybody else felt "amazed" and "glorified God," from that moment on, the Pharisees and Sadducees counted Jesus as their enemy.

This story shows that men do not come to God through human wisdom. The religious leaders were right in believing that only God can forgive sins; but when Jesus paired His ability to heal with His ability to forgive, they should have put two and two together and said, "Since that lame man is walking, it proves that Jesus *does* have the authority to forgive. Why…He's God our Savior!" This miracle should have been one of the first incidents to lead these religious leaders to faith, but instead it became one of the first events leading them to oppose and eventually kill Jesus. Instead of embracing Him as their Savior, they left the house plotting how to destroy Him.

Neither their opposition nor their unbelief, however, could change the truth. Jesus had the power and authority to forgive sins, which made Him the Savior. He *still* is, and He always will be.

A Savior Like No Other

One of the most glorious names given to Jesus in all of Scripture is the title Savior. The Bible declares that Jesus "is able to save completely those who come to God through him, because he always lives to intercede for them" (Hebrews 7:25 NIV). This verse magnifies several aspects of Christ's great work of salvation.

Jesus is omnipotent

The fact that Jesus saves at all speaks of His omnipotence. Almighty power throbs in Christ's salvation. No priest or king, politician or psychiatrist, parent or religious leader was ever able to save, not even partially or temporarily. Jesus *only* can save. The Bible says of Him, "Salvation is found in no one else, for there is no other name under heaven given to mankind by which we must be saved" (Acts 4:12 NIV).

I was buying some groceries one day, doing my honey-do jobs. I didn't have much in my cart, but the young woman who waited on me asked if she could take my groceries to my car. As she and I walked across the parking lot, we met a man just bouncing along who stopped and stared at me.

"How you doing?" I asked.

"Good," he replied. He stared some more, and then added, "Excuse me, but are you Johnny Hunt?"

"Yeah," I said.

"Praise God!" he answered. "I've been an atheist all my life, and

the other day while riding across Bethany Bridge, God saved me."
The memory clearly fired him up. "I'm going to come and tell you
about it," he promised.

When I got home, I told my wife the story. "Where's Bethany
Bridge?" she asked.

"I don't have a clue," I said. "But I'll tell you one thing: that man
will never forget where it is."

The fact that Jesus can visit some little bridge in Georgia and
there save a man who's been an atheist his whole life doesn't surprise
me. Do you know why? Because Jesus is able. He's omnipotent and
saves us with almighty power. He *completely* saves us, past, present,
and future. When Jesus Christ saved me, He saved me for forever.
My salvation has nothing to do with my ability to serve Him but
with His sufficiency to save me. Jesus saved *all* of me for eternity.

Maybe you have a son or a daddy at home, or a mom or daughter, or a friend at work, and you think, *God can't save him,* or *Jesus
just can't reach her.* You need to rethink that! Jesus is able.

Jesus operates like no one else

The New King James Bible translates Hebrews 7:25 to say that
Jesus "is able to save to the uttermost." I like how one old preacher
said it: "He saved me from the guttermost to the uttermost." Jesus
plucked me out of the gutter and gave me a prospect brighter than
the sun. I was lost in sin, under its power and penalty, and Jesus
Christ bought me out of the devil's slave market. He saved me, just
as He promises: "For 'whoever calls on the name of the Lord shall
be saved'" (Romans 10:13).

And don't forget the prospect of where you're going! We best
magnify Jesus' salvation not by what He saved us *from,* but what He
saved us *to.* Have you seen the bumper sticker that says "Christians
are not perfect, just forgiven"? I might want to add a parenthetical

statement: "And for those who don't understand, let me say that I will be perfect one day." *That* is my prospect.

A lady once said to me, "You know, preacher, I'm in the same category you're in. I can't sing, either." I thought, *Thank you very much.* She added, "But I think we're all going to sing on the other side."

Yes, praise God, we will all sing in heaven. But I'm singing on this side too! You don't have to be able to sing to *sing*; you just have to have a song. When I got saved, the Holy Spirit put a song in my heart, and I'm still singing it. Too many people in our churches can sing, but they don't have a song.

Do you have a song? Do you know your prospect? Do you know where you're heading?

Anyone can be the object of Jesus' saving power

Jesus Christ can save *any* sinner from *any* condition—and those He saves, He saves completely and for all eternity. Our Lord emphatically declared, "All those the Father gives me will come to me, and whoever comes to me I will never drive away" (John 6:37 NIV).

Decades ago, when I pastored Long Leaf Baptist Church, one night I went out soul-winning. I dropped by Buddy and Belinda Joyner's house and presented the gospel of Jesus Christ to them. They both got down on their knees and asked Jesus to come into their hearts.

Like any old Baptist boy would do, I returned to the church, eager to share the news. Someone asked, "How's it going?"

"Buddy and Belinda Joyner just got saved!" I said.

"Well, brother Johnny," a man said, "did you know it's not Buddy and Belinda *Joyner*? It's Buddy Joyner, but Belinda's got a different last name. They're living together."

"Is that right?" I said.

"Yeah, so I hate to pop your bubble," he said, "but they didn't get saved. They can't get saved until they break off what they are doing wrong, and then they can come to Jesus."

Don't you believe it! If that were true, no Christian on the planet should ever sing again the old hymn "Just as I am, without one plea." To come to Jesus, you don't *stop* anything. The reason you need Jesus is that you lack the power to change your own life. So you come just as you are. Jesus takes care of the rest.

About three days later, my phone rang. I heard Buddy's voice say, "Can we have breakfast?" I met him at a local restaurant, and he said, "Brother Johnny, I need some help. You didn't know this, but Belinda ain't my wife."

"Well, I heard," I replied.

"I'm really sorry, but for five years we've been living together. We're used to each other's salary helping to pay the rent and all that. But did you know that ever since the other night, after you left, we can't sleep together? She's in one room, I'm in another, and we're in a pickle. We need to know what to do. We can't live like that anymore."

Did some outward law tell Buddy what he needed to do? Oh, no. Jesus took that old, cold stone from Moses's hand and laid it aside, and with His finger He wrote the wonderful law of God on Buddy's heart.

I immediately got on the phone and called one of my wealthy members. "Doug," I said, "I know you have a real big house, and I have a dilemma. Can you give Buddy or Belinda a place to live for a while?"

"I can take either one of them," he answered right away. And that day he took Belinda into his home. I did the wedding about three months later.

Years later, I heard from Buddy. "Belinda sends her love," he said. "We're serving Jesus and have been ever since that night you left our house."

Anybody can be the object of Jesus' saving power. *He* does the saving, not us. No system of legalism, whether Judaic or Christian, ever brought a man to God. Sometimes I witness to someone and he says, "Brother Johnny, I've been coming to your church. I've been doing better lately. I'm going to clean up my act, and then I'll join your church."

You can guess how I respond. "You don't need to clean up your act and join the church," I tell him. "You need to come just as you are, right now, and let Jesus Christ clean up your heart and soul."

Listen, it isn't about you "getting better." You aren't any good and you deserve to go to hell. That's not a message you'll hear often today; we worry more about offending people than about helping them. But I'd rather tell you the truth and offend you than have you sit on the end of a pew and let it rock you to hell.

Christ died for you *because* you were no good. We are all sinners. We've all missed the mark. Jesus took your place on the cross, and that's why we call Him "Savior."

Salvation is completely of the Lord

Is our salvation rooted in our efforts to serve Jesus or in His ability to save us? It's *all* Him. Salvation is of the Lord.

He's the rescuer. *He's* the completer. *He's* the high priest (see chapter 5). *He's* the One who ever lives to intercede for me. *He's* the one who pleads on my side. Every time I sin, Jesus says, "Put it on My account." That's why the Bible says, "The blood of Jesus Christ His Son cleanses us from *all* sin" (1 John 1:7, emphasis mine).

We can no more keep ourselves saved than we can save ourselves in the first place. Constantly, eternally, and perpetually, Jesus intercedes for us before His Father. If you ask some people if they're going to heaven when they die, they'll say, "I hope so." They speak like that because they believe if they get into sin before they die, they won't make it. But that would highlight their ability to obey rather than Christ's sufficiency to save, and God won't have any of that.

He Meets Our Need

Our Savior, Jesus, meets our need like no one else ever could. The writer of Hebrews says that Jesus "truly meets our need—one who is holy, blameless, pure, set apart from sinners, exalted above the heavens" (Hebrews 7:26 NIV).

Jesus fits us like a neoprene glove. He's totally suited to us and meets our needs completely. He "feels" right. I've worn Him long enough to know He's exactly the right Savior for me. Notice five things the writer of Hebrews says about our Savior.

1. Jesus is holy

The Bible describes Jesus Christ as holy. That means He fully satisfies all the righteous claims of a holy God. Who declared Jesus Christ holy? God did.

And what is holiness? Our holy God is set apart from sin, morally perfect, infinitely righteous. The prophet Habakkuk said to the Lord, "Your eyes are too pure to look on evil; you cannot tolerate wrongdoing" (Habakkuk 1:13 NIV). And it's this holy God who says to you and me, "You shall be holy, for I am holy" (1 Peter 1:16 ESV). God demands holiness in the life of every believer.

But how does that help us? How can *we* be holy? In ourselves, we can't comply. In ourselves, we're the opposite of holy. *In Christ*, however, we're holy because Christ in us satisfies all the holy demands of a righteous and holy God. Our salvation doesn't rest on how well we live for Him, but on the fact that He lives in us.

2. Jesus is blameless

Jesus is both upwardly holy and outwardly blameless. No malice or craftiness has ever lived in Him. He is guileless, innocent, and guiltless. Jesus healed, but He never harmed. No one ever has or ever will be able to convict Him of sin.

3. Jesus is pure

Inwardly, Jesus is undefiled and unstained. No sin ever tainted Him and no evil ever corrupted Him. Someone may say, "But during His earthly ministry, wasn't Jesus called a friend of sinners? How can anyone be a friend of sinners and not end up defiled?" Jesus' contact with sinners never defiled His character or warped His conduct. Jesus had lots of contact, but no contamination.

4. Jesus was separated from sinners

This may sound like a contradiction, but it's not. How could Jesus have contact with sinners but still remain separated from them? This speaks of His sinlessness. He is in a different class from everyone else, distinct, unique. But while He stayed separated, He did not remain isolated. Even as He interacted with sinners, He remained separate from them, distinct.

Simon Peter understood this from the very beginning. When Jesus showed up one day at Simon's workplace, the big fisherman allowed Him to preach from his boat. After Jesus had finished, the Lord instructed Peter and his friends to let out their nets into the lake, even though the men had worked the whole night before without catching anything. They complied, and caught so many fish that their nets began to break. Peter immediately sensed how separate and distinct Jesus was, and cried out, "Depart from me, for I am a sinful man, O Lord!" (Luke 5:8 ESV).

Jesus did *not* depart, but instead replied, "Do not be afraid; from now on you will be catching men" (v. 10 ESV). And from that time on, Peter and his fishing buddies "left everything and followed him" (v. 11 ESV). Separated, but together.

Sometimes I go to the race track, where I hang out to talk about Jesus. What a preacher's paradise! Thousands of unsaved people show up, and I come to hand out gospel tracts, books, and tapes and to brag on Jesus. One night, twenty-five thousand people turned out. Several nights, we've had twenty thousand. That's a lot of fish to catch! So I go out to the race track and preach early Sunday morning before I go to church and preach in some worship services.

5. Jesus is exalted above the heavens

Through His resurrection from the dead, Jesus was "declared to be the Son of God in power according to the Spirit of holiness" (Romans 1:4 ESV). While He was always King, in His resurrection He wears the crown of life as the King of kings and Lord of lords. His exaltation above the heavens speaks of His sovereignty:

> Therefore God has highly exalted him and bestowed on him the name that is above every name, so that at the name of Jesus every knee should bow, in heaven and on earth and under the earth, and every tongue confess that Jesus Christ is Lord, to the glory of God the Father (Philippians 2:9-11 ESV).

You could not have a greater Savior!

How Jesus Saves

The Bible lays out a very clear, simple road to salvation. John wrote, "To all who did receive him [Jesus], to those who believed in his name, he gave the right to become children of God" (John 1:12 NIV). Three words in this verse, all action verbs, outline the process of how Jesus saves.

Believe

Did you know that John mentions the name "Jesus" 247 times?

Why mention His name so often? Because to believe in His name is to believe in what His name signifies. It is to believe that Jesus can save you from your sins.

The very name Jesus means "God saves." Before the Lord's birth in Bethlehem, an angel told His foster father, Joseph, "You shall call His name JESUS, for He will save His people from their sins" (Matthew 1:21). Believing in the name of Jesus implies personal surrender and commitment to Him.

May I ask, when have you personally surrendered and committed your life to Jesus Christ? Have you "believed in His name"?

In ancient times, one's name was more than just a personal designation. It was a reflection of one's character and attributes. When we believe in Jesus' name, we yield ourselves to be possessed by the One in whom we believe. When a man says, "I'm giving my life to Jesus Christ," he's expressing his faith in Jesus. He's surrendering himself to Christ, acknowledging the Lord's rightful position and the man's subordinate place before Christ's divine character.

One translation puts it this way: "To those who had yielded him their allegiance, he gave the right to become children of God." People tell me, "Oh, I know all about God." But they don't know Him personally. As a result, Jesus doesn't have their allegiance—everything else does. They give Jesus the leftovers of their time. They give Him little pieces of their talent and scraps (or nothing) of their treasure. Why? Because they know *about* Him, but they don't *know* Him. When a man comes to know Jesus, he surrenders allegiance to Him. All of that is wrapped up in the little word "believe."

Receive

It's not enough to believe that Jesus is the Savior. He must become *your* Savior. And the only way that happens is for you to receive Him.

When my wife gives me a present at Christmas, I believe it's a gift, but I'll never know what that gift is until I open it and receive it as my own. That's what you do when you receive something—you take it and it becomes your personal possession.

A lot of people know *about* God's gift, but have never *received* the gift. Oh, it's been given! But it's meant nothing to them. It's still wrapped and they have no idea what lies inside. They've never taken the time to wrap their hands around it, open it, and receive it. Have you received the gift of Jesus' salvation?

Become

I used to go out at night, handing out gospel tracts. I'd been saved only a little while when somebody bought me fifty orange-colored tracts called *The Four Spiritual Laws*. The final law said, "You must individually receive Jesus Christ as Lord and Savior."

The Bible says you must *individually* receive Jesus. No one else can do this for you. At some time in your life, you must receive Him individually. And when you do receive Him, He gives you the right to *become* a child of God.

The term *right* can be translated "power" or "authority," but don't believe for a moment this means you have the power or authority to become a son of God at will. The word *right* does not refer to the ability to say, "I'll become a child of God anytime I want to." Salvation is of God, which means becoming a child of God is not within your strength or ability.

Salvation is a divine initiative, not a human one. John insisted that God's children are "born not of natural descent, nor of human decision or a husband's will, but born of God" (John 1:13 NIV).

If you think, *I'm not ready to make this decision right now, but when I'm good and ready, I will*, let me explain something to you. Do you know why you're not ready? It's because only God can get you ready to take that step. This isn't a matter of you picking and choosing. Salvation is of the Lord, and He's the one who initiates.

While you're sitting in your favorite chair, minding your own business, He can choose to suddenly touch you. Maybe you didn't intend to do business with Him, but He can step into your world, speak to you, and initiate your conversion. Maybe you're fighting back tears right now. Maybe you're shaking a bit. If so, He's saying to you, "Come to Me, all you who labor and are heavy laden, and I will give you rest" (Matthew 11:28).

Salvation is not of human descent any more than it is of human initiative. It is not "of blood," in the Bible's language. Why not? God has no grandchildren, only sons and daughters.

"But my daddy was one of the finest Baptist preachers this country has ever known," you say. Well, God bless your daddy. But the question is, are *you* a Christian?

Since salvation doesn't come through human desire or by the will of the flesh, that means no amount of wishful thinking can make someone a child of God. One's own efforts simply cannot produce salvation. So, are you a Christian?

"Well, I sure hope so."

That's just wishful thinking. *Hope* so? I *know* I'm a Christian. I've been born again. Jesus has changed my life. I met Him. I know Him. He walks with me, talks to me, reveals Himself to me in the heavens and in my heart. So again, are you a Christian?

"Well, Brother Johnny, you and I believe a little different here, but I'm not a bad person."

I'm not talking about good or bad. No man is good enough to go to heaven on his own merits. Anyone who goes to heaven gets there because of God's grace, not because of his own goodness. Jesus "saved us, not because of righteous things we had done, but because of his mercy" (Titus 3:5 NIV).

If you're a parent, you probably want your children and grand-children to be saved. But if they ever are saved, it won't be because of your will, but because of God's will. Salvation is of divine origin, not of human desire.

My brother had a baby named Frieda, who died tragically by some form of crib death. Afterwards, some religious friends came by to comfort the parents. They meant well, but they asked, "Was the baby baptized? If she was not baptized, she cannot go to heaven." Listen, nobody goes to heaven by human effort. Salvation is not of the will of man. Your parents may have had you baptized as a baby, but that does not make you a child of God. When babies die, they automatically go to heaven because of God's grace, not because of some priest or a preacher or ritual.

Your parents probably wanted you to know God one day, but your infant baptism happened because of their decision, not yours. *You* have to receive Christ. Neither is it enough to go through cate-chism, check off the list, and say, "I believe this about Him, I believe that about Him." It's not what you believe *about* Him, it's *knowing* Him. You have to know Him.

Do you know Him?

Those who receive Christ are granted the privilege of becom-ing children of God, the moment they believe. One snowy Sunday night, my sweet wife and I got in our car and drove less than two blocks to Long Leaf Baptist Church. We went in and sat down on a pew near the front. I already knew I was going to respond to a gospel invitation, so I didn't want to have to walk far. When the preacher gave the invitation to receive Christ, I went down to the front and gave my life to Jesus Christ.

The moment I believed in Jesus and received Him as my Savior and Lord, God granted me the privilege of becoming His child. I didn't "grow into" becoming a child of God. I became one of His children supernaturally, at that very moment. I became a child of God right then, right there, forever.

Our Obligation

Those of us who have believed, received, and now belong to Jesus have an obligation. Remember, Jesus can save only those who come to Him in faith. He is able to save all, but not all will be saved because not all will believe.

While the Bible clearly speaks of divine election—we didn't choose Him, He chose us—I believe it also teaches that a man can say yes or no. One of the saddest verses in the New Testament says, "The Pharisees and the lawyers rejected the purpose of God for themselves" (Luke 7:30 ESV). Yes, you can reject God's purpose for you.

God will save to the uttermost *all* who will come to Him. The late Adrian Rogers once said, "Since we don't know who the elect are, why don't we just go around and witness and nominate everybody?"

While we cannot *make* people believe or obey, our responsibility doesn't end until we have urged them as strongly as we know how to trust in the Savior. A lady said to me one day, "I'm really concerned about one of my loved ones. I'm not sure if he's saved or not."

"Why don't you know if he's saved or not?" I asked.

"I've never asked him," she said.

I believe we have an obligation to ask. Do you know how I know where my dad stands with Jesus? I asked him. My mom is in heaven now. Do you know how I knew where my mother stood with Jesus? I asked her. It's my obligation.

I speak with strangers. I talk to my friends about Jesus. I ask them. I share Christ—and so should you.

So Let Me Ask You Again

Have you ever asked Jesus Christ to be your Savior and Lord? Do you know for sure that you're on your way to heaven? Does Jesus live inside you, empowering you moment by moment to do the will of God?

If you want Jesus Christ to come into your life, then I urge you to receive Him today. Even now, He may be speaking to you, drawing you, working in your heart. Would you like to receive Him? If you do, then I suggest you pray in your heart to God something like the following:

> Lord Jesus, I need you. I'm sorry for my sins. Come into my life and into my heart. I want to individually receive you as my Lord and Savior. Forgive me, cleanse me, save me. Make me into one of Your children. I pray in Jesus' name, amen.

If you prayed a prayer like that, congratulations! Welcome to the family of God.

5

A HIGH PRIEST WHO BREAKS THE MOLD

The Old Testament has no concept of sinful people being cleansed from their sin, only of having their sin temporarily covered. In His forbearance, God allowed the blood of goats and bulls shed in sacrifice to "cover" the sins of His people, until a perfect sacrifice could be made that had the power to totally cleanse guilty men and women.

God arranged for priests to serve as intermediaries between His people and Himself, thus reminding the nation that no sinner could directly approach a holy God. The Lord further stipulated that the priests of ancient Israel had to come from the family of Aaron, and that only the high priest could offer the highest sacrifice under the old covenant. This sacrifice took place only once a year, on Yom Kippur, the "day of atonement" (see Leviticus 16). For one year, God in His forbearance would pass over the sin of the people; but the sacrifice had to take place every year.

When Yom Kippur arrived, the high priest entered the innermost part of the temple, the Most Holy Place, in order to sprinkle the blood of an innocent animal on a golden slab (called the mercy seat) that sat atop the ark of the covenant. Underneath the mercy seat and inside the ark lay the broken law of God—God's way of symbolically showing us that the Messiah's blood covered the broken law. Even though all of us have sinned and so have broken the law, God was willing, even before Christ, to pass over the sin of His people. Of course, the blood of bulls and goats could cover their sin only temporarily, until the final and perfect sacrifice was made.

Because the high priest was as much of a sinner as anyone else, he had to make an offering for himself and his own sins before he could even enter the Most Holy Place (much less make a sacrifice there). On his way to the ark, the high priest had to pass through three areas of the temple. First, he took the blood of an innocent animal and went through a door into the outer court. Then he went through another door into what was called the Holy Place. Finally, he made his way through a thick curtain into the Most Holy Place, the inner sanctum, where the ark of the covenant stood.

Because the high priest was not allowed to sit down as he carried out his solemn duties, the law permitted no chairs in the temple, emphasizing that the sacrifice had to be completed without delay. As soon as the high priest completed his annual task, he left the Most Holy Place and did not return for another year.

This solemn sacrifice on Yom Kippur began with Aaron in Moses' day and continued through the centuries until the Romans destroyed both Jerusalem and the temple in AD 70.

Did you know that eighty-three high priests served God under the Levitical system? Every one of them died. Just like us, they had clay feet. No Hebrew high priest had the power to live forever.

Every high priest who served under the old economy died and was buried.

Not so Jesus! As He did in so many critical categories, Jesus broke the mold.

Jesus Christ, Our High Priest

Do you consider yourself a Christian? If so, the Bible explicitly commands you to "fix your thoughts on Jesus, whom we acknowledge as our apostle and high priest" (Hebrews 3:1 NIV). In other words, you need to make a careful observation, direct your attention to something crucial. God is telling you and me, "Put your mind on Jesus and let it remain there."

While the Bible has a lot to say about Jesus as our high priest, I want to highlight seven characteristics that should change the way we think about our Lord.

1. Jesus is our great high priest

Many religions, instead of having a pastor or a minister, have a priest. The Bible calls Jesus Christ our *great* high priest (Hebrews 4:14). There's no high priest quite like Jesus, the best high priest who ever lived.

Did you know that Scripture never bestows this title of "great high priest" on another? The Bible refers to many priests and high priests, but never has anyone other than Jesus Christ been called our great high priest.

Why is He so great? For one thing, He is not a high priest in the order of Aaron (eighty-three dead men in that category). Instead, He serves as high priest in the order of Melchizedek. Jesus fulfills the ancient prophecy of Psalm 110:4 (NIV), which says of the coming Messiah,

The Lord has sworn
  and will not change his mind:
"You are a priest forever,
  in the order of Melchizedek."

2. Jesus committed no sin

Unlike every other high priest, Jesus never had to make a sacrifice for His sins, for the simple fact that He never committed any. The Bible tells us that He "was in all points tempted as we are, yet without sin" (Hebrews 4:15). Do you think a harlot ever came after Him? I do. Do you think the enemy ever tried to get Him to tell a lie? Oh, yes. He was tempted in every way that we are, and yet He never sinned.

Certainly, the devil and his helpers did their worst. They loaded their best guns and began their attack. They hit Jesus with every missile from the pit they could muster, and used every shell and every automatic weapon. They brought everything they had, and smoke poured from everywhere. But when the smoke cleared, Jesus looked Satan square in the eyes and said, "Is that all you got, bud?"

I would say that spells V-I-C-T-O-R-Y. Jesus had won! When it was all over, Jesus took everything hell could throw at Him and He ended up the victor. That's our great high priest.

3. Jesus is suited for us

There's nothing like being fitted for something, and the Word of God declares that the Lord Jesus Christ is perfectly suited for us. Hebrews 7:26 says, "For such a High Priest was fitting for us, who is holy, harmless, undefiled, separate from sinners, and has become higher than the heavens." Regardless of our needs, Jesus Christ is sufficient to meet the demands and challenges we face.

4. Jesus is able to save

We serve a High Priest who can present us faultless before God. Hebrews 7:25 says that Jesus "is also able to save to the uttermost those who come to God through Him." Jesus is able to save!

Jesus always completes what He begins: "being confident of this very thing, that He who has begun a good work in you will complete it until the day of Jesus Christ" (Philippians 1:6). Paul adds that Jesus "is able to keep you from stumbling, and to present you faultless before the presence of His glory with exceeding joy" (Jude 24).

5. Jesus is a caring high priest

How wonderful to know that we have a High Priest who personally cares for His family! The writer of Hebrews magnifies this caring aspect when he calls Jesus "a merciful and faithful high priest" who "because he himself suffered when he was tempted, he is able to help those who are being tempted" (Hebrews 2:17-18 NIV). No wonder Peter says, "Cast all your anxiety on him because he cares for you" (1 Peter 5:7 NIV).

6. Jesus sympathizes with us

Many people think of God as far removed from human life and concerns, yet the Bible makes it clear that in His humanity, Jesus experienced our feelings, our emotions, our temptations, and our pain.

Jesus knows what it is to suffer disappointment. He knows what it is to be criticized. He knows what it is to be ridiculed. He knows what it is to be betrayed. He knows what it is to suffer grief. He knows what it is to experience pain. And He knows what it is to suffer death.

When His friend Lazarus died, Jesus wept. Although He knew Lazarus wouldn't remain dead long, Jesus felt deeply moved and touched by the infirmities of His friends.

It's important to note that the Bible calls Jesus a "sympathizing" High Priest, not an "empathizing" one. To empathize would mean that Jesus felt as we do because He did the same things we did, including our choices to sin. To sympathize says, "Although I've never done that and I'll never go there, your pain still deeply moves me." Jesus cleansed sinners while remaining separate from and free of sin. As the sinless Son of God, He didn't empathize and say, "Yeah, I know how you feel because I got drunk one time too." He did, however, sympathize with those who had fallen into sin. Thank God, Jesus is a sympathizer and not an empathizer!

7. Jesus is a bridge maker and mediator

The word *priest* carries the idea of "bridge builder." Only Jesus Christ can build a bridge between God and man. He made a way for us to reach heaven by making Himself into our bridge over troubled water.

As God, Jesus was able to reach up and take hold of the hand of His heavenly Father. In His humanity, Jesus can reach down to us and grab our hands. And as the bridge builder, Jesus Christ brings us and God together…and so changes our lives for eternity.

Jesus' Two Key Roles as High Priest

As our High Priest, Jesus plays two critical roles, each of them equally vital. In one capacity, Jesus puts us in a right relationship with God; in the other, He keeps us in a dynamic relationship with His Father. We need both.

1. Jesus atoned for our sins, once for all

None of the eighty-three high priests who preceded Jesus ever finished the work of atonement. They had to keep returning to the temple, year after year and century after century, to make temporary sacrifices that could never take away sins. Jesus, however, entered the true temple in heaven and offered *one* sacrifice that took care of our sin problem permanently.

How? He offered the perfect sacrifice of Himself.

The Bible tells us, "Unlike the other high priests, he does not need to offer sacrifices day after day, first for his own sins, and then for the sins of the people. He sacrificed for their sins once for all when he offered himself" (Hebrews 7:27 NIV).

Jesus is the only high priest who did not have to make a sacrifice to enter the Most Holy Place. He *was* the sacrifice. Every other high priest in Old Testament days had to offer a sacrifice for his own sins, and only then could he take a spotless lamb and offer its blood on the mercy seat for the sins of others. But Jesus is both the priest *and* the sacrifice. He offered Himself for us.

The blood of Jesus, the God-man, had the power both to meet God's standard of righteousness (infinite perfection) and to wholly identify with the guilty parties (humans). Thus Hebrews 9:12 (NIV) says that Jesus "did not enter by means of the blood of goats and calves; but he entered the Most Holy Place once for all by his own blood, thus obtaining eternal redemption." When Jesus Christ, God's Son, went to Calvary and shed the eternal blood of God on the cross, that blood not only covered our sin, but it washed us clean. If you have placed your faith in Jesus, you're cleansed by His blood. I love how the old hymn says it:

> What can wash away my sins?
> Nothing but the blood of Jesus.
> What can make me whole again?
> Nothing but the blood of Jesus.
> Oh, precious is the flow

that makes me white as snow.
No other fount I know.
Nothing but the blood of Jesus.

Jesus, our great high priest, went just once to Golgotha, where He made a perfect sacrifice for us. On the cross He said, *tetelestai*, "It is finished" (John 19:30). That word had an interesting usage in first-century prisons. I've visited some ancient jails in Jerusalem, and guides say that most prisoners were released because someone had paid for their freedom. The jailer would enter the prison and nail a sign at the top of the man's cell: *Tetelestai* ("paid in full").

When Jesus Christ died on the cross to purge our sins, He did it once and for all. He presented Himself in the heavenly Most Holy Place as our sacrifice, then sat down on His throne at the right hand of God.

Tetelestai, "paid in full."

2. Jesus is always interceding for us

Although Jesus' atoning work has finished for all time, He continues to work on our behalf. We are told that Jesus "always lives to intercede" for "those who come to God through him" (Hebrews 7:25 NIV).

Of course, Jesus couldn't do this unless He lives forever. He couldn't promise to perpetually intercede for us unless He had conquered death—and that is exactly what He did on the cross. Jesus Christ, our great high priest, lives forever. That means that when He makes a promise, He will forever remain alive to make it good. Hebrews 7:24-25 (NIV) puts it all together: "Because Jesus lives forever, he has a permanent priesthood. Therefore he is able to save completely those who come to God through him, because he always lives to intercede for them."

Jesus holds His priesthood permanently. It's unchangeable, unalterable. No one will ever dethrone Him, and thank God He will never resign. He lives forever as our high priest. And where does He perform His intercessory duties? The Bible declares that Jesus "has passed through the heavens" (Hebrews 4:14).

There was a time when we could have followed the tabernacle in the wilderness, or we could have visited the temple in Jerusalem. Neither of them any longer exists. Since the Jewish people have no temple today, there are no sacrifices, no priests, no high priest. The Most Holy Place still exists, but it's in no earthly tent, tabernacle, or temple in Jerusalem. The real thing is in heaven.

When we speak today of going into the Most Holy Place and into the presence of God, we speak of the throne room of our Lord in heaven, where Jesus ever lives to intercede for us. Jesus was both priest and sacrifice—that was His destiny.

Shortly before Jesus left this earth, He prayed to His heavenly Father, "I have brought you glory on earth by finishing the work you gave me to do" (John 17:4 NIV). And what was his work? Calvary. Jesus prayed, "I am coming to you now, but I say these things while I am still in the world" (John 17:13 NIV). Jesus came to earth and did what God sent Him to do, and then went right back to heaven where He came from. So, how does that help us?

The Bible answers, "Let us then approach God's throne of grace with confidence, so that we may receive mercy and find grace to help us in our time of need" (Hebrews 4:16 NIV). The high priestly office of Jesus speaks of a time of nearness. God invites us, "Draw near."

Before the time of Jesus, God simply didn't say, "Hey, typical renegade man who came to faith, come near." Instead, He said, "This mountain is holy. If you so much as touch it, you will die. This ark of the covenant, which represents My presence, only the Levitical priest can touch. If *you* ever touch the ark (or even the wagon on which someone mistakenly carries it), I'll wipe you out."

That same God now says, "Come near."

Suppose a recent convert approaches timidly and whispers, "I'm new. I just started studying my Bible. Who are you?"

God replies, "Abba, Father. Just call me Daddy. And come on, son."

James, the half-brother of Jesus, tells us, "Draw near to God and He will draw near to you" (James 4:8). The Lord Jesus left the throne of glory and went to Calvary that He might one day sit upon the throne of grace.

The Old Testament, before the cross, knew nothing of the throne of grace. Under the old covenant, you and I were condemned to die and were on our way to hell. In the Old Testament, no ordinary Israelite could approach the Most Holy Place, where God sat enthroned. Only the high priest could do that, and then only once a year.

But because of Jesus, you and I can approach the throne of grace *at any time, as often as we wish, for whatever we need.* And God tells us, "Come boldly. Come with confidence." The Lord gives you and me freedom of expression, freedom of speech, and the ability to converse with Him without hesitation.

Just come!

Jesus, Our Advocate

Through His role as high priest, Jesus Christ gives us free access to the Father. That privilege alone ought to amaze us. But the Bible teaches that Jesus does even more. He's not only our high priest; He's also our defense attorney.

The apostle John declared, "My dear children, I write this to you so that you will not sin. But if anybody does sin, we have an advocate with the Father—Jesus Christ, the Righteous One" (1 John 2:1 NIV). The reason we can come to Jesus Christ is because of that adjective, "righteous."

I am not righteous in and of myself, and neither are you. The only righteousness we can claim is that which has been imparted to us, imputed to us, placed into our account by Jesus Christ. We don't go to heaven by our own righteousness; we go to heaven clothed in a robe of righteousness purchased for us on the cross and given to us by grace through faith.

The word translated "advocate" is the Greek term *paracleton.* Four times in the Bible it refers to the Holy Spirit, and once it refers to Jesus. How can it refer to both Jesus and the Holy Spirit? It can do so because the Holy Spirit is God and Jesus Christ is God, and the Bible reveals God as a Trinity, three Persons in one Godhead: God the Father, God the Son, and God the Holy Spirit.

The Holy Spirit convicts us of sin so we'll run to our advocate, and our advocate takes us into a heavenly courtroom where we see at least four individuals.

There's the judge; see Him up there on the bench?

There's the prosecutor; he's the one pressing charges against me.

I have my advocate, my defense attorney, standing there at my side.

And then there's the defendant: me.

God is the judge; the prosecutor is Satan; I am the accused; and the attorney for my defense is Jesus. My advocate will intercede with the judge on my behalf. Don't you just love it when the prosecuting attorney makes his case against you, and then you see your attorney approaching the bench to say something to the judge, as though he knows the judge far better than anyone else? I can almost hear the courtroom scene:

"All right, Almighty God," Satan says, "Johnny Hunt's one of your preachers. You saved him many years ago and he's studied the Bible for over forty years. But did you see how he acted just then? Did you see what he did?" I can hear the devil quote Scripture concerning the penalty for sin: death.

"Yes, Father, this is all true," replies my defense attorney, the Lord Jesus. "Johnny *is* guilty of that sin. But Father, I went to the cross and died for that sin. When Johnny was twenty years old, he placed his faith in Me and I applied My atonement to him. He received My forgiveness. His sins are forgiven. I put My robe of righteousness on him, he's covered by My blood, and he's forgiven because he's My child."

The scene gives me goosebumps…but let me go a step further. What I just pictured was the courtroom of heaven, but in the modern legal world, the defense attorney takes a very different tack. He defends his client on the merits of the defendant's case. The defendant tells him, "Hey, I am guiltless. I did not *do* this crime." That's how defendants on earth want their attorneys to argue for them, based on their innocence.

That is *not* what happens in heaven. When I go into God's throne room, my defense attorney speaks to the judge, defending me, but not on *my* merits. Rather, He bases my defense on *His* merits. As our advocate, Jesus admits we're guilty, but He insists that He's already paid in full for our crimes. He died the death we deserved and rose from the dead so we could live the life He lived.

Why would you not want such a scene playing out *all the time*?

In the modern legal world, no attorney involved in a case can be related to the judge. Neither can the defense attorney be related to the defendant. In our legal system, you can't hire your brother to defend you, and the defense attorney you hire can have no legal relationship to the judge.

But in heaven, the advocate is the Father's Son and the defendant is the brother of the defense attorney (see Hebrews 2:11-12). Not only is my attorney related to the judge, but I'm also related to my lawyer!

Do you see how high the deck is stacked against the devil?

But it's precisely here that you and I can get in trouble. We try to be good enough. We think we can defend ourselves.

We can't.

We need an advocate, Jesus Christ, the Righteous One. He pleads our case before His Father and before our Father.

A Very Different Life

When you know you have in your corner a high priest who cannot die and an advocate who cannot lose, your confidence ought to shoot to the stars. At least three major things ought to change forever.

1. You gain stability in life

Jesus is God in the flesh. In His humanity, He becomes aware of your needs; and in His divinity, He is able to meet your deepest needs. Knowing all this ought to give your life great stability.

Nevertheless, when many men get in trouble or suffer great pain, they tend to run away from God. But why? When you know you have an immortal high priest and an invincible advocate, any trials, tribulations, or disappointments you suffer ought to push you *toward* God.

If you were to ask me, "When has the Lord Jesus Christ felt most real to you?" I would reply without hesitation, "In my times of greatest difficulty."

My dad left when I was seven, so Mom became both Mom and Mister Mom. She was the one who gave me dating money. She was the one who worked two jobs to provide for six children. (I still wonder how she did it, God bless her soul.) She's been with the Son of God for many years, and I look forward to seeing her again.

But what a dark morning I faced after my mom died! A man came to my house and said, "God told me to come by and give you two words: You'll be all right, but God's going to use *God* and *time*." When you suffer a crushing loss, it takes both God and time to heal. I've never lost anyone closer to me than Mom. But during those dark, painful days, Jesus the Son of God, the great high priest, my advocate, was magnificently, wonderfully good to me.

How many men have said, "I just lost my job. How could God do that to me? I'll never go back to church"? Oh, my friend, don't run from Him! Run *to* the mercy seat. When bad news hits, don't make it worse by taking yourself away from the one person who can do you the most good. Draw near.

Jesus is touched with the feelings of your infirmities. He suffers with you. He concerns Himself with what concerns you. God often allows you to go through some valley because He wants to prove His faithfulness to you. He wants some of His children to be able to say, "I know God cares for me, because there was a day I had nothing to eat. Somebody knocked at the door, and I thought, *Who is that?* And standing there was somebody saying, 'God spoke to me and told me to empty my cupboard and bring it over to your house to feed you and your family. I don't understand it, I don't even know who you are or what your need is, but that's what God told me to do.'"

How can such knowledge *not* give you stability in life?

2. You don't need to come to Jesus more than once

When I ask some men, "Have you ever invited Jesus Christ into your heart as your personal Lord and Savior?" they reply,

"Oh, I do that every day." Their answer reveals that they just don't understand.

Jesus Christ is God, you have sinned, and without Him, you are on your way to hell. Jesus died for your sins, and by faith—once for all and forever—you place your faith in the Lord Jesus Christ. You invite Him *once* to come into your life and to be your personal Lord and Savior.

At that moment, Jesus comes into your heart and rescues you, delivers you, and empowers you to become what you ought to be. Do you know how many times you need to ask Him to do that? Just once. Do you know what Jesus does the instant you ask Him to save you? He saves you "to the uttermost," which means forever and completely (see Hebrews 7:25). He never saves any man half-way. He doesn't get you part of the way there and then you have to do the rest. You get it all or nothing at all. That's why you ask Him just once.

Have you ever, for that one time, asked Him to become your Lord and Savior?

3. There's nothing left for you to add to your salvation

You can add nothing to the salvation Jesus supplies, nor can you take anything away from it. Occasionally I'll hear a man say, "It's not that I don't want to become a Christian. I just feel like there's something I have to do."

Listen, there's *nothing* you have to do. Jesus has already done it all. He paid the price. He doesn't need your help. You'd just mess it up, anyway.

Remember that, long ago, God put us in a perfect garden and gave us perfect hearts. What did we do? We messed it up and got kicked out. The only way we could return to the garden is for the perfect one to pay the perfect price—and Jesus did that on the cross.

"I'm Changed! I'm Changed!"

I played pool professionally for four years before Jesus saved me. I still like the game and have a pool table in my house. Most of my sticks cost about $20, although I have one that costs about $150.

Years ago someone asked me to share the gospel with a man who makes high-end pool cues. The four sticks he was making at the time cost $20,000 each, and he'd sold at least one cue worth $50,000. I just wanted to hold that thing! Fifty grand for a pool stick?

After the man showed me around his carpentry shop, I asked if he'd come to the place in his life that he knew for certain he had eternal life. Would he go to heaven when he died? I, and a friend who hadn't been saved long, began to talk to him about Jesus. The late Vance Havner used to say that the most exciting Christian in the world is the man who gets saved before he meets his first theologian. There's some truth to that claim.

"Johnny," my friend said, "let me explain to him how he can be saved."

"Go ahead," I replied.

"When I was younger and was thinking about becoming a Christian," he began, "somebody told me, 'If you really want to become a Christian, you need to do just like you do in business: cut out the middleman. Just forget about Jesus and get right on to God.'" My friend then quoted John 14:1, which says, "Let not your heart be troubled; you believe in God, believe also in Me."

He continued: "I said, 'God, I want you to save me. God, I want you to help me.' But my marriage had fallen apart and I was drinking real bad and I was in a time of despair. I didn't care to live any longer. I didn't even want to get out of bed in the morning.

"One night, while lying in bed, I said, 'God, I ask you in Jesus' name. I come to you in the name of Jesus. Please come into my heart.' And I want to tell you, God invaded my heart in the person of Jesus Christ!"

The more my friend talked, the more excited he got. He grew red in the face, stood up on his tiptoes, and almost shouted, "I'm telling you, I'm changed! I'm changed!"

You can be changed too. That's what can happen when you ask Jesus Christ to become your Lord and Savior—and to top it off, you get a great high priest and an unbeatable advocate in the bargain.

Why wait?

6

HOW TO ABIDE IN JESUS

Why are you here? For what reason has God put you on this planet?

While a lot of Christian men can quote Jesus' famous words about having life "more abundantly" (John 10:10), they still struggle to figure out why they're here. For many men, that unresolved struggle leads to a crisis of identity.

It doesn't have to be that way.

No Christian man needs to have an identity crisis. Jesus tells us very clearly who we are and why we are here. In short, He declares that He is the vine and we are the branches. We're here to bear fruit to the glory of God.

But how does that work? How do we bear fruit to the glory of God? And what does it mean that Christ is the vine and we are the branches? Let's get some answers...and so get the fruit-bearing started.

Branches in the Vine

Most of what we need to know about bearing fruit for God's glory we learn in John 15. Jesus begins by saying, "I am the true vine, and My Father is the vinedresser. Every branch in Me that does not bear fruit He takes away; and every branch that bears fruit He prunes, that it may bear more fruit" (vv. 1-2).

How do we become a branch in the vine? You and I become a branch by trusting Jesus Christ as our Lord and Savior. We don't initiate it; He does when He brings us under conviction by the Holy Spirit to show us our need for Jesus. If you're a Christian, you are a branch in the true vine, who is none other than the Lord Jesus.

As the life of Jesus Christ comes into you and as you yield to the true vine, you simply rest in Him, as a branch does in its vine. As the sap from the source of your life invades your life, Jesus eliminates old and useless things, much like old, dead leaves fall off a tree. New things grow in their place. Weaknesses get replaced with strengths.

The Bible calls this fruit-bearing. Day by day, God sends moisture up from beneath and the sun from above in order to grow you as a Christian.

"Abide in Me, and I in you," Jesus commanded. "As the branch cannot bear fruit of itself, unless it abides in the vine, neither can you, unless you abide in Me" (John 15:4). He means, "You're going to be a living branch, receiving your substance and the very source of your life through Me. And through that living relationship with the true vine, you will produce fruit."

Not only will you produce fruit, but Jesus makes it clear that your purpose on earth is to produce *much* fruit. "I am the vine, you are the branches," Jesus declared. "He who abides in Me, and I in him, bears much fruit; for without Me you can do nothing" (v. 5). To emphasize His point, He later added, "By this My Father is glorified, that you bear much fruit; so you will be My disciples" (v. 8).

Are you bearing "much fruit" through and for the Savior? If you're not, then you cannot fulfill the purpose for which He put you on earth. Neither can you enjoy the abundant life Jesus promises to those who abide in Him. Your prayer life also suffers. I know this because Jesus also said, "If you abide in Me, and My words abide in you, you will ask what you desire, and it shall be done for you" (v. 7). Are you asking and *not* receiving? If so, the reason may be that you're not abiding.

What keeps us from abiding in Jesus? Certainly, we don't fail because the task is too complicated; it's as simple as remaining connected to the true vine. You don't have to go to seminary to learn how to abide in Jesus. Really, all you have to do is observe a fruit tree growing.

Fruit Trees Don't Grunt

Can you imagine going out to an orchard and hearing the fruit trees grunt? Maybe an apple is growing on some branch, but the apple hasn't yet turned red. The branch is doing all it can to produce more life and sweetness in that apple—but you'll never hear the branch grunt. It simply abides where it is, receiving its sustenance from the tree; and in time, the apple very naturally gets red and juicy.

By faith, you and I have a living relationship with Jesus Christ. You are a *living* branch connected to a *living* vine. And just as a branch gets its life from the vine, so a believer gets his life from Jesus Christ, the true vine.

I have known many believing men who have not grown enough to realize that the genuine source of their life is Jesus Christ. They therefore seek other outlets and other sources to bring them true meaning. None of those other sources ever works because Jesus Christ *alone* is that source. Until these men learn to abide in Jesus, their lives will continue to lack true meaning. Nothing they do will really count for God.

Is it hard to bear fruit? Does it take tremendous effort to abide in Jesus? Frankly, I've never seen a branch struggle. Have you ever walked past a fruit tree and said, "Would you look at that branch over there, struggling to bear fruit! See how the poor thing strains." Of course not. It produces fruit because it's connected to the source.

In an exuberant kind of way, the tree just pushes this life, this power, through that branch. Before you know it, you see leaves. A little later, buds form and flowers start blooming. People smell the fragrance of those flowers, and shortly afterwards, fruit shows up.

Our lives should follow a similar pattern. Someone should be able to look at your life and say, "Would you notice how green that branch looks! There's life there." And then comes the flower, with its sweet fragrance. When we're full of Jesus, we ought to smell, act, and live in ways that attract people. We are living branches growing out of the true vine.

When people begin to smell the fragrance, they move a little closer. Eventually they say, "You're different. You smell different, you look different, you act different, you talk different, you walk different. You go to different places. What is it about you?" When they taste the fruit you've produced, they get what you have—and then they, too, become branches in the true vine.

It is the will of God for every Christian man to be tied into the true source of life, the Lord Jesus, and so bear fruit for the glory of God. Once you accept this simple fact, you're on your way to making your life both meaningful and useful.

The Pruning Process

Those who lack a living union with Jesus Christ cannot bear fruit to the glory of God. They cannot do so because they have no connection to the genuine source of life. Spiritual fruit is the natural result of being connected to the divine life. One can manufacture religious substitutes, but such substitutes always fall far short of God's fruit.

When a fruit tree fails to produce fruit, do you know what a farmer does? He prunes it, cuts it back, until it can start producing. "Every branch in Me that does not bear fruit [My Father] takes away," Jesus said, "and every branch that bears fruit He prunes, that it may bear more fruit" (v. 2). If you're a Christian, you can be sure that one of two things is happening:

- You are producing fruit to God's glory.
- God is pruning you so you can produce more of His fruit.

If you can go out there and do nothing for the kingdom of God, then you may not be part of His kingdom at all. If you're a Christian, either you're bearing fruit or God is at work in your life to enable you to produce fruit (or more fruit). But an extended time of willful idleness never characterizes the life of a genuine believer.

If a branch is doing nothing at all, the only disciplinary action Jesus mentions in John 15 is to cut off the branch and throw it in the fire. Such Christians are "disqualified for the prize," in Paul's terminology (see 1 Corinthians 9:24-27). If a branch refuses to produce fruit, the vinedresser may simply decide to remove it from the earth (see 1 Corinthians 11:27-32).

Why did God save you? So that you might bear fruit in this world. You live on a hungry planet, with people starving for spiritual reality. Very often, when weird movements take place across our nation, you may find yourself thinking, *Maybe they know more about real life than I do.* No, they don't. They're just looking for real life. They're hungry, even starving, for spiritual reality.

Jesus wants to use *you* to show them where to find it.

Bearing Fruit for Others

No branch bears fruit for itself. Branches bear fruit for others to eat.

God wants you to bear fruit because we live in a spiritually hungry world. God has *never* grown spiritual fruit on a branch for its own consumption. Fruit exists to nourish others.

If you are full of the Spirit of God, you are a branch connected to the true vine. The gift of life goes from Jesus Christ to others through you as a branch. Fruit comes through your life, and people around you consume that fruit. The effectiveness of God's work within your life makes them curious and greatly influences them toward the Lord.

As we're united to Jesus and we abide in Him, His life flows through us and in us. In that way, we bear fruit. As we make ourselves available to Jesus, He makes Himself available to us. This is the will of God for every saved man. God wants to use *you* for His glory.

Six Kinds of Spiritual Fruit

Spiritual fruit comes in many varieties. The six kinds of spiritual fruit I'm about to describe are all mentioned in Scripture, but this is no exhaustive list. I see it simply as a helpful place to start.

1. The principle of soul-winning

When a man invited me to church many years ago, little did he know that he'd just invited the guy who would become his next pastor. At the time, I was managing a pool room as a high school dropout and teenage alcoholic, with no direction or purpose in life.

One day a carpenter said to me, "Johnny, I wish you'd come to church and hear the story of Jesus." When I showed up a few Sundays later, Jesus Christ changed my life.

I went off to college and then to seminary. After I graduated, that very church called me back and I pastored there for six of the better years of my life. God brought a lot of fruit during that period.

As I got ready to leave that church to pastor elsewhere, someone checked our church records and discovered that in the half century of the church's history, it had baptized more people the year I came to faith than in any other year. Do you know why? Forty-five of my friends got saved as a result of me getting saved. I began to tell my friends what Jesus had done in my life.

Was it hard to do that? Not if you're connected to the vine. It's simply the principle of soul-winning.

First come the green leaves, then the flower, then the fruit. Paul referred to the process in Romans 1:13, where he told the Roman church of his desire to visit, "that I might have some fruit among you also, just as among the other Gentiles." What kind of fruit did the apostle have in mind? He longed to win Gentiles to Jesus Christ.

Scripture gives us at least five pictures of this soul-winning principle.

A hunter. Proverbs 11:30 says, "The fruit of the righteous is a tree of life, and he who wins souls is wise." The word "win" calls to mind a hunter taking his prey. Sometimes we "track down" a lost soul in order to take him for Christ.

A fisherman. This one comes from Mark 1:17, where Jesus said to Peter and his friends, "Follow Me, and I will make you become fishers of men." Jesus compared evangelism to catching fish. We need to keep a line out. I travel a lot, and when I do, I try to keep a line out. You just never know when you're gonna get a bite or when you may snag something that leads to an opportunity for sharing the gospel.

An ambassador. One of my favorite New Testament passages is 2 Corinthians 5:20, where Paul writes, "Now then, we are ambassadors for Christ, as though God were pleading through us: we implore you on Christ's behalf, be reconciled to God." Here Paul compares an evangelist to an ambassador.

What do we know about ambassadors? They live in a foreign

land, representing their own king or country. If their nation gets into trouble, their king calls them home.

I'm an ambassador for Christ. I live in this world, but it's not my real home. I represent Jesus to those who don't yet know Him. I live in this world, but I am trying not to live as though I am of this world.

In my years as a pastor, sometimes church people would write me unsigned notes. One note asked, "How can you vote no on the liquor referendum, and then play golf at a golf course that serves beer?" The answer is, I am Christ's ambassador, representing Him to those who don't yet know Him. God did not call me to enter a monastery, sit in a corner, and never share my faith with anyone. God's called me to be salt and light in this world. I'm to be a soul-winner.

Don't ever get so spiritual that you say, "I don't go anywhere that does anything wrong." Have you ever read where Jesus went? His enemies called Him a drunkard because He went where the drunkards were, to win them to the Son of God. May God help us to go where the lost world is, and there be salt and light! I'm an ambassador for Christ, and I'm here until my King calls me home.

A harvester. Jesus once told His disciples, "Do you not say, 'There are still four months and then comes the harvest'? Behold, I say to you, lift up your eyes and look at the fields, for they are already white for harvest!" (John 4:35). As He spoke, He and His disciples watched a crowd of unsaved Samaritans coming toward them. *They* were the harvest Jesus had in mind.

A fireman. In Zechariah 3:2, the Lord rebuked Satan and said about a certain man He intended to use, "Is this not a brand plucked from the fire?" I still have a deep conviction that lost people are going to hell and that we need to get out there and pluck them out of the fire. I'm a fireman for Jesus.

Some years ago, a missionary couple from Uganda stayed in our home. Someone asked the husband, "What's it like out there in the bush? Travel maps tell us to stay out of Uganda. You live among people who regularly carry automatic weapons, which they use to kill tourists and visitors. Aren't you afraid for your wife and two little children?"

"Oh, no," he replied. "We're there by the sovereign will of God. God placed me out there." He smiled and then asked, "May I tell you what overcomes my fright?"

His interviewer nodded.

"First of all, God has not given me the spirit of fear. But second, what outweighs my fear is the fact that these men, if they never hear the gospel, will go to hell when they die."

We're firemen, you see.

2. The principle of the sanctified life

Holiness refers to the beauty and the character of God displayed in our daily lives. Holiness means growth in godly behavior, becoming increasingly like Jesus. As we share the life of Christ, we share the character of Christ.

Romans 6:22 says, "But now having been set free from sin, and having become slaves of God, you have your fruit to holiness, and the end, everlasting life." The theme of Romans 6 is victory over sin, and the fruit of this victory is a holy life.

Holiness cannot be manufactured but must come from within, from Almighty God. Jesus Christ is the true vine, sending His life up through the branch. As you yield to Jesus, holiness automatically starts to become part of your life. As a branch of a holy vine, you bear holy fruit. When you respond properly, you fill up with love, joy, and peace.

Every man of God is to be holy and to live a holy life. It is the will of God that you live a sanctified life.

3. The principle of sharing with others

If you plant an apple tree, you're right to assume that one day it will grow, have leaves, flowers, and fruit. If that doesn't happen, you'll find an expert to help you fix the problem, because apple trees are there to produce fruit for sharing with others. Branches exist to bear fruit.

A church I pastored once had to raise $1.2 million within thirty days. We wanted to buy a piece of property we saw as crucial to our mission, but to that point, we typically had income of only $400,000. How would we get that money? We didn't know, but in faith, we believed we would somehow obtain what we needed.

The bank called and said, "Johnny, your church is debt free. Our bank will loan you the money." We had no Plan B. The Holy Spirit had said, "Here's your Plan A: Trust me. I'm going to give you the $1.2 million. And by giving you that money, I'm going to make my name strong in your area."

In the middle of this episode, somebody told me, "Preacher, you're leading the church out on a limb. You know that, don't you?"

When a pastor friend of mine heard this comment, he retorted, "Brother, lead them out on a limb. That's where the fruit is." I've never forgotten his counsel.

Giving to God, and in His name to others, is the result of who we are and what we are. When a branch receives life from the vine, it cannot help but give. The branch *exists* to give. For a branch, living and giving are almost synonymous. This is why the apostle John wrote, "If anyone has material possessions and sees a brother or sister in need but has no pity on them, how can the love of God be in that person?" (1 John 3:17 NIV).

A believing man cannot selfishly hold on to whatever material blessing God may have given him. Can you imagine going through an apple orchard, looking up and seeing a beautiful apple, but when you reach up to grab the fruit, the tree's branches reach out, slap your hand, and say, "We ain't giving you that apple. It's ours!"? How crazy would that be?

Jesus has given you life, and He wants you to share what He gives you. If you're a branch, it makes no sense to say, "No, I want to hold on to it."

If you're not His son, of course, that's a different story. If you're not a branch, then you have nothing to give. A trunk doesn't give fruit; a branch does. You might hang down around the base of some tree, but maybe you've never been grafted into the true vine. Maybe you've hung around the tree because you like the way some of its branches sing. Maybe every now and then you like to hang around an exciting branch that, at least, doesn't bore you. But the truth is, you're just hanging around the tree; you've never been grafted into the vine.

Once God grafts you in, you'll not only rejoice at what God is doing in some preacher, but that preacher will rejoice in what he sees God doing in you as you share your resources with others.

4. The principle of the Spirit

The Bible instructs Christians to develop personal qualities it calls "fruit"—qualities such as love, joy, peace, longsuffering, temperance, self-control, and meekness. The apostle Paul called this cluster of qualities "the fruit of the Spirit" (see Galatians 5:22-23).

I know I can't produce love, joy, peace, and the rest of these qualities on my own. If I'm vitally connected to the true vine, however, and the vine is the source of all love, joy, peace, longsuffering, temperance, self-control, and meekness, then these spiritual qualities will inevitably start appearing in my life.

Since I'm connected to the vine, the vine's life gets sent right on through me as a branch, and in time, my life begins producing spiritual fruit. Qualities such as love, joy, and peace start to bloom and grow in me, and people begin to say, "I like hanging around him. I always feel better after spending some time together. Our conversations encourage me."

As these qualities show up in your life, they emit such a sweet aroma that people who don't yet know Jesus take note. When they start to see fruit growing, they'll want some of their own...and so God's kingdom expands.

The world, of course, has substitutes for these Christian graces, but it cannot duplicate them. Unsaved people can enjoy love, but they can't produce the deep *agape* love that comes only from the heart of Jesus Christ. The world manufactures entertainment and even short bursts of happiness, but it cannot manufacture the deep joy that comes from Jesus Christ. The same is true for each of the spiritual qualities the Bible calls fruit.

Although the world can manufacture faint echoes of spiritual fruit, it can never reproduce the real thing. God produces real apples and genuine cherries; the world can make only wax table decorations.

5. The principle of service

The Bible lists good works as another type of spiritual fruit. Such works don't save you, but a saved man should regularly produce them. Paul told us that we should be "fruitful in every good work" (Colossians 1:10). Jesus Himself instructed us to "Let your light so shine before men, that they may see your good works and glorify your Father in heaven" (Matthew 5:16).

These good works are tailor-made for each believer. Wherever you live, work, go to school, shop, hang out, or spend time, God has tailor-made certain fruit that He wants to produce in your life to meet the needs of starving people in your corner of the world. Men sometimes say to me, "Johnny, I wish I could bring you down to where I work and let you minister to the people there." While I'd love going down to minister to those people, I can think of something much more exciting, and that's *you* going to where you already are and ministering to those people.

If you're a believer, the same Holy Spirit who produces fruit in my life also lives in you, producing the same fruit. Let Him do His work! God has people in your life *right now* who need to taste Christ's fruit through you. I'll never be able to minister to them, but you can.

Almighty God enables you to do unique good works, tailor-made to your situation in life. Ephesians 2:10 tells us, "We are His workmanship, created in Christ Jesus for good works, which God prepared beforehand that we should walk in them." Each believing man has his own ministry to fulfill. We don't need to compete with other believers in the will of God.

6. The principle of the praise of the Spirit

Yet another kind of spiritual fruit in your life is the praise of your lips. Hebrews 13:15 instructs us to "continually offer the sacrifice of praise to God."

A "sacrifice of praise" means that you give thanks to your Lord. While Old Testament worshipers brought the fruit of the field for sacrifice to God, New Testament worshipers bring the fruit of their lips for praise to God.

One of the main reasons God commands us to regularly gather for worship is to praise and thank Him. "Thank You, Jesus," we should be saying. "You woke me up again this morning, gave me a good week, and kept me alive. The obituary columns were full every day this week, but I'm still alive."

God has numbered each of our days (see Psalm 139:16). The only reason you're still breathing is because God gave you the breath to breathe, so praise His name and thank Him for His goodness to you.

What kind of praise should we offer? I can imagine all kinds of praise in our churches, other than anything cold and dead. I've heard people say, "I feel uncomfortable in that church because they applaud. Some folk even holler 'amen' and 'glory!' I think I'll find a church more conducive to my preference of worship." I'd say, go back to Hebrews 13:15 and make sure that your attitude toward worship is based in the Word of God.

Every church ought to be a thankful, grateful, praising body. The words spoken, sung, or even shouted ought to praise and glorify God. At the same time, though, forced praise is empty praise. Just as you don't have to force a tree to produce a certain kind of fruit, so you shouldn't try to force a certain kind of praise in church.

If I were to walk into a church and someone said, "Just raise your hands and praise the Lord," I'd think, *You don't have to force me to do that.* Or maybe at another church someone says, "Notice that the bulletin says we don't applaud here." Others might say, "Please understand, we do not raise our hands here." Why force it, one way or another? Fruit just *is*; you don't force it either way.

Please don't tell me what I can or can't do in His presence. He's God and He owns this world. If He puts it on my heart to stand and shout, then I'm going to stand and shout. You don't force praise into some predetermined mold. I've gone to church some days not feeling well. But when the fruit of praise passed my lips, something changed. I didn't force it, nor did I determine ahead of time what it had to be. But in genuine, unforced praise and thanksgiving, I met God. And through it, He changed my world.

Results vs. Fruit

A big difference exists between results and fruit. For one thing, while results don't necessarily create more results, fruit always has the potential to bear more fruit. Fruit produces seeds that can be planted to produce more fruit, while results often are one-and-done.

Second, Jesus wants our fruit to remain, not disappear. "I chose you and appointed you that you should go and bear fruit, and that your fruit should remain," He said (John 15:16). Results don't always remain, but spiritual fruit *always* remains. I'm interested in producing fruit that remains.

One night years ago I flew to Asheville, North Carolina, to do a joint service for two churches. A man in his fifties got saved, along with a little girl and two little boys. After the service, a young lady approached to speak with me.

"I don't expect you to remember me," she said, "but my mother told me that I shouldn't leave without telling you the story." I noticed some other young women had joined her. "Do you see these girls standing around me?" she asked.

"Yes," I said.

"Do you remember preaching in Southport, North Carolina, in 1987, in the month of June?"

"Yes, I did the state convention. Best I remember, it was a thousand-seat building and we had eleven hundred teenagers there."

"I want you to know that my girlfriends all got saved that week," she continued, "and they're here tonight to thank you. I also want you to know I was already a Christian. I took them with me so they could get saved. God not only saved them, but God called me to full-time Christian service. I just graduated from seminary. It's been eight years since I saw you, and now I'm the children's minister of this church."

That's fruit that remains!

This young woman and her friends were not the "results" of my ministry, but they certainly were "fruit" from the ministry of the true vine. I didn't struggle to see her get saved; I was just a branch, connected to the vine.

If you feel concerned about whether Jesus really drew a certain person to Himself, then write down that person's name and in a year find out where he is. And for the record, I never get as concerned over how many people respond to some message I give as much as I do over how many of them are still walking with Jesus a year later. I want fruit that remains.

Prepare for a Bumper Crop

Jesus came to earth that you might have life and have it more abundantly. So, how can you have that abundant life?

Make sure you're saved. Let no question remain in your mind whether you belong to the true vine. Settle that question for good, and then yield yourself in total submission to Jesus.

Let the Lord do what He chooses to do through your life. Remember, if you're a branch, you can't do a thing on your own. Jesus said emphatically, "Without Me you can do nothing" (John 15:5). But with Him?

Prepare yourself for a bumper crop.

Part 2

TRANSFORMED BY JESUS

7

CHANGED FROM
THE INSIDE OUT

A friend once wrote an article about New Year's resolutions that got picked up by *USA Today*. Approximately 75 percent of the adults surveyed for the article said they believed every person's life had an ultimate purpose and plan. Almost 90 percent of respondents said they thought it was important to pursue a higher purpose and meaning in life, and 67 percent agreed with the statement, "A major priority in my life is finding my deeper purpose."

Do you agree with that statement? Do you believe *your* life has a higher purpose and meaning?

The Bible makes it clear that finding and fulfilling your life's purpose as a Christian man ought to energize you. It ought to launch you out of bed each morning. Everything you and I do should revolve around living out God's purpose for our lives.

But what *is* that life's purpose? Do you know God's purpose and calling for your life? Where is your life heading? Are you moving forward? Do you know where your current direction will take you?

Christian men have no higher calling than to become like Christ. God created you and me to have a growing relationship with Him, and Jesus made this possible by applying His righteousness to our account through His work on the cross.

What would be the downside if you were to become like the One who died for you? How might your life benefit from becoming increasingly like Jesus?

A Certain Destiny

Let's first establish that God's purpose and plan for us really is to become like His Son, Jesus Christ. It turns out, that's very easy to do.

The apostle Paul declared that all Christians are "predestined to be conformed to the image" of God's Son (Romans 8:29). The apostle John declares that our ultimate destiny is to be like Jesus: "Beloved, now we are children of God; and it has not yet been revealed what we shall be, but we know that when He is revealed, we shall be like Him, for we shall see Him as He is" (1 John 3:2). Think of it! When Jesus Christ returns to this earth, all those who have placed their faith in Him will be *totally* and *completely* conformed to His likeness. What a day that will be!

Until that day, however, Scripture declares that God wants us to continually cooperate with His Spirit to move us closer and closer to the way Jesus thinks and acts and operates. Paul told a group of Christian believers that he labored very hard for them, like a woman giving birth, "until Christ is formed in you" (Galatians 4:19). He told some other Christians that "the life of Jesus" should be displayed even in their bodies (2 Corinthians 4:10-11). As we walk with Jesus, Paul declared that we are progressively transformed into the "image" of Jesus, "from glory to glory, just as by the Spirit of the Lord" (2 Corinthians 3:18). He explained that God gave us apostles, prophets, evangelists, pastors, and teachers to help us grow together as Christians, "till we all come to the unity of the faith and of the knowledge of the Son of God, to a perfect man, to the measure of the stature of the fullness of Christ" (Ephesians 4:13).

Believing men are to reflect Jesus' attitudes (Philippians 2:4-5) and His actions (1 Peter 2:21-23). John claims that the man who says he abides in Jesus "ought himself also to walk just as He walked" (1 John 2:6). We are to "imitate" Jesus (1 Corinthians 11:1; 1 Thessalonians 1:6), as the Lord Himself told His disciples after He washed their dirty feet: "I have given you an example, that you should do as I have done to you" (John 13:15).

Do you want to become increasingly like Jesus? That is God's goal for you in this life, and it's also His ultimate purpose for you in the life to come. And how does the Lord plan to accomplish this miracle? He intends to change you from the inside out, using the same divine tool He used to bring you into His family in the first place: grace.

Endowed with Moral Power

God's grace does not merely set you free from the penalty of sin; it also endows you with moral power. It makes a decisive difference for good in your life. Listen to the apostle Paul:

> For the grace of God that brings salvation has appeared to all men, teaching us that, denying ungodliness and worldly lusts, we should live soberly, righteously, and godly in the present age, looking for the blessed hope and glorious appearing of our great God and Savior Jesus Christ, who gave Himself for us, that He might redeem us from every lawless deed and purify for Himself His own special people, zealous for good works (Titus 2:11-14).

Jesus doesn't save you only from your past, but He purifies you to be a part of His own special people, eager to do what's right. God wants you and me to be on fire to do good works.

Every Christian man has been given a radical new nature that enables him to become increasingly like Christ. When God saved me, He not only called me to Himself, He also enabled me by grace to become conformed to the image of Jesus. I need more than God's call; I need His help! And God gives it to me through His grace. He enables you and me to reflect our new nature in Christ through a radically new way of living.

When a man is genuinely saved and given new life in Jesus, a transformation occurs. God changes him from the inside out. A metamorphosis begins, not only of his nature but of his manner of living. The Christian's new nature, new disposition, and the indwelling Holy Spirit all mean a redeemed man simply cannot continue to live in gross sin, bereft of any outward evidence of his new holy and righteous nature. Paul wrote in Galatians 2:20, "I have been crucified with Christ; it is no longer I who live, but Christ lives in me; and the life which I now live in the flesh I live by faith in the Son of God, who loved me and gave Himself for me."

John MacArthur has said, "By his divine grace, Jesus Christ completely reprograms our computers, as it were. He throws away the old disc and deletes the previous programs, all of which were permeated with error and destructive viruses, and graciously replaces them with his own divine truth and righteousness."[4]

The Goal of Grace

Almost a century and a half after its publication, the number one song in religious circles around the world today is still "Amazing Grace" by John Newton, first published in 1779. What makes grace so amazing? What is the goal of grace?

Remember how Titus 2:11-12 puts it: "The grace of God that brings salvation has appeared to all men, teaching us that, denying ungodliness and worldly lusts, we should live soberly, righteously, and godly in the present age." The same grace that saved me also teaches me. Before I ever heard a sermon against getting drunk, the grace of God already had taught me that I was a drunkard. God started preparing me to change my life before I ever heard a gospel sermon.

What does Paul mean that grace "teaches" us? He means that grace instructs us, trains us, disciplines us, educates us, nurtures us, and chastises us. The "teaching" of grace has two sides, one negative and the other positive.

1. Grace teaches us to say no

Before I came to faith, I said yes to a mountain of ugly things. How did I learn to say no? Grace taught me. It not only *told* me, it *enabled* me. Grace teaches us that we must come to a conscious, willful repudiation of all thoughts, words, and actions that oppose true godliness.

The verb "teaches" is in the present tense, indicating a continuing process. No one ever graduates from the school of God's grace. There will never come a time on this earth where you can say, "Thank God, I finally graduated from all that grace wanted to teach me." So long as you breathe, you will continue to receive instruction in Christ's school of grace.

Grace teaches, in part, by warning us. One of the most famous lines of "Amazing Grace" says, "'Twas grace that taught my heart to fear, and grace my fears relieved." One reason why I love the old hymns so much is that many of them were written by great preachers who taught great theology. God saved John Newton out of the miserable life of a slave trader and made him into a preacher and theologian with a broad understanding of God's Word.

Grace also teaches by enabling us. When I was twenty years old, I accepted a man's invitation to visit his church—and immediately I got under conviction. God began dealing with me about my sins and the Holy Spirit began calling me to Himself. It all made me very nervous. A lady standing beside me must have noticed, because she said, "Wouldn't you like to be saved today?"

I really wanted to say yes, but back in those days I was timid and shy, and so I replied, "No, not today."

In the next few moments I heard the preacher say, "There's a man here whom God's speaking to. Let's pray that God will bring him back tonight and save him." Gulp! On the way home, I told my wife that the preacher was talking about me, which led to an interesting conversation.

Back in those days, I loved to gamble, and I won a lot of money playing pool. I would go to the Red Fox Saloon, drink embalming fluid with a bunch of guys, and come home loaded a couple of nights a week. I was completely irreligious. No one in my family *ever* went to church. After that first visit to church, I said to my wife, "Janet, tonight I'm going back to that church, and I'm going to give my life to Jesus Christ."

But one thought plagued me. *What if God doesn't change me? I mean, look at me! If God doesn't change me, I'll come with a Christian label, but I won't have the power to live a new life.*

I knew very well how deeply into sin I'd fallen, and I wanted out. But I also knew I didn't have the strength, on my own, to begin a new, clean life. So I told Janet, "If He doesn't change me, honey, you leave me, because I'll be right back at the saloon." I actually spoke those words.

But guess what happened? That night, I encountered the living Jesus Christ, who saved me and changed me. Since that day, Janet has never once had to come down to the saloon to retrieve me.

Before then, I'd never heard anyone teach the Ten Commandments, but in the first few weeks after my conversion, the grace of God taught me to clean up my language and stop taking the Lord's name in vain (a nasty habit of mine). And He didn't just tell me to clean it up; He empowered me to clean it up.

What does Paul mean that we must "deny ungodliness"? The word "deny" carries the idea of a conscious, purposeful action of the will. It means to say *no!* It's to confess and consciously turn away from anything sinful and destructive and to move toward that which is good and godly. The word "ungodliness" refers to a lack of true reverence for and devotion to God. The original Greek word describes the opposite of godliness; it speaks of defiance toward God's person or hostility toward God's sacred place.

In the church, we hardly ever see defiance toward God's person, but you'll often hear someone say, "I'm a Christian, but I am not going to church." That's defiance toward God's place. If you claim to be a Christian, you'd better learn to get together with God's people, or you'll be one miserable dude when (if?) you get to heaven.

The word "ungodliness" shows up as the adjective "profane" or "godless" in Hebrews 12:16 to describe a man named Esau, the eldest son of Isaac. John Phillips said, "Profane means that there was no sacred enclosure in his life where God could dwell."

If you could open Esau's life and see the spot where Jesus Christ wanted to live, you would not have seen any sacred enclosure where the sacred could dwell. *No place for God!* Can you be in church and have place for lots of religious activities, but have no place for God? Absolutely.

William Barclay, one of the greatest Bible word scholars ever, said, "The word for godless...was used for ground that was profane, in contradistinction to ground that was consecrated. The ancient world had its religions into which only the initiated could come. 'Godless' was a word for the person who was uninitiated and uninterested, in contradistinction to the man who was devout. It was applied to Jews who had become apostates and had forsaken God."[5]

What is an apostate? An apostate is someone who comes very close to making a commitment to Jesus Christ but never quite takes the leap. Eventually he turns away, leaves, and never returns. The term is related to our word *threshold*. Maybe someone is in church, active, and moving toward God. Maybe the man gets as far as the threshold, the place where you enter…and he stops and turns away. That man could be called "godless," regardless of the amount of time he'd spent in church doing religious activities.

Could it be that we have thousands of men in our churches who came to the threshold, but who never quite entered in? When we get to eternity, we'll find out why they never spoke about their faith, or gave, or displayed the fruit of the Spirit in their lives. In fact, they had never crossed the threshold. They had never fully embraced Jesus. They had never fully bought in to the gospel.

They were godless.

Godless describes the man whose mind recognizes nothing higher than the earth, for whom nothing is sacred, and who has no reverence for the unseen. A godless man has no awareness of or interest in God. He is completely earthbound in his thoughts, aims, and pleasures.

Esau's problem was that he treated spiritual things as of no account, and then proved it by selling his birthright to satisfy his appetite. The entire Old Testament might have been written differently had Esau obeyed God. Rather than speaking of Abraham, Isaac, and Jacob, we might be speaking about Abraham, Isaac, and Esau. Although Esau was the firstborn, he cared nothing for its significance. Esau had the right to become the family priest, but the role didn't interest him. He cared nothing about landing in the genealogical tree of Jesus Christ. We trace the family line of Jesus Christ back to Jacob, but could it have been traced back to Esau? As the firstborn, Esau could have inherited a double portion of his father's property, but he preferred immediate gratification instead of waiting for the best. And so the Bible calls him "godless."

Are you sacrificing the eternal for the temporal? Do you care for earth more than for heaven? We have many men in the church who supposedly live for the Lord, but then just check out. In the South, we have a word for those who hang around for a while but then stop living for Jesus. We call them backsliders. So how long can a man remain backslidden?

Suppose a man makes a profession of faith and remains in the church for six months, but then for the next thirty years he lives as a drunkard, a fornicator, a thief, or a robber. In his case, whatever happened to enabling grace? Did God not give him the promise He gave me? Did the man receive something that didn't work? Or did he never really receive it at all?

Suppose another man grew up in a Christian home. In preschool he sang "Jesus Loves the Little Children" in the choir. When he grew older, he got active in Awana, where he could quote scores of Bible verses and learned all about Christian character traits. As a middle schooler, he traveled with a mission group to Cleveland, Ohio, where he gave out gospel tracts on the street. In high school, he joined the senior high choir and took a mission trip to Argentina.

Did attending Awana make that man a Christian?

Did joining the student choirs make him a Christian?

Did going on a mission trip make him a Christian?

Those are all good things, aren't they? Don't we feel good about them? That's the wrong question. The right question is this: Does that man have a sacred enclosure in his life where God lives? All of the other stuff is good, but it's not God.

But what if a man walks down an aisle in response to an evangelist's appeal? Is that man saved? It all depends on his motive. If he really gave his life to Jesus, then his subsequent life will show it. If not, his grace is not amazing; it's pitiful. That man has no sacred enclosure for God.

Do you have a sacred enclosure for God? Deep in your own heart, are you godly or ungodly? Do you look more like Abraham or his grandson Esau?

Esau grew up with great light. It was the duty of every godly daddy to tell his sons the sacred stories so they wouldn't forget how good God had been to them. I can picture Esau as a little boy getting placed on his granddaddy's knee and hearing Abraham say, "Let me tell you about Mount Moriah." God gave Abraham spiritual insight to look into the future, and I'm sure he spoke of it. Esau had every opportunity, as much as any person in his time, of knowing and following God. He didn't come from a godless family. And yet, somehow, Esau did not have a sacred enclosure for God. Despite his godly heritage, Esau was a godless man.

How do you know if a man really belongs to God? If a saved man strays from God, he normally doesn't stray for long because grace teaches, trains, and chastises him. Grace takes him to the woodshed.

But what if that man sins as freely as he breathes and never says, with tears of brokenness, "Look what I'm doing to my Savior"? Then that man has no sacred enclosure for God. He's godless.

Decades ago, when I worried aloud to my wife about whether I could become a Christian, she told me, "Johnny, He'll change you. Go ahead tonight when Mr. Gibson gives the invitation. Go down front, honey, and give your life to Jesus Christ. God will change you." And He did!

I wish I could say that I never sinned after I came to faith, but that'd be a lie. I sin, but I can't sin and be happy about it. I always feel dirty afterward. I can't wait to get right with God.

When God calls you to a new life, He doesn't call you merely to move away from something; He also calls you to move toward something else. It's not just what you deny, it's also what you embrace.

2. Grace teaches us to say yes

A born-again man is no longer under the dominion of Satan and of sin. He's been radically changed and given a new nature. He's called and enabled to live a godly life. God gives him the power to reflect his new nature through a radically new way of living.

When a man trusts Christ, he becomes a witness to the work of Christ in his life. If he should witness to someone how Jesus has changed his life, he will testify not only with his lips, but his life will also do some talking. Observers will see a significant change in him. When a man is genuinely saved and given new life in Jesus Christ, he undergoes a radical transformation. A metamorphosis takes place.

God changes you from the inside out. You begin to feel differently within. You act differently, you think differently, and essentially God makes you into a different person. God gives you His nature, His disposition, and because of the indwelling Holy Spirit, you simply cannot continue to live in rebellion and sin. God's righteous nature becomes a growing reality inside of you.

If you're going to make an impact in your lifetime, it won't be because of what you quit doing; it will be because of what you start doing. The chaff will blow away and the fruit will blossom, once the new man becomes dominant in your life. Titus 2:12 says that every converted man "should live soberly, righteously, and godly in the present age."

What does it mean to live "soberly" or sensibly? We must develop a sound mind. A saved man has control over the issues of his life and exercises self-restraint over his passions and desires. No Spirit-filled man lets himself get out of control, for he is being tutored and taught by grace. He is under the control of Jesus. The believing man is enabled to be conformed to the mind of Christ, which governs his passions and desires.

This doesn't mean that once you place your faith in Jesus Christ, your passions and desires disappear, never again tempting you to sin. Your passions and desires don't vanish, but they do come under the enabling control of Jesus Christ. That's why it's wrong for a man to say, "Wow, I don't know how I just did that." I know *exactly* how he did it. Give me about thirty seconds apart from Jesus Christ and the enabling power of His grace, and I'll do the same thing. I understand why Charles Spurgeon said about men on death row, "But by the grace of God, there go I."

Paul also calls us to live "righteously." Our faith in Christ ought to change our relationships with believers and nonbelievers alike. The term denotes conduct that cannot be condemned. People can talk about you, lie about you, they can even theorize about you, but they can say nothing truly damaging about you, because you have lived a righteous life that cannot be condemned. *Thayer's Greek-English Lexicon of the New Testament* says that the root of this word is "right." God wants us to live right, observing both divine and human laws.

As I thought about this verse from Titus, my wife and I pulled up to a stoplight. No cars were coming and I said, "I'm going to run it."

"You'd better not," she warned me.

Immediately I thought, *If I do run it, I won't be able to discuss this text with integrity.*

The word "righteously" means to conduct yourself in such a way that no one has any reason to condemn you. Had I run that light (which I didn't), and a police officer had seen me, he would have had all the reason in the world to condemn me. Righteousness requires of us a light and a truth in all of our dealings. It means we live with integrity.

I've tried to teach men about integrity, but it's not an easy word to define. A dictionary will tell you it means wholeness, completeness, truthfulness. Thayer says it means whole in every area of your life, complete and truthful in every area of your life.

Maybe a man looks good at church, but he's a shady car dealer at work. He's an excellent lawyer, but he cheats on his taxes. He's a reliable mechanic, but a dishonest student. No, a righteous man is right in *every* area. We are to live in such a way that in no area of our lives or conduct can others rightfully condemn us. People should be able to speak about us without using a comma: "I believe he loves Jesus, *but*..." Why shouldn't they be able to use a period or an exclamation point instead?

The Bible warns us not to "give place to the devil" (Ephesians 4:27), especially since Satan needs only one area to bring us down. We are therefore to live soberly, sensibly, righteously. We're to live as godly men.

If an ungodly man has no sacred enclosure for Jesus Christ in his life, then to be godly means I'm devout. Someone ought to be able to say, "He is a devout Christian, committed to Jesus." We are to *live* godly. The verb speaks of a man's regular manner of life. If you're married, your wife should be able to say of you, "He's a godly man." Listen, if you can be a godly man at home, then you can be a godly man anywhere. But if you're not a godly man at home, then how can you be a godly man anywhere else? What makes you think you can suddenly start to act in a godly way on a business trip? Deep in the spirit of his will, a godly man consciously denies ungodliness. An attitude of supreme devotion to God has replaced his old attitude of indifference.

Finally, Paul says that we are to "live soberly, righteously, and godly *in the present age*." That means right now. God expects this of us *now*. Those who receive the teaching of the grace of God are enabled to live in this way *at this moment*. His grace in us therefore becomes a powerful testimony to the saving and transforming power of Jesus Christ. When people watch us, they ought to be asking, "What in the world is the difference? How does that man say no?"

God saved us in order that He might demonstrate His glorious grace to others. He produces in us the desire to do what is right and good, thereby giving glory to our Lord Jesus Christ. As that happens, we righteously impact the lives of nonbelievers, in His name. For that reason, the Lord Jesus Christ commanded us to live in such a way "that they may see your good works and glorify your Father in heaven" (Matthew 5:16). *Really?* Absolutely.

Janet's grandmother, Selma Allen, was a wonderful, godly lady. Before my conversion, she persistently kept after me to go to church. Sometimes we would accompany her to a Sunday service. When someone would make an appeal for the morning offering, I'd reach in my pocket, hoping that I had a one dollar bill. I'd think, *Ain't no way I'm giving them a twenty.*

That all changed after I came to faith in Christ. How did I change from trying to make sure I gave God the smallest thing I had to where I want to give him more and more and more? What made the difference? Back then, grace hadn't yet appeared in my life. But when God made His grace known to me and brought me to faith, that same grace began to teach me to do what's right in every area of my life. He's still teaching me, thank God! And His grace will continue to teach me until I see Him face-to-face.

The Priority of Pursuing

Despite all of the apostle Paul's accomplishments, he made it clear that he considered himself still "on the way" in his Christian life. He admitted, "I press on, that I may lay hold of that for which Christ Jesus has also laid hold of me" (Philippians 3:12).

The Greek word translated "press on" was often used of a sprinter. It also referred to a person who acted aggressively and energetically. Paul *pursued* his relationship with Christ with all of his might. Since he wanted to be holy, he pressed on to become more holy. He strained every spiritual muscle to win the prize set before him. And what was that prize?

To be like Jesus.

To become more like Jesus, you have to press on. You have to keep moving when you decide you want to get up early in the morning to spend the first hour of your day with your Lord. That may be a new challenge for you; maybe it's never been part of your routine. But if you want to be more like Jesus, then you need to do some of the same things He did, and one of the things He did regularly was to rise early and spend some unhurried, uninterrupted time with His Father.

What would it take for you to have an unhurried quiet time with Jesus? Would you need to get up fifteen or thirty minutes earlier than usual? I know I need that time with the Lord. It helps me to start off my day right. I journal, I read, I pray. And I don't always feel like doing any of those things. Many times I feel like spending more time in bed. But I press on. I keep moving.

A Total Change Within

God changes us from the inside out. His Holy Spirit takes up residence within us and from there starts a total renovation of our character, our behavior, and our lives.

Where I was a drunkard, God freed me.

Where I was a liar, God gave me truth.

Where I was profane, God made me holy.

God's grace affects my conversation. If I get angry with some-body, I don't talk to him the same way I used to. The Bible says, "Let your speech always be with grace, seasoned with salt" (Colossians 4:6). Grace affects *everything* in your life, enabling you to live a holy and godly life. That's the moral power of grace.

God calls us to demonstrate His saving power in our lives. By this, we show Him to be a loving God; and by this, we glorify Him and draw others to Him. That's what grace does!

I never took a course that taught me how to live sober, but grace taught me.

I never took a course on how not to take God's name in vain, but grace taught me.

I never took a course on how to stop street fighting, but grace taught me.

I never took a course on how to speak to my mother, but grace taught me.

I never took a course on how to treat my wife, but grace taught me. Grace taught me how to treat Janet like a lady. I'm ashamed of the way I treated her before I got saved. The Spirit of God would have quite a time with me if I tried to talk to Janet like I used to before I got saved! But He forgave me. He not only pardoned me of my foul mouth, but He purged me of it. He cleansed me of it and washed away my sin.

The grace of God in Jesus Christ is our teacher. It's our guide, our counselor. The moment we get saved, we immediately come under the tutelage of God through the Holy Spirit and His Word.

Grace is God's primary tool to change us...from the inside out.

8

KEEP THE BALL
IN PLAY

Major League Baseball and its rabid fans keep records on nearly everything that happens in almost every ballgame ever played. One statistic, however, gets only part-time attention, and then only unofficially. If you were to ask, "Who holds the record for hitting the most foul balls in one at-bat?," you'd get several conflicting answers.

Roy Thomas, who played from 1899–1911, unofficially fouled off twenty-two balls in one at-bat, twenty-four in another appearance at the plate, and in yet another at-bat, "maybe" twenty-seven. That's a lot of foul balls!

In the modern era, two players apparently share the unofficial record. On June 26, 1998, Ricky Gutierrez fouled off fourteen times before he struck out. Six years later, on May 12, Alex Cora fouled off fourteen consecutive pitches before hitting a home run on the eighteenth pitch thrown to him.

But no doubt the most interesting (and painful) unofficial record in this category belongs to Richie Ashburn, who played in the big leagues from 1948–1962. As an outfielder for the Philadelphia

Phillies, Ashburn earned a reputation for fouling off pitches in order to prolong his at-bats. In one inning, he fouled off fourteen pitches. One of his foul balls in that plate appearance hit a spectator in the face, breaking her nose. The game continued as medical personnel carried her away on a stretcher—and Ashburn promptly hit another foul ball that struck the poor woman *again*.

Who could blame the lady if she never showed up for another game?

While foul balls in baseball may prolong a difficult at-bat, I don't know of *any* player who'd choose to hit a foul ball rather than get a hit. Two foul balls means two strikes, and if an opposing player catches a foul ball before it touches the ground, the batter's out. Although hitting a lot of foul balls can give a batter more chances to get a hit, and perhaps tire out the pitcher, they're largely a waste of energy.

In life, foul balls have far fewer positive traits. We all hit them occasionally, but they don't help us move forward. They tire *us* out while giving the enemy of our souls a better chance to tag us out. While thinking along these lines in a morning Bible study, I said, "All of us in life have hit foul balls." A man in the audience immediately turned around—it turned out to be Otis Nixon, formerly with the Atlanta Braves—and said, "I've hit a lot of foul balls. It's better than striking out."

True enough…in baseball. In life, though, I pray that God would help us to live more productively than that. Instead of consistently hitting out of bounds, let's learn to keep the ball in play. Let's make it a habit to move our Christian brothers around the bases. Remember, we're in this thing to win—and foul balls simply don't align us with God's Word. To the contrary, they get us off trajectory, and too often they take us out of the game altogether.

From the Outside to the Inside

When I came to faith in Jesus, God saved me and gave me a new nature. The moment I believed, God transformed the inner me. Now, I want the transformation that already took place inside me to become evident on the outside. I want the watching world to be able to see the positive changes in me that the Lord has produced. I want my life to progressively align with the wealth of knowledge I'm gaining from the Word of God.

This outward transformation is made possible by an inner change *in my mind*. I don't always think right. I need God to continually take my foul thoughts, change their trajectory, and give me a line drive in fair territory. The Spirit gives Christian men the power and the desire to transform their minds. A simple formula describes what happens:

Transformed hearts + renewed minds = aligned lives

While the Bible lays out a clear process for renewing our minds (which we'll see in a moment), it also warns us that we have a battle on our hands. Ever since Adam, the natural, carnal mind is at war with God. It refuses to submit to Him and has no interest in obeying His instructions; in fact, it *cannot* obey since it lacks any power to do so. None of us with a mind "set on the flesh" can please God (see Romans 8:5-8). *That's* our problem.

So what's the solution?

Paul writes, "And do not be conformed to this world, but be transformed by the renewing of your mind, that you may prove what is that good and acceptable and perfect will of God" (Romans 12:2). Without renewed minds, we will live our entire lives on earth without ever pleasing the One who made us and redeemed us for His purpose.

The central question is, do you and I want to please God? Do we want to know and do His good, acceptable, and perfect will? If we do, then we need to learn how to cooperate with the Spirit of God in the process of renewing our mind. A renewed mind is a spiritually sensitive mind, and the Bible says, "To be spiritually minded is life and peace" (Romans 8:6).

Who doesn't want *that*?

The How of Renewal

The primary tool God uses in this fight is the Word of God. David said to the Lord, "Your word I have hidden in my heart, that I might not sin against You" (Psalm 119:11). When we put God's Word in our hearts, the Lord uses what's there to bring about remarkable changes in our behavior.

If you want to transform your mind, you must learn how to think biblically. In practice, that means you need to learn to think like Jesus. But how can you think Jesus' thoughts without knowing Jesus' words? In the Gospels, we see Jesus at work and hear Him speak. If we want to become like Him, we have to become intimately familiar with His story as told in Scripture.

As we listen to Jesus' words, meditate on His interactions with others, read of His miracles, and see His power over sin and the devil, in effect, we gaze upon His life. As we are "beholding" Him, we "are being transformed into the same image from glory to glory, just as by the Spirit of the Lord" (2 Corinthians 3:18). The more we behold Jesus' glory, the more we reflect that glory.

In Greek, the word translated "beholding" is in the present middle tense, which means God doesn't *make* you behold Jesus' glory. You don't change because the Lord forces you to change. You change because you continually desire to behold His glory, and that glorious sight changes you. To keep growing in Christ, to continue the process of spiritual transformation, you must keep on beholding Jesus, right up to the time of your homegoing. Our bodies may decline and our physical strength may wane, but the glory of Jesus can continue to shine through our lives.

I long to be further along tonight than I was this morning, and tomorrow I want to be further along than today. I'm still being changed, step by step. I won't get transformed into the likeness of Christ by New Year's resolutions, trying harder, or promising to do better next time. I can change, from one degree of glory to another, only by continuing to behold the glory of Christ Jesus.

Do you want to get in on this? You can—but you have to choose it. The Spirit of God changes us as we willingly surrender and respond to Him in obedience. He does not force us to obey; He empowers us to obey. There is a very large difference! John Piper, commenting on Romans 12:2, put it this way: "What, then, do we do in obedience to this truth? We join the Holy Spirit in His precious and all-important work. We pursue Christ-exalting truth."[6] We *pursue* it. It's a personal, with-all-our-heart pursuit.

Are you pursuing Christ-exalting truth? Are you striving to get to know the Bible, the Word of God? Are you praying that the truth you learn in Scripture enables you to humbly embrace the changes that God wants to bring about in you?

As the Holy Spirit transforms your mind through God's Word, He transforms your living. Over time, you become "fully mature in Christ" (Colossians 1:28 NIV). Oh, you'll still have room for growth. In this life, you and I will never get to the point where we have no room for further spiritual development. Renewal of the mind and conformity to the likeness of Christ take place gradually. It's not as though you get up one morning, spend an hour with the Lord, and say, "Well, there it is! I'm *there*. Praise the Lord, I made it!" No, it's an extended process (the Bible calls it "sanctification") in which the mind gradually gets adjusted to thinking more like Christ.

A Twofold Process

As the process of sanctification unfolds in your life, keep in mind two equal but distinct truths about how it works.

1. The instant you put your faith in Jesus, God completely dealt with the penalty of your sin. Jesus suffered both death and separation from God *for you.* That issue is taken care of totally, once and for all. Nothing more can happen there or ever will happen there. You are "in Christ," and that means God sees you as though you're as righteous as Jesus Himself. Some Bible teachers call this *positional truth.*

2. In your experience on earth, God did not change you once and for all, forever. When you came to faith, you did *not* immediately become the person you'll be in eternity. That's why the Lord calls you to increasingly live out the eternal life He's already given you. Some Bible teachers call this *experiential truth.*

This twofold reality about sanctification explains why Paul told his Philippian friends, "Work out your own salvation with fear and trembling; for it is God who works in you both to will and to do for His good pleasure" (Philippians 2:12-13). God wants you to work *out* what He's already worked *in.* He doesn't, of course, leave you on your own to do this. He works in you so that you can accomplish His will, thereby giving Him great pleasure through your eager obedience.

Through sanctification, God graciously redirects your worship and affection away from worldliness and toward Jesus' image. I once read an article by G.K. Beale titled, "We Become What We Worship." Have you ever been around somebody who talks all the time about one specific issue? He never stops harping on it. It's always on his mind. When you're around a man like that, you can be pretty sure he's worshiping that thing. It consumes his attention, his time, and his devotion. Eventually, he starts becoming like that thing.

As you become increasingly like Christ—as you become conformed to His image—you are sanctified. In that way, your life becomes less and less about you and more and more about Him.

I sometimes hear men say things like, "I just can't stand Brother Billy. He really gets on my nerves, you know?" Does that look like a foul ball to you? It does to me—and I've hit more than my share. Engaging in that kind of bad behavior puts your mind on the wrong trajectory, and if you stay there, you'll remain in foul territory. Every now and then, God will speak to you and me and whisper to our hearts, "Son, you need to get in fair territory." At those moments, in Christ-honoring humility, we must learn to say, "You're right, Lord, and I'm wrong. Forgive me, and help me to do what pleases You." God can work in our hearts as we embrace godly choices, but He doesn't make us embrace any of them (although He can make things awfully uncomfortable for us until we obey).

When your life aligns with God's Word, you stay in fair territory and your actions bring glory to your Lord. As you stop hitting foul balls, you find your life's calling…and that's when the real fun begins.

Construction Materials for a Christian Mind

Transformed hearts and renewed minds ultimately lead to an aligned life. This process of renewal begins inwardly but manifests itself outwardly. If Christ is working inside of us and is really changing us, His inward work will change us outwardly. We can't keep it inside!

It's ludicrous to talk about being a Christian if the Spirit of God has not invaded your life and begun changing it. It'd be like saying you're an active Major League Baseball player even though you're blind and paralyzed, or that you're going to fly from Atlanta to Boston without your feet ever leaving the ground. The idea is both ridiculous and impossible.

In order to change your behavior on the outside (to match Jesus), you need to first change your thinking on the inside (to match Jesus). You need to construct a biblical mind. How does God build a biblical mind in us? He uses the blueprint of the Bible along with the right building materials. In Philippians 4:8, God lists for us the materials for constructing a biblical mind:

> Finally, brethren, whatever things are true, whatever things are noble, whatever things are just, whatever things are pure, whatever things are lovely, whatever things are of good report, if there is any virtue and if there is anything praiseworthy—meditate on these things.

In considering this list, this saying comes to mind: "You are not what you think you are, but what you think, you are." Scripture leaves no doubt that our lives are the product of our thoughts. It's something like a computer: garbage in, garbage out. Put the wrong thing into someone's mind and out will come the error you put in. Jesus said, "What comes out of a man, that defiles a man. For from within, out of the heart of men, proceed evil thoughts, adulteries, fornications, murders, thefts, covetousness, wickedness, deceit, lewdness, an evil eye, blasphemy, pride, foolishness" (Mark 7:20-22). Notice that "evil thoughts" appear first on Jesus' list. A troubled mind makes a convenient depository for seeds of doubt, despair, and wickedness.

Adrian Rogers put it this way: "The devil had rather get you to think wrong than to do wrong, because if you do wrong but you still think right, you'll get right. But if you do wrong because you think wrong, you'll continue to do wrong because you think you're right."[7] Since the devil wins if he can get hold of your mind, let's take a closer look at the building materials for constructing a biblical mind.

True

When the Bible speaks of truth, it refers not only to the Christian's accurate apprehension of reality, but to every phase of his conduct. I should not only *think* truth, I should conduct my life in a way that reflects truth.

The "belt of truth" holds everything together in Paul's description of the Christian's armor in Ephesians 6. The ancient belt didn't just go around the waist, but extended down to a man's loins. The image speaks of integrity and truth keeping everything together.

You can have everything in the world going for you—you can be intellectual, you can be wealthy, you can have great influence—but if you buy into a lie, you'll have nothing in the end. When a man thinks falsehoods, before long his outer life reflects the inner lies he's accepted.

Noble

The word translated "noble" means honorable, or that which claims respect. The Greek term carries the idea of serious as opposed to frivolous. Believing men shouldn't camp on what is trivial, temporal, mundane, common, or earthly. Rather, they must train their minds to think about whatever is heavenly, worthy of adoration and praise.

Honorable thoughts produce honorable people. When you think dishonorably about a man, you often find yourself telling ugly rumors and lies about him. Someone may say, "But you don't know what he did to me!" May I remind you of what you did to

Jesus? And yet, He forgave you. I'm grateful to God that He did not give me what I deserved.

Years ago, a friend said to me, "We say that we're to love the sinner and hate his sin, but there's one thing wrong with that. The emphasis is on somebody else and not a reflection on ourselves. Why don't we say, 'We are to love the sinner and hate our sin?'" If I'm going to think biblically, it's not what I say about others, but what God has helped me to see about myself. *Then* I can start thinking as Jesus does.

Just

This term is the root of the word *righteous*, or doing what is right. It speaks of a man who faces his duty and does it. It speaks of right relationships and proper action, of fair and equitable dealings with others.

What things cause us to be right with God and with each other? We ought to contemplate them. What is in perfect harmony with God's eternal, unchanging standard as revealed in Scripture? Faithful, believing men dwell on things consistent with God's Word.

To be "just" is the opposite of doing what's convenient. My favorite Bible verse is Proverbs 20:7: "The righteous man walks in his integrity; his children are blessed after him." Am I living toward Christ and others in such a way that my conduct can win God's approval? A just person wants to do the right thing. Are you there? If not, are you willing to get there? Is that a passion of your life?

Pure

The original Greek term refers to all sorts of purity: pure thoughts, pure words, pure deeds. Purity is often defined as "holy, morally clean." Lightfoot says the word suggests "stainless."[8]

Did you know that some thoughts leave a stain that is difficult to erase? At least 35 percent of all downloads on American computers is pornography. Forty million Americans regularly visit porn sites. Every second, nearly thirty thousand users are watching Internet porn. Americans spend more than thirty billion dollars annually on porn, more than received by the entire Christian church in America. Americans spend more on porn each year than they do on Major League Baseball, the NFL, and the NBA combined. In that sort of filthy environment, how can a Christian man keep his thoughts pure?

The ancient Philippians lived in an impure environment where "anything goes" would have made an appropriate slogan. How did they combat it? They had to fill their minds with pure thoughts. Peter told his Christian friends to "gird up the loins of your mind" (1 Peter 1:13). He pictured the thought life as a flowing robe or gown. We're running a race and he said, "Pull up your gown and tie it with a rope so it won't impede your progress."

Moral purity has been a problem since ancient times. Men both then and now were and are under constant attack by a thousand temptations to violate sexual purity. How do you combat it? John says one way is to think of Jesus' return: "And everyone who has this hope in Him purifies himself, just as He is pure" (1 John 3:3). Because Jesus Christ is pure, Christian men must purify themselves. One way they do that is by reminding themselves that Jesus could return at any time.

Lovely

This Greek term is used only here in the New Testament. It could be literally translated "friendly toward." It means pleasing, agreeable, dearly prized, and worth the effort to have and embrace.

Something lovely speaks of that which is full of love. And so I pray, "Lord, help me to construct a mind that will be sweet, gracious, generous, patient, and loving."

Good report

The term means "laudable, well reported of, reputable, spoken of in a kindly spirit." When I leave this world, I want it to be said, "Pastor Johnny was an honorable, respected man of God." I intend to build my life on doing what's right—not what's most popular, not what's most palatable, but what is right. I want to earn a good reputation, and I'll do that as I continue to build a Christlike mind.

Virtuous, praiseworthy

Does your mind every now and then find itself wandering to places that are neither virtuous nor praiseworthy? Maybe it's a fractured relationship or an activity that, if widely known, would cause you a great deal of embarrassment or even shame. Don't let your mind go there.

Instead, fill your consciousness with images and thoughts that, if projected on a screen in front of your loved ones, would prompt them to express gratitude and praise. Why forfeit victory by focusing your attention on corrupt or disgraceful thoughts? Commit yourself to follow Jesus' example and seek the praise of your Father in heaven, especially in your thought life.

Two Critical Bookends

The two bookends of proper thinking are *learning* truth and *implementing* truth. It's not enough merely to know truth or to have curiosity about God's construction materials for a biblical mind. You must implement those materials by meditating on the truth you learn. Dwell on it. Welcome it. Turn it over and over again in your brain.

If you want to build a biblical mind, this is not an option for you. It's a divine command. To meditate on these things means to evaluate them carefully, consider them deeply, ponder them with a view toward putting them into practice.

Christian men must learn to stop dwelling on trivial, temporal, mundane, common, and earthly things, and instead make it a habit to marinate their thoughts on heaven-centered truth. We must train ourselves to think on things worthy of adoration and praise, things that promote godly character. If this begins to happen in your life, you'll act differently from most men. Your behavior will cause you to stand out in a crowd. As a consequence, you will build great self-respect and self-confidence.

When Paul writes, "Think on these things," he again uses a present middle imperative, which means, once more, you have a choice to make. You must *decide* to "think on these things." If you choose not to do so, your mind will go places it shouldn't go. We are responsible for our thoughts and we *can* hold them to a high and lofty ideal.

Imagine a lock and key. The key that unlocks a man's capacity to think biblically is truth. Jesus is truth. The Bible is truth. God has given you truth. The lock of obedience opens only with the key of truth. Many times we find ourselves locked out from the divine resources intended to give us victory simply because we refuse to obey. While it's easier to retain truth than it is to implement it, God wants us to release that truth and so lead us to freedom. Once we take the key (called *truth*) and place it in the lock (called *obedience*), the storehouses of God's resources swing wide open to us.

Again, you must choose. Will you choose to build a biblical mind, or will you say, "I know how I'm supposed to act, but I'm ticked off. I'm hurt." Author Kent Hughes has written, "I have great sympathy for those whose past has been a series of bad choices. I understand that, if over the years, one has chosen the impure and the negative, it is very difficult to change; but as a biblical thinker, I give no quarter to myself or anyone else who rationalizes his present choices by the past."[9]

Don't allow yourself to say, "I'm without hope. I've thought this way for so long that I see no chance of changing." That is simply not true. The Spirit of God can stop the bleeding in your life right now.

He Changes Our Wants

Several years ago, I preached at a friend's church in another state, and someone dear to me whom I hadn't seen in a very long time came unexpectedly to the service. At the close of the evening, I said, "Is there anyone in this room who would like to repent of their sins, ask God to forgive them, and place their faith in Jesus Christ?"

I saw a long arm rise up in the air, attached to a body with a very familiar face.

You can hardly imagine what it meant for me to see my first cousin there, after all those years. I had witnessed to him many times, but he'd never responded. I told the audience, "You can put your hands down." My cousin put his hand down. "Anyone else?" I continued.

His hand shot up again. James Ray wanted to make sure he'd been seen.

That night my cousin gave his life to Christ after a lifetime of alcohol abuse. He and I had been inseparable from five years of age until about age fifteen, remaining best buds that whole time. He'd married young and I had followed suit. After that, we basically went our separate ways and decades had passed. James Ray put his faith in Jesus just after his sixty-first birthday.

A couple of years later, I planned to visit his town again. By then, James Ray had developed cirrhosis of the liver and his kidneys had begun to fail. He weighed about ninety pounds. I called him to say I'd be visiting his area.

"Oh, please come and see me," he said.

"I wouldn't think about coming without seeing you," I answered.

When I arrived at his mobile home, I found him covered in blankets, with the oven on and its door down to help keep him warm.

"James Ray," I said, "tell me what's going on."

"My kidneys are failing and there's nothing else they can do, so I'm going to be leaving any minute."

"James Ray, are you ready to meet Jesus?"

"I am, but I want you to answer some questions for me. Can you take your Bible and tell me what's going to happen when I draw my last breath?"

No one had ever asked me those questions, but I did my best to answer them all. At the end, I said, "James Ray, when you get to heaven, tell my mom I said hello."

As I recall that heart-wrenching scene, my mind flashes back to a friend who got converted while still active with the Hell's Angels. I went to hear him give his testimony, as did a lot of other Hell's Angels—a rough-looking crowd. "If I'm wrong and the Bible's not true," he told us, "I still have lived a better life since I committed my life to Jesus. If I die and it's all over with, I'm still glad I made my decision. But if I'm right and the Bible's true, Romans 8:16 says that once you become a Christian, God's Spirit bears witness with your spirit. He comes to live in us. He changes our wants."

Indeed, God changed the wants of both my cousin and my friend. While my cousin had just as genuine a conversion as my Hell's Angel friend, however, James Ray's "wants" didn't change until almost the very end. A man can be overwhelmingly forgiven on his way to heaven, but that doesn't mean God removes the consequences of the way he's chosen to live for decades.

My friend, you can get past your past and the way you've thought over the years. We are free to have a Christian mind. It is within our reach! And it is our duty.

Will you choose it? Will you choose to keep the ball in play?

9

THE GREATEST POWER IN THE WORLD

My wife once took me to a NASCAR event and to a chapel service held before the race. I got excited when I found out that the speaker would be James Dobson, the founder of Focus on the Family. He was still recovering from a heart attack that he had thought would take him to heaven.

During his hospital stay, Dr. Dobson said he had a lot of time to ponder what's most important to a man. When you believe your time on earth is growing short, three key issues bubble to the surface:

1. Who do I love?
2. Who really loves me?
3. Will I spend eternity with the ones I love?

As he pondered those three questions, Dr. Dobson realized he didn't know whether his son, Ryan, even knew the Lord. After his release from the hospital, Dr. Dobson felt a consuming passion for his wayward son. The love of God and his own broken heart drove him to make sure that Ryan would spend eternity with him. As father pursued son in the love of God, the Lord did a wonderful work in the life of Ryan Dobson, and today Ryan is a minister of the gospel of Jesus Christ.

This story reminds me that love is an action verb. It *acts* on behalf of those it loves—and if you're a Christian man, God calls you to let the love of God be the driving force of your life.

God's Love: What Is It?

If most people know one Greek word from the New Testament, it's *agape*, a term that refers to self-giving, God-like love. The word suggests the absorption of every part of one's being in one great passion.

Have you ever heard somebody say, "I just want to love God with every fiber of my being"? Well, God loves us with every fiber of His being. Every fiber of His being overflows with *agape* love, and God keeps on loving, even when He disciplines us.

The word has little to do with mere emotion. It indicates a deliberate love, exercised by an act of will. It chooses its object and, through thick or thin, regardless of the attractiveness of the object, goes on loving, continually and eternally. God's *agape* love thinks not of itself but of the objects it loves.

God's *agape* love depends on nothing outside of itself. It's not affected by the worthiness or unworthiness of the one loved. God has chosen to pour into us His love—unconditional, sacrificial, submissive.

God's love is unconquerable, considerate, charitable, and benevolent. It demands expression. It seeks an object to serve and then sacrifices for it. God's love makes it a practice to do good. It doesn't wait to be asked to join an opportunity to do good, but seeks out opportunities to express itself.

Jesus reflected God's *agape* love when He said, "It is more blessed to give than to receive" (Acts 20:35). And so God's love reaches out to those who do not deserve it: "God demonstrates His own love toward us, in that while we were still sinners, Christ died for us" (Romans 5:8). This divine love forgives undeserving people. It knows how to start over and repeatedly sacrifices itself for others. It's a love that genuinely cares.

The love of God endures when all else fails. It is completely indestructible. While other things pass away, His love lasts. It's permanent. It's not going away. It will never dry up, run down, cave in, or blow away. I love the Song of Solomon, which says,

> Many waters cannot quench love,
> nor can the floods drown it.
> If a man would give for love
> all the wealth of his house,
> it would be utterly despised.
> (Song of Solomon 8:7)

Nothing matches God's love. "And now abide faith, hope, love, these three," wrote the apostle Paul, "but the greatest of these is love" (1 Corinthians 13:13).

God's Love: We're to Express It

It should surprise none of us that love is the supreme characteristic that God demands to see expressed in His people. When asked to name the greatest commandment, Jesus replied, "'You shall love the LORD your God with all your heart, with all your soul, and with all your mind.' This is the first and great commandment. And the second is like it: 'You shall love your neighbor as yourself'" (Matthew 22:37-39). It doesn't matter how much you and I know. People want to know that we genuinely care.

The only acceptable love that God ever receives from us is the love that He's poured into us. He pours it in that we might pour it out.

And who do we love? We love both those who love us and those who don't love us. We love our enemies, even those who hate us.

"Well, I can't do that," you say. I agree with you; you can't. But when you allow God to pour His love into you, you'll be surprised at the capacity you gain to love others. I say surprised, not proud, because 1 Corinthians 13:4 insists love is not proud. There is no room for pride in the love of God.

Men who express God's love through their lives don't strut around. Pride short-circuits the effects of *agape* love. Pride *always* precedes loveless living. It can't express genuine love because love requires a focus off of self and on others.

Pride negotiates for its own benefit. Its sense of superiority slices into a man's soul like a surgeon's scalpel. Pride produces both bitterness and resentment because it thinks that by giving free reign to these negative emotions, somehow it pays back the offender. The proud man actually believes that when he drinks the poison of unforgiveness, the person he hates will die.

Love listens; pride talks. Love forgives; pride resents. Love gives; pride takes. Love apologizes; pride blames. Love understands; pride assumes. Love accepts; pride rejects. Love trusts; pride doubts. Love asks; pride tells. Love leads; pride drives. Love frees; pride binds. Love builds up; pride tears down. Love encourages; pride discourages. Love is peaceful; pride is fearful. Love clarifies with truth; pride confuses with lies.

Love and pride are mutually exclusive. Love dies when pride comes alive.

If you struggle with pride, what can you do? The only antidote to pride is humility. Humility is a veritable hotbed of love.

Humility invites love to take up permanent residence in a man's heart. Humility understands that love is reserved for everyone. Love forgives even the worst of sinners, as humility knows it needs help in receiving *agape* love. A humble heart yearns for love from the Lord Jesus Christ.

Love releases the power of God's Spirit in us because the love of God has been shed abroad in our hearts by the Holy Spirit (see Romans 5:5). It edifies and builds up. Love builds up your home. It builds up your marriage. It builds up your life. The love of God takes joy in promoting others.

This kind of *agape* love does not originate in our nature, but comes from the very heart of God. It is supernatural in origin. You do not have *agape* love until you fall in love with God and the Lord instills within your heart His love.

I once attended a Southern Baptist convention where the greatest song performed was sung by the worst voice I'd ever heard. The man had recently been converted and had come to the convention with a choir and orchestra from his church. He'd just left a horrible life of sin, but God had radically changed his life and he wanted to sing about it. He couldn't carry a tune in a bucket, but when he finished, I didn't see a dry eye in the place. I had to dab away tears too.

Is it easy to love others with God's *agape* love? Frankly, no. It's easier to be orthodox than to be loving. I've known some men who had a stranglehold on doctrinal truth, but were as mean as rattlesnakes. It's easier to be active in church than to be loving. If you don't believe me, let me ask a few questions.

Do you ever have trouble loving somebody because you don't think they deserve it?

When did you last get on your knees and pray for your enemies?

Have you ever prayed for those who spitefully used you or who said nasty things about you?

Remember, "love does not envy" (1 Corinthians 13:4). There's no meanness of soul in *agape* love, while jealousy has a viciousness shared by no other sin.

Love "does not behave rudely" (v. 5). It has good manners. It's not blunt or rude or brutal. Love cares about the other person's feelings and takes them into account before it speaks or acts.

One Sunday, in the middle of a sermon, I learned an unforgettable lesson about failing to care for another's feelings. I'd told a story about an exchange between Janet and me, and as I finished, my wife found a mic, grabbed it, came up on the platform, and said to the congregation, "Y'all just heard Pastor Johnny tell a story about us. How many of you'd like to hear my version?" The audience cheered so loud, it embarrassed me. I'd forgotten that love *never* overlooks the other person's feelings. I hope I won't forget again! (Ever since that day, anytime I mention Janet's name in a sermon, I'm fearful of a mic close by.)

Love "thinks no evil" (v. 5). The original term used here was an accounting word for "ledger." Love does not store in memory the wrong against it and retrieve that memory whenever needed. You don't even have a ledger.

Have you ever heard bad news about somebody and rejoiced over the report? Maybe you even said, "It couldn't have happened to a better guy." When you heard that some unpleasant man crashed or his marriage blew up or he'd landed in legal trouble, did you feel good about it? Listen to Proverbs 24:17: "Do not rejoice when your enemy falls, and do not let your heart be glad when he stumbles." Don't throw a party when you hear bad reports about difficult people. If God's love has taken up residence in you, then you want to see the best for everybody.

Love hides the ugliness from public view. It does not drag it out into the light. Aren't you glad for great marriages that can keep some things between themselves and the Lord?

Love "suffers long" (v. 4). That means you have a long fuse, not a short temper. It means that God is building patience into your life. A lot of little things used to bother me about Janet, and in former days, I let her know about them. I've always thought she takes along too much luggage whenever we take a trip. We go overnight and it looks to me like she brings enough for a week. I used to rag on her about it, until love taught me that's just who she is. We've been married just under fifty years, and if my harping strategy had a chance of working, it would have kicked in by now. It hasn't. So I leave it alone.

"Get my luggage," she says.

"Yes, dear," I say. And I think, *Pick it up. Carry it. Don't criticize.*

If you're married, speak to your wife today and say to her, "I'm not going to say anything else about _____." Harping on it doesn't work, but love does. Love may not "cure" her of the habit that bugs you, but it'll sure cure you of being bugged.

Love sees the bright side. It believes the best in people, just like Jesus when he saw Simon Peter, the wavering one. Do you remember what Jesus called him? *Petras,* "rock." What a confidence booster! That was a prophecy, not a statement of then-current fact.

It has been said that the only thing God will reward at the *bēma,* the judgment seat of Christ, is what we've done that was motivated by God's love. If that's true, then what kind of reward can you expect?

Once you genuinely receive the love of your heavenly Father, you can't help but dispense it to others. As you receive love, you become capable of giving it, even eager to give it.

The pinnacle of spiritual development is to love God with our total being and to love our neighbor as ourselves. The strongest men in the world are those who love the most.

This Love Is Strong, Not Weak

Even as Jesus pours His love into us, He also makes us fearless and strong. Paul put it this way: "For God has not given us a spirit of fear, but of power and of love and of a sound mind" (2 Timothy 1:7). The greatest power in *any* man's leadership is love.

Jesus founded His conquering kingdom on love: "For God so loved the world that He gave His only begotten Son" (John 3:16). As a result, millions around the world would willingly die for Him. And just for the record's sake, more have died for Christ in the last one hundred years than in all the nineteen hundred years preceding. That takes strength.

God's love in us is not sentimental emotion, but the outpouring of a man's total being to another in blessing. Maybe one morning you get up and the love of God begins to remind you that a man has something against you. Before you know it, the love of God will say to you, "Call him." It takes real strength to obey. But you reach out with the love of God and you touch him…and then God begins to move. Only then do you realize the real force and power of God's love. You see it in mighty action.

Love outlasts any potent spiritual gift you might have. Maybe you say, "I can't sing now, but when I get to heaven, I'll sure be able to sing!" But heaven will not be about how well you sing. If you think it is, you're missing it. Heaven will be about loving God with a perfected, strong love, and loving one another with God's omnipotent love.

The bottom line is, God magnifies love. At the end of the day, the Lord desires that you and I love Him with a fierce, strong, and growing passion. The only way anyone will ever know if we really love God is if they see us using our gifts and graces to love and serve others. The strongest man on earth is the one who best channels the mighty river of God's love into the lives of those who most need it.

One Fruit, Many Varieties

Just as an apple tree expresses its life in bearing apples, so the Christ follower expresses his life in bearing the spiritual fruit of love. What does a healthy apple tree do? It produces apples. What does a Christian man full of the love of God do? He expresses and bears the love of God.

In the ancient world, the Greeks prized what a man knew, his intellect. The Romans worshiped a man for what he could do, his power. But the apostle Paul stressed what a man is, his character. And so he wrote these amazing words: "But the fruit of the Spirit is love, joy, peace, longsuffering, kindness, goodness, faithfulness, gentleness, self-control. Against such there is no law" (Galatians 5:22-23).

Notice that Paul speaks of the fruit of the Spirit in the singular—the *fruit* of the Spirit, not *fruits*. I agree with many theologians who believe that all eight qualities Paul mentions above are expressions of love. Each of these eight qualities should express themselves through every man who receives God's love. These eight traits are so critical that I want to linger over them, both in this chapter and in the next one. I believe it's that important.

Don't forget that none of us can produce the fruit of the Spirit; only Jesus can do that. While we have the ability to manufacture plastic fruit, no man can manufacture the fruit of the Spirit. Spiritual fruit grows only when a branch remains vitally connected to the vine. In God's family, we are those branches and Jesus is the true vine. As the Holy Spirit pours out the love of God in our hearts (see

Romans 5:5), the fruit of the Spirit grows on us, the branches. The fruit we produce gives nourishment for others, who taste in it the love of God. And so God's kingdom expands.

Joy: Love's Music

Joy is love's music. Tell me something that's sweeter than a home filled with joy. If love is absent, you can forget joy.

God's love can keep a man cheerful in all circumstances. Do you know what the reformers said when they referred to the love of God that brought them joy? They said God gave them a "happy soul."

Is your soul happy? Your soul speaks of who you are, the seat of affection, everything that you represent. Do you have that kind of joy? Jesus told His disciples, "These things I have spoken to you, that My joy may remain in you, and that your joy may be full" (John 15:11). A friend of mine has taped to his desk a saying written by his godly uncle, who served the Lord vocationally for over seventy years and who lived to be just a couple of months shy of one hundred: "Joy is the indisputable proof of the Holy Spirit."

The word translated "joy" in John 15:11 can also mean contentment. When God fills us with His joy, we become content. Are you content? If contentment eludes you, then you lack His joy.

Our self-centered nature has led us to believe that happiness and joy come only when we get what we want. But how many illustrations from real life do we need to see that getting what we think we want does *not* meet our needs? When some of the wealthiest people in the world finally obtain what they've clamored for, they get a divorce. Before you know it, they've walked down the aisle so many times that you've lost count. Is that happiness? Is that joy?

Some men think, *If I could just get that new car* or *a bigger house* or *healthier children* or *a bit of fame*, they'd find contentment, happiness, and joy. But those things never bring joy, because joy comes not from getting but from giving out the love of God. Do you want joy? Then learn to dispense God's love like you're giving out candy.

When the love of God prompts me to give, sometimes I get the holy giggles. Does that sound crazy? Maybe what's wrong with you is that you're in what you call your "right mind," and that kind of mind is about to wreck your life. I wish you could let your hair down!

One Sunday, someone said something terrible to me, and I laughed.

"That's not the response I expected," the man said.

"You'll never make it in this ministry without a sense of humor," I replied. I'm not referring to making jokes or even about having a pleasant outlook on life. This is better than humor; it's joy.

Every time we have the chance to flesh out the love of God to others, our joy cycle revs up all over again. It goes from one wave of joy to another. Why not let God be a source of spiritual refreshment to you and to others?

A farmer once had a helper who filled his buckets of grain only three-fourths full. The farmer said to him, "The buckets are never full until they're running over."

I want God to fill my cup of joy to overflowing. I want my bucket and my heart to overflow with the joy of the Lord. I don't want merely to get by; I want to thrive. A Christian man who never gets filled with the spiritual blessings of God will never run over with joy and so refresh the lives of others.

I like the old acronym J-O-Y. How do you get joy? By living according to the acronym: **J**esus, **O**thers, **Y**ourself.

When Paul tells us to "rejoice always" in 1 Thessalonians 5:16, he uses the same Greek word elsewhere translated "joy." How is it even possible to always have joy? It's possible because joy is not happiness.

While happiness is based on circumstance and happenstance, joy is based on a relationship. I need something that controls me, regardless of my circumstances. I need joy! Someone has said, "Joy is the flag flown high from the castle of my heart, for the King is in residence there."

When Jesus Christ told us in John 15:11 that He wants us to have "full" joy, He immediately added, "This is My commandment, that you love one another as I have loved you" (v. 12). There is a straight line between our love for one another and our experience of joy. As a minister and as a people person, I've observed that at least 90 percent of the time when people lose their joy, they've done so because of a fractured relationship.

As people observe your life, do they see joy or discouragement? If you find yourself constantly asking people, "What are you so happy about?" could it be because you so often feel discouraged?

Habakkuk 3:17-18 features what I call a "hymn of faith." The prophet had seen the coming destruction of his homeland, and he knew that God's fearful time of judgment had arrived. So how did he respond?

> Though the fig tree may not blossom,
>   Nor fruit be on the vines;
> Though the labor of the olive may fail,
> And the fields yield no food;
> Though the flock may be cut off from the fold,
> And there be no herd in the stalls—
> Yet I will rejoice in the LORD,
> I will joy in the God of my salvation.

He says, "Everything that I'd hoped for has disappeared. None of the good I wanted has happened. But because of my relationship with God, I still have joy, real joy, wonderful joy."

How did the apostle Paul manage to rejoice when his missionary activities landed him in jail? He rejoiced even in prison because no jail could stop his prayers. No prison warden could cut him off from his living connection to Jesus. Paul had learned to rejoice and be content in every circumstance, not at every circumstance.

Some things bring me no joy. But when I take that circumstance and bring it to Jesus, God can still give me joy. When you get your relationship right with Jesus, you can rejoice in the Lord anywhere and always. Writing from prison, Paul told his Christian friends, "Rejoice in the Lord always. Again I will say, rejoice!" (Philippians 4:4). That's a command, not a suggestion. How can anyone command joy? Only because true joy, deep joy, flows out of a growing relationship with Jesus Christ.

Peace: Love's Agreement

Peace is love's agreement. We can have both peace *with* God and the peace *of* God when we agree that He's right and we're wrong.

Before I got saved, I was at enmity with God. A wall separated me from a relationship with Him. But when I came to faith, Christ Jesus tore down the wall and made me one with others who also have come to know Him. As a result, peace rules in our hearts. We agree with God and with one another.

The word *confession* means to agree with God. When I confessed my sin, repented, and placed my faith in Christ, peace with God became a reality in my life. Peace *with* God comes to every man as a result of a loving relationship with the Savior. It's like making a peace treaty after a war ends. The only way that peace treaty with heaven ever gets signed is to acknowledge that Jesus made perfect provision on the cross so that you and I could be cleansed and forgiven through His sacrifice.

The peace *of* God refers to an inner tranquility you can have, even in the midst of a confusing and disintegrating world. You can have this peace because you know that God remains in charge. The fruit of the Spirit produces peace. I'm at peace with God and I have the peace of God. I have an inner tranquility that God gives me.

One time before a Sunday service, our church's deacons knelt with me to pray. We typically prayed at that time for the service and for me as I prepared to minister the Word, but that morning we knelt and prayed over a dear man in our church suffering with cancer. His numbers didn't look good. We prayed that the peace of God would rule in his heart, overwhelmingly, regardless of his outward circumstances.

If you think, *I might have peace once my circumstances change*, you have a shrunken view of God. Regardless of your circumstances, the love of God can be poured into your heart where God's peace can rule even in the midst of chaos. Despite all kinds of unpleasant stuff happening around you, you can learn to say, as the kids' song says, "I've got the peace that passes understanding down in my heart." This kind of peace is not based on outward circumstances but depends on a living, vibrant relationship with Almighty God.

The Lord pours His peace into you, and it simply has to find expression through your life. Even when the world falls apart, God remains in charge—and that truth brings you peace.

God's peace goes even a step further. It brings peace to others in a world of turmoil. Did you know that God has given you a ministry of reconciliation (see 2 Corinthians 5:18-21)?

Every now and then when I officiate at a funeral, the family of the deceased clearly has no peace. I see turmoil everywhere, with contentious people pulling at me from all sides. How do I respond? I open my Bible and lift up Jesus. And more often than not, I watch as God comes over that place, settles in, and brings His peace. I've never seen anything else like it.

Is that your experience?

How Can I Pray for You?

One day a dear friend and I had lunch at a restaurant. When our server came to our table, I noticed her name tag said "Jennifer." So I said, "Jennifer, we're getting ready to pray to thank the Lord for our food. Anything we can pray for you about?"

She instantly got all choked up. "Pray for me. I'm a single mom with two special needs kids."

"Ma'am," I asked, "have you heard of Night to Shine?" (The Tim Tebow Foundation sponsors Night to Shine, a celebratory prom for special needs young people ages fourteen and older. The nationwide program centers on the love of God.)

Jennifer and I began to talk about her situation. I had ordered club soda with lime, and by the time I left the restaurant, I'd put down three full glasses. Jennifer couldn't do enough to serve me. Every time she walked by our table, she'd say, "God bless you! God bless you!"

The devil's convinced too many of us that if we open our mouths to represent the King who made us, we'll cause offense or make somebody angry. But you can care for someone through praying. You can minister the love, joy, and peace of God to them. I prayed that God would move in Jennifer's heart.

At some point that afternoon, I told her, "Let me share something else with you, Jennifer. My momma was a single mom, raised six kids. Two of them became preachers, both my sisters are serving the Lord. My oldest brother is a deacon in the Methodist church, and I have one brother in prison." I just told her our family story.

When I meet someone in need like Jennifer, I talk about the love, joy, and peace of God. I testify how faithful Jesus is, about how much He loves her and will forgive her, minister to her, and even use her. God can give anyone His love, joy, and peace even in the most trying of circumstances.

How can this happen? Remember, love is an action verb. It's never passive. Love calls you to action, and then goes to work on your behalf and for the benefit of others.

10

DO YOU LOOK LIKE YOUR FATHER?

Most of us have a soft spot in our hearts for family resemblances. We like it when someone says to us, "Boy, I can really see you in your son's face. There's no question who *his* daddy is!"

I've thought about this glee over family resemblances when the Bible calls Jesus "the express image" of His heavenly Father (Hebrews 1:3). I've pondered it when Jesus Himself told His disciples, "He who has seen Me has seen the Father" (John 14:9). And I've wondered why no theologian has ever written a book on the attributes of God solely by using incidents from the life of Jesus Christ. I can't help but think such an approach would make an otherwise abstract topic come fully alive.

As I write, Easter is just a few weeks away. My mind drifts toward Passion Week and Calvary and all that our Savior accomplished for us on the cross. As I dwell on the events of that season, it strikes me that Jesus exhibited *every one* of the varieties of the Spirit's fruit that Paul listed in Galatians 5.

Love, of course, moved God to make provision for our salvation, and love led Jesus to die in our place to make that salvation possible.

God took great *joy* in bringing many sons to glory, and Jesus accepted the shame and agony of the cross for the joy set before Him.

God used Easter to give us *peace* with Him, and the Prince of Peace, Jesus, made it a reality.

In this chapter, I want to briefly discuss the remaining six varieties of the Spirit's fruit—longsuffering, kindness, goodness, faithfulness, gentleness, and self-control—in order to remind us that these qualities must increasingly characterize us as men of God. The more they take up residence in us, the more we look like Jesus.

But as I thought about these qualities, and as I looked ahead toward Easter, it struck me powerfully that even in the last hours before His death, Jesus exhibited every one of the six divine qualities we'll note in this chapter. Consider:

- He demonstrated great *longsuffering* when His disciples kept falling asleep in Gethsemane, even though He'd asked them to join Him in prayer at His most trying hour.

- He displayed stunning *kindness* when He referred to Judas as "friend," even though this disciple-turned-betrayer came to the garden only to deliver Jesus to His enemies.

- He embodied inconceivable *goodness* when He willingly went to the cross on our behalf; no wonder we call it Good Friday!

- He revealed breathtaking *faithfulness* when, while gasping for air, He made provision for the ongoing care of His widowed mother.

- He showed amazing *gentleness* when He told a criminal hanging next to Him—a man who moments before had insulted and scorned Him—"Today you will be with Me in Paradise."

- He exhibited enormous *self-control* when He refrained from calling for legions of angels to free Him. These mighty beings would have wiped out, most eagerly, everyone on the planet in order to save their Lord from harm.

As we briefly consider these six qualities, remember that Jesus Christ perfectly displayed each one in His life on earth, thus perfectly reflecting His Father's divine nature. Now it's our turn. We won't reach perfection, of course; but at least let's get on the road. Through our lives, let's give people a taste of what awaits them in heaven.

Love's Endurance: Longsuffering/Patience

When you love people, you suffer long with them. You develop a longer fuse. You endure slights with unruffled temper. You become long-tempered, patient. Love suffers *long*.

When someone wrongs you, you deal with them patiently. That's not easy. You must firmly resist the old self and graciously accept unjust criticism. A man of God is known for his longsuffering perseverance. The word more literally means "to remain under," which calls for endurance. It refers not to complacent waiting but to a determination that continues even in hard places.

To be longsuffering refers to a victorious, triumphant, unswerving loyalty to the Lord in the midst of trials. Such patience enables a man of God to stick with his calling no matter the cost. When God calls him to do something emotionally difficult, he remains loyal to it. People will say about him, "Now, there goes a patient man."

People are watching. When you persevere, endure, and display a longsuffering spirit, someone will approach you and say, "You modeled the Christian life for me during that hard time. You mirrored what the Word said in such a way that you showed me the character of Jesus. What an encourager you have been for me!"

Not everything Jesus calls us to endure is pleasant. But if we'll stay under it until God is through with us, amazing things can happen. God loves to honor the courage of a man who remains patient while in a hard place.

Love's Service: Kindness

When you serve someone, you express God's love through your kindness. To be kind refers not to sentiment but to service. We express the love of God by acts of kindness done for others. We reflect Jesus' kindness by offering our help even in the small things, thus making someone's life better.

The original Greek word translated "kindness" speaks of a practical warm-heartedness. Through it we show our concern and care. We take care to be friendly.

One way to show kindness is through generosity. We know a family from South America who moved to a closed Muslim country. In that difficult place, they're serving as incognito missionaries within the government. After they moved, something happened in their home country that prevented money from flowing from there to their new place of ministry. When you have no money, serving in one of the world's most dangerous countries, you're in trouble. At the same time, God has given them an incredible platform for ministry. So what can anyone do?

Some of my friends said to one another, "We have to pray. We need to help them somehow." Do you know what kindness does? Kindness goes to the throne of God and says, "King Jesus, what do you want me to do?"

Some Christian men will just forward an email describing situations like this and say, "I think the church needs to do something."

You are the church! Sometimes we have this mistaken idea that the church is "out there" and we're "over here." No, you and I are right in the midst of it. *We* are the church, and if kindness dwells in our hearts, we won't leave needy people to fend for themselves. We'll find a way to help.

In this case, we made sure that somebody willing to put their life in jeopardy by living for Christ in a dangerous country, separated by many hours of flight time from most of their children, would get some help from us. Why? Because the love of God in our hearts prompts us to express that love through kindness.

Jesus came to us from heaven because of His kindness. Nehemiah called God "abundant in kindness" (Nehemiah 9:17). The prophet Joel declared God is "of great kindness" (Joel 2:13). The kindness of God sent us a Savior; God saved us because of His kindness and love (Titus 3:4). Today, the kindness of God sends believers all over the world from their places of safety, helped along by kind individuals, churches, and organizations.

Love is kind. If I'm not kind, I'm not letting the love of God flow through me.

Am I always kind? I wish I could answer yes, but I can't. At times, I have been the opposite of kind. At times, I have not responded as the Spirit of Jesus instructed me. At those times, I didn't let the love of God flow through me.

So what happened? In His kindness, the Spirit of the living God convicted me of my sin, gave me the grace to repent, and said, "Try it again, son."

Love's Deportment: Goodness

Goodness refers to the manifestation of Godlike virtues in a man. We begin to take on those virtues as the Holy Spirit fills us with the love of God, and soon our lives begin to express divine goodness.

Goodness is Joseph fleeing from Potiphar's wife when she tried to seduce him (see Genesis 39).

Goodness is Moses interceding for a rebellious nation when God threatened to wipe it out and start over (see Exodus 32).

Goodness is Joshua sparing the lives of Rahab and her family after she hid the Hebrew spies sent on a reconnaissance mission to Jericho (Joshua 6).

Goodness is Jesus showing compassion to a woman caught in adultery, yet without condoning her sin (see John 8).

Goodness is Peter giving a lame man something very different, but far better, than what the man had requested (see Acts 3).

Goodness is Barnabas befriending Saul and introducing him to the church, even though no Christian wanted anything to do with him (see Acts 9).

Goodness is a high-profile man on his knees, asking God for guidance and strength to do the right thing.

One evening at a program to honor special needs kids in our area, I watched as a man who had sold his company for a lot of money got down on his knees to shine the shoes of the young participants. That's the goodness of God at work.

A friend of mine who eventually succumbed to dementia said, long before his mind started slipping away, "There are no big shots in God's kingdom, and if there are any that think they're big shots, they ought to be shot with big shots." A good man is never too big to bow low.

Goodness is a man on a modest income choosing to serve a needy people group, when he could easily have risen to a more prestigious position had he chosen to promote himself.

Many years ago, I bought a plane ticket to visit four missionary families serving on various Indonesian islands. When I discovered I had cancer, I couldn't go. A friend took my ticket and went in my place. After he returned, he said something I've never been able to get out of my mind. "Pastor Johnny," he said, "the house where they live with their children would be equivalent to a storage house we might have behind our homes." He got emotional and added, "Now, they don't know it. They've not even noticed it." My friend thought we needed to do something about their situation. That's what the goodness of God will do.

Goodness can't help but express itself. You can't keep it inside of you; it has to get out. It spreads all over you and rubs off on everybody you come into contact with. If you're not influencing family and friends through your goodness, it's because you're not letting the love of God be poured out in your heart by the Holy Spirit.

I thank the Lord for the goodness of God expressed to me by so many followers of Jesus. We have a good, good Father! Goodness opposes everything evil and immoral and drives the Christlike person to depend on God to strive to bring about a better world. A man bearing the spiritual fruit of goodness has a strong disposition to hate what is evil. He may pray, "God, help me to hate what You hate and love what You love."

If the fruit of goodness is blossoming in your life, then you have a compulsion to follow after what is good. You have a great desire to gain the wisdom to judge rightly in all things. You have a longing to increase in thoughtfulness and sensitivity in all your dealings with everyone you meet.

The Greek word translated "goodness" in the New Testament never even appeared in secular Greek writing. Neither the Greeks nor the Romans grasped the meaning of *agape* love or of its offspring, goodness. They saw love and goodness as qualities to be avoided, traits that would make a man either feebleminded or weak. But God said, "Goodness is one of my attributes."

If we worship Jesus, His Spirit will infuse us with divine love, and that love will be expressed in goodness. Goodness finds its anchor in the love of God. Goodness produces a deportment that is kind but just, tender but tough, fair but firm.

Could people rightly say of you, "He's a good man"?

Love's Measurement: Faithfulness

Faithfulness means staying true to something. For a follower of Christ, it means staying true to your trust, to your commitment to others, to yourself, and above all, staying true to God.

Faithfulness is Noah building the ark despite the jeers and criticism of his neighbors (see Genesis 6). That kind of criticism has slowed down many a Christian. It's kept many men quiet in a hostile business environment. Many believing students have remained seated while skeptics got up to blaspheme our great God.

Faithfulness is Abraham's willingness to sacrifice his only son because he believed God would deliver Isaac and through him fulfill the Lord's promise (see Genesis 22; Romans 4:20-22; Hebrews 11:17-19).

Faithfulness is keeping your promises. It's paying your bills. It's honoring your appointments. People know that your word is your bond. The attitude of *agape* love behind faithfulness gives vitality and credibility to a man's influence.

Faithfulness accomplishes what fame or force cannot. Manipulation cannot obtain what love-fueled faithfulness can.

The question is often asked, what do you do when faithfulness doesn't work? I'd say, "Increase your dosage." Faithfulness *does* work, although often not on our timetables. Don't give up on God and don't abandon faithfulness in favor of expedience.

Where can you show your faithfulness today? Who in your life most needs to see your faithfulness?

Love's Mood: Gentleness

Gentleness expresses love in a considerate, meek way. The word is closely related to humility. Together, gentleness and humility give enormous strength to your work and ministry.

Men often get the wrong idea about both gentleness and humility. Picture a muscular stallion, broken by its handlers. That horse still has all the strength he ever had, but all those muscles have been brought under the direction of a master. The bit is in the horse's mouth, the reins are in the rider's hands, but that is still one powerful horse.

Gentleness/humility allows you to meet criticism with meekness and a pleasant spirit. It strengthens your soul and honors God. It is love's prevailing attitude, its temperament and disposition. A gentle man knows he's been the object of undeserved, redeeming love, and therefore he doesn't lash out when he's wronged. It's amazing what a gentle man can take.

Somebody once asked the evangelist D.L. Moody, "Are you saying that a humble man doesn't think much of himself?"

"No," Moody replied, "a humble man doesn't think of himself at all." Humility means being nearly unconscious of yourself.

A gentle man is kind, meek, and humble. He sees the minimum of self and the maximum of God. A gentle man, although consumed with the greatness of a noble cause, recognizes that, in and of himself, he makes no contribution to its success. He knows God could accomplish this great thing just as well without him.

Suppose somebody said to Bill, "Bill, thanks for your generous contribution to our initiative. Look what's happening. By the grace of God, we are ready to help more destitute children than ever before in the history of our organization. Your generosity inspired others to give, and now we can expand our work into some of the most needy countries on earth. Even more great opportunities are on the horizon, thanks to you!"

It would be so easy for Bill to throw out his chest and say, "Well, thanks. Last year was a tough year for me, but…" In that moment, I believe the Holy Spirit would likely say to Bill, "What are you talking about? Don't you remember what you read in your devotions just the other day in Malachi 2:2: 'If you will not hear, and if you will not take it to heart, to give glory to My name,' says the LORD of hosts, 'I will send a curse upon you, and I will curse your blessings'? Bill, if you fail to give glory to My name now, I'll curse your blessings. The fact that you were able to give at all wasn't because of you; that was Christ in you. So get on your face and give God the glory for what *He's* done."

How can a man filled with God's Spirit take credit for the Lord's work? A man ruled by the spirit of gentleness takes delight in staying in the background and giving God the glory due His name.

John Bunyan said it better than anyone I've ever read. Listen to these profound words from one of his poems:

> He that is down need fear no fall;
> He that is low, no pride;
> He that is humble ever shall
> Have God to be his guide.

Love's Mastery: Self-Control

A self-controlled man does not let his desires master his life. He allows all aspects of his life to be brought under the mastery of the Holy Spirit. Holy discipline characterizes the life of a self-controlled man.

The Greek word translated "self-control" means "to grip or to take hold of." It indicates that God empowers a man to take control of himself.

I heard Truett Cathy, founder of Chick-fil-A, say, "The reason the average person cannot lead others is that he has not learned to lead himself." Self-control should result in an attitude of humility and caution. It develops strong character and gives a man courage.

How do you develop and exercise self-control? You build it into your life through conscious dependence on God, paired with a life of Spirit-filled discipline. You mind especially the little things. Jesus said, "He who is faithful in what is least is faithful also in much; and he who is unjust in what is least is unjust also in much" (Luke 16:10). When you're faithful in the little things, you demonstrate your capacity and fitness to handle much more.

You can help build your self-discipline if you make some important decisions ahead of time. When my daughters reached the age of ten or eleven, I started teaching them how to remain pure. I told them, "If a boy ever says to you, 'Get in the back seat with me,' don't you dare get back there!" It becomes a lot easier to do the right thing when you make up your mind ahead of time to follow a certain course of action.

When young Daniel found himself in King Nebuchadnezzar's palace, tasked to serve the Babylonian king, he "purposed in his heart that he would not defile himself with the portion of the king's delicacies, nor with the wine which he drank" (Daniel 1:8). Do you think such a decision took self-control, especially when he saw many other young men gladly accept the dainties presented to them? When the right time came, Daniel had a reasonable alternate plan for his overseers. They accepted his suggestion, and at the end of a test period (which Daniel also proposed), he "appeared better and fatter in flesh than all the young men who ate the portion of the king's delicacies" (Daniel 1:15). Daniel's self-control and predetermined commitment to honor his God, even as a young man, led directly to his long and celebrated career in the upper echelons of Middle Eastern power politics.

Make godly decisions ahead of time. On the way to a hard meeting, decide that you need God's help to enable you to navigate the stormy waters. You could pray, "O Lord, clothe me with humility. Fill me with the Spirit of God, help me to exercise self-control, and put a watch on my mouth so that my tongue utters no words that tarnish Your glory."

To exercise self-control requires that you rule over your own spirit. "The devil made me do it" is not only bad theology, it's both false and stupid. Proverbs 16:32 says, "He who is slow to anger is better than the mighty, and he who rules his spirit than he who takes a city." When you control your thoughts, you control your actions. It's amazing what happens when the love of God rules in your heart!

When you allow the Spirit of the living God to help you develop self-control, your whole world changes. You stop making unreasonable demands of others. You give others the benefit of the doubt. A true friend exercising self-control picks up where he left off, even after a long period of not speaking with his buddy. Such a man doesn't say, "Well, *there* you are. Finally! You haven't called. You haven't written. You haven't emailed. What kind of friend are you, anyway?" You might want to say all of those things. You might feel all of those things. But the fruit of the Spirit growing within you allows you to exercise self-control. So what do you say? "Man, it's great to speak with you again! It's been too long."

Proverbs 25:28 says, "Whoever has no rule over his own spirit is like a city broken down, without walls." When you lack self-control, the enemy can invade your space anytime he wants to, raid your goods, and smack you around. How are you going to stop him? You've let the protective walls around you crumble into dust. The love of God doesn't want that to happen, so the Spirit comes into your life, builds self-control into your character, and gives you the strength to persevere.

When the fruit of the Spirit blossoms in your life, even tough times give you the opportunity to shine for God. Through His Spirit, "we also glory in tribulations, knowing that tribulation produces perseverance; and perseverance, character; and character, hope" (Romans 5:3-4). God builds Christian character through perseverance—but what man needs perseverance if he has no problems?

When you exercise self-control in the middle of your troubles, you persevere through them, and as a result, God produces a Christlike spirit in you. Hope breaks forth because you can see God at work within you. You realize that God's Spirit is making you into a better man, a more godly leader, and this realization gives you the hope that great things lie ahead.

Paul told a young pastor, "Exhort the young men to be soberminded" (Titus 2:6). What does a sober-minded person look like? The word suggests the exercise of self-restraint. A sober-minded man develops self-control with the power to govern all his passions and desires. I admit that every time my big mouth has landed me in trouble, the cause was my failure to restrain my passions. I took off the governor.

Suppose you rent a truck to move to another part of the country. You want to get there as quickly as possible, but the truck's owner has installed a governor that will hardly let you reach the speed limit, and it takes forever to get anywhere. Only when you go downhill can you achieve a little speed because the governor restrains how fast you can go.

When we're filled with the Holy Spirit of God, the Spirit serves as a restrainer. In fact, the Scripture even gives Him that name. Writing about the time of the end when God begins wrapping up all of human history, Paul declared, "The mystery of lawlessness is already at work; only He who now restrains will do so until He is taken out of the way" (2 Thessalonians 2:7). When that day comes—the time when the Lord takes out of the way the Restrainer, the Holy Spirit—all hell will break loose. Do you think things look out of control in our nation right now? Just wait until the Restrainer, the Governor, the Holy Spirit, gets removed from this earth. It'll be anything goes.

Self-control allows you to govern all your passions and desires. As the Spirit fills you with His love, and as you cooperate with Him to grow the fruit of the Spirit in your life, you develop self-control, self-discipline, self-restraint. You become sober-minded and you learn to more effectively manage your life.

If you want to become a man of God, you must train yourself to cultivate balance and self-restraint. Do you want God to give you more opportunities to grow, more freedom to explore? There's truth in the old saying: "The more freedom granted, the more self-control needed." Paul wrote, "It is for freedom that Christ has set us free" (Galatians 5:1 NIV).

Many men, however, prefer to live under law: Do this, don't do that, sit here, don't go there. But when you live in freedom, you have more choices to make. What should you do with your free time? How should you set up your schedule? You need a governor, a restrainer, to control your passions and desires. As you abide in the true vine, the spiritual fruit of self-control supernaturally grows. But you have to abide.

Paul put it this way to the out-of-control church at Corinth: "Everyone who competes for the prize is temperate in all things" (1 Corinthians 9:25). To be "temperate" means you exercise self-control. The apostle told his Christian friends that pagan athletes exercised restraint in order to win a race or a match, hoping to obtain a victor's crown made of perishable laurel leaves. Followers of Christ, however, run in the race of life for an imperishable crown.

Paul told them he ran, but not with uncertainty. He fought, but not like a shadow boxer. Instead, "I discipline my body and bring it into subjection, lest, when I have preached to others, I myself should become disqualified" (1 Corinthians 9:27).

To succeed in the Christian life, self-control has to become part of who you are. As the Spirit works in your life, you become increasingly sensible and sound-minded. You gain self-mastery, which directs your behavior.

One time I visited Argentina to speak on leadership. Someone at the conference said to me, "You're here teaching leadership; I'm surprised you're not teaching theology."

"There's a Bible institute here that teaches theology," I replied, "and I've noticed in my travels around the world that the average leader does not get in trouble because of his theology. The average leader gets in trouble because of poor relationships and a lack of understanding about how life works. Many leaders don't know how to relate well and get along with people."

Do you know what I taught that week? I spoke a great deal about self-control, about learning to be sensible and how to gain self-mastery, leading to sound-mindedness and godly behavior. The Old Testament would use the word *prudence* to describe the same issue. To exercise self-control means to develop a quality of mind that keeps your life safe. Self-control produces the kind of security that comes from getting all things under God's control.

When I serve as a guest speaker and a lot of leaders fill the room, do you know what they usually ask after my talk? Most of them ask the same thing: "What's the number one thing that you think leaders need to know?"

I always name the same thing. "Keep it close and clean. Guard your heart, for out of it are the issues of life. Guard it diligently. Develop self-mastery. Don't let your life spin out of control."

The great principle that brings all of this together is Proverbs 29:18, which says, "Where there is no revelation, the people cast off restraint." You might have memorized this verse in the King James version, which renders it, "Where there is no vision, the people perish." The verse means that without a prophetic revelation—without God's Word speaking into a man's heart—that man casts off restraint. He lacks self-control. He has no vision of his future beyond the immediate gratification of his flesh.

Dietrich Bonhoeffer rightly said that the devil is not trying to get you to deny God; he just wants you to temporarily forget God. In that temporary forgetfulness, just for a moment, Satan can tempt you to make a decision that can alter the rest of your life. It can change the way others view you, and not for the better. He can put you on the sidelines.

When we cast off restraint, we throw off the controls, we let loose. We hand over the reins of our life to another. Instead of letting Christ and the Spirit of God control us, we give the reins to someone else. When we give into the temptation to lust, lie, steal, gossip, or whatever else our flesh wants to do, we shelve self-restraint and give in. You will not succeed in life without developing self-control.

The longer I live, the more I'm convinced that *nothing* means as much in a godly man's life as moral purity. It's the truth! And you cannot remain morally pure without developing self-control.

Emulating Beats Delegating

Not very often do I make a tweet-worthy statement, but I did a while ago. Two or three younger guys were standing around when I said something that prompted them to immediately pull out their smartphones and tweet it. I had said, "Delegation is never a substitute for emulation."

Every once in a while, my wife will kiddingly say to me, "All you ever do is go to your office, get on the phone, and tell everybody else what to do."

"It's a gift," I reply. "It's called delegation."

But delegating tasks is never a substitute for emulating Christ. While I definitely get more done by delegating, delegating doesn't much help me to grow more like Jesus.

I want people to see a strong family resemblance between me and my Lord. I want them to say, "Boy, I can really see Jesus in you." If you were to look in a mirror today, how much of Jesus would you see staring back?

Part 3

WINNING IN JESUS

11

FIGHT THE GOOD
FIGHT OF FAITH

Andre Ward retired from professional boxing in 2017 as a two-time world champion in the light heavyweight division. He put down his gloves for the last time after compiling a record of 32-0; he hadn't lost in the ring since 1998, when he fought as a thirteen-year-old amateur.

The highlight of his career—the accomplishment he put at "the top of the list," counted as his "highest achievement" and his "crowning moment in boxing"—came in 2004 when he won Olympic gold. No American has managed that feat since then.[10]

Ward announced his retirement on Twitter under the heading, "Mission Accomplished." He wrote, "As I walk away from the sport of boxing today, I leave at the top of your glorious mountain, which was always my vision and my dream. I did it. We did it."

Why did Ward retire at the relatively young age of thirty-three? In a word, the sport took too great a toll on his body. "I am leaving because my body can no longer put up with the rigors of the sport and therefore my desire to fight is no longer there," he explained.

"If I cannot give my family, my team, and the fans everything I have, then I should no longer be fighting."

Ward's decision surprised many observers, but not those who knew him best. He said he chose to step away from boxing to give more time to his family, to his community, to his church, and perhaps to a new career in broadcasting. "Boxing is just a season," he told one interviewer. "This isn't my life. It's what I do, it's not who I am." Nevertheless, he declared he had given the sport "everything I am."[11]

I think that had the apostle Paul lived in our day, he might have thoroughly enjoyed following Andre Ward's career. Paul's writings make it clear the apostle loved watching athletic events, especially boxing and running. I suppose Paul would enthusiastically commend Ward not only for his stellar boxing accomplishments, but for his excellent outlook on life.

The Announcement

Paul announced his own "retirement" in his final letter: "I have fought the good fight, I have finished the race, I have kept the faith" (2 Timothy 4:7). It seems only natural that as Paul faced his death, he should turn retrospective and think back over his long career. He pictured it both as a boxing match and as a long-distance race.

The Fight

Note that Paul does not say he had fought well but that it had been a worthwhile fight. The struggle had called forth his best, worthiest efforts. The original Greek of the sentence reads, "The good fight I have fought." It takes the emphasis off the "I."

Paul made no comment about having done his best in the contest, only that he had fought in the noblest, grandest fight of them all: the ministry of the gospel. No other fight compared to that one. No other mission could rise to greater importance.

The apostle also called it "the" fight, not "a" fight. This suggests Paul believed the Lord had set him apart for a very specific fight. His fight did not look the same as Peter's fight. Timothy had a different kind of fight than either of them. In fact, *all* of us have fights designed specifically for us—different challenges, different highlights, different hardships, different needs. Each round has its own character and feel. While the core of the fight remains the same for us all—making known the gospel of Jesus Christ—how we fight, where we fight, and a host of other details change, often markedly.

The Race

Paul saw his race much as he saw his fight. He did not commend himself for having run the full distance, but simply declared that he had followed the specific course laid out for him by his Lord. Like Andre Ward, he could have tweeted, "Mission Accomplished."

Long before he sat on death row, Paul had said, "But none of these things move me; nor do I count my life dear to myself, so that I may finish my race with joy, and the ministry which I received from the Lord Jesus, to testify to the gospel of the grace of God" (Acts 20:24). Now in a dank Roman prison, Paul knew he was about to finish the divine purpose for which God had placed him on earth. He had finished the race marked out specifically for him.

Do you know the race that God has marked out specifically for you? As God's athletes, a set course has been given to each of us. God Himself has chosen our path and marked out the way He wants us to go. If a man claims he's started the race, but we never see him on the course, is he really in the race? This race demands progression.

It's Your Race Too

Paul chose the analogy of a runner to picture every Christian's spiritual growth. Simon Peter said it this way in the last verse of the final letter he ever penned: "Grow in the grace and knowledge of our Lord and Savior Jesus Christ" (2 Peter 3:18). Both Paul and Peter, in their last written correspondence, emphasized the necessity of growth in the Christian life. How else could we become more like Christ? Like a runner in a race, you and I have to keep going because the ultimate goal is to be conformed to the image of Christ.

Do you *want* to become more like Jesus? I know that you will never remain faithful to the race unless you love where it's taking you. If you don't love where you'll end up, you'll quit. For the Christian, the finish line is unquestionably to become more like Christ. The prize at the end of the fight and the reward at the race's finish line is to be like Jesus.

Do you like that destination? Do you genuinely desire to become more like Jesus Christ?

There's far more to your relationship with God than merely extracting eternal life. Once you're saved, Jesus infuses you with His life, intending it to overrule everything else. From then on, a man of God finds his greatest joy and fulfillment in letting Jesus have His way. Does that sound like you? Regardless of where you are right now, regardless of how well or poorly you've boxed or run to this point, Jesus still wants to fulfill His dream for your life.

You don't know my story, you might be thinking. *Do you really think He has a purpose and a dream and potential for* my *life?* Absolutely! But to make this happen might require a midcourse correction.

I love the Chinese proverb: "If you don't change the direction you're going, you're likely to end up where you're headed." Don't come to the end of your life and say, "This is *not* how I expected my life to turn out." Take a look at the road you're traveling right now.

Peer all the way to the end of the line. If you don't like what you see there, then change your path.

Christ's dream for you includes a compelling life purpose, a continual source of joy and peace, an intimate relationship with His Father, a mind filled with timeless wisdom that only God can give, and a heart overflowing with love for Him and for others. And that's not an exhaustive list.

We've all embarked on a lifelong journey. Our best efforts here will result in an incomplete product, for none of us will be fully transformed until we pass from this life into the next. Today, however, we have the opportunity to shift from a life focused exclusively on success on earth to a life centered on service to God and His creation. That's the match we're fighting, the race we're running. We're called to be Christ followers, not merely Christ admirers. Christianity is not a religion for consumers but a relationship for participants.

Are you in?

The Faith

As the apostle's life on this planet came to a close, Paul said he had "kept the faith" (2 Timothy 4:7). It's as if some valuable treasure had been entrusted to his care for delivery to someone on the other side of the world.

Paul faithfully guarded his Lord's deposit. He carefully stewarded the commission he had received. He would fully agree with Jude, who urged some Christian friends "to contend earnestly for the faith which was once for all delivered to the saints" (Jude 3).

How do we contend for the faith? I once spoke to a weekend conference of eighteen hundred women. One participant asked me during a break, "What would you do, Pastor Hunt, if your husband wouldn't come to church?"

Well, who's the church? *We* are the church. The God who used to live in a temple vacated it because His people desecrated His name. Subsequently, He moved into us and said, "I will never leave you nor forsake you" (Hebrews 13:5). God doesn't plan to ever check out, for the kingdom of God is within us (Luke 17:21).

So I told the woman, "You mean, he won't come to the church where we meet. But *you're* the church, so take church to him. In a sweet, kind, unannoying way, weave your faith into every conversation, every opportunity you have at home. Work it in. Give God the glory." That's one way to contend for the faith.

Another way to contend for the faith is to live it out. Ravi Zacharias is one of the world's foremost Christian apologists and a good friend of mine. He says that the world is in desperate need of *seeing* Christians whose lives change because of their relationship with Christ.

Ravi has spoken on the campuses of many Islamic universities around the world to present his case for Christ. As he watches the crowds listen to his message, he's told me it's as though the Islamic theologians in the audience are saying in their hearts, *I hope what he's saying is true.* They already know that what they've embraced doesn't work.

But can you guess the major obstacle that keeps these men from putting their faith in Christ? It's not theological. These Islamic leaders want to know if this relationship with Jesus Christ can indeed be lived out. They wonder, because when they observe the average professing Christian, they see very little difference between the way he lives and the lifestyle of anyone else.

Paul kept the faith. So must we.

The Prize

Although none of us can earn any part of our salvation in any way, that doesn't mean God saves us so that we can sit around. Paul gives us a wonderful example. He wrote: "By the grace of God I am what I am, and his grace to me was not without effect. No, I worked harder than all of them—yet not I, but the grace of God that was with me" (1 Corinthians 15:10 NIV).

When some false teachers tried to claim that they had more authority and credibility than Paul, the apostle wrote, "I have worked much harder, been in prison more frequently, been flogged more severely, and been exposed to death again and again. Five times I received from the Jews the forty lashes minus one," and then he goes on to detail a long list of his labors for Christ (2 Corinthians 11:23-24 NIV).

Now, at the end of his life, Paul looked forward to receiving a reward for all of this hard work. He had kept the rules and deserved a prize. So he said, "Finally, there is laid up for me the crown of righteousness" (2 Timothy 4:8). Paul had been faithful to God's calling and so he looked ahead with assurance to a rousing commendation from his Lord.

The crown (*stephanos* in Greek) was a victor's crown. God will award the crown "of righteousness" to righteous people who live righteous lives. At the ancient Greek games, officials would display in some public spot the prizes to be awarded the winners. Not only did they honor the winning athletes, but when those winners returned home with their crowns or precious awards, the townspeople gave them a joyous procession and a reception.

Paul has this in mind as he looks ahead to his fast-approaching audience with Jesus, his Lord. He sees the Greek games as a dim foreshadowing of all that victorious Christians can anticipate from Christ. And so he writes elsewhere, "Do you not know that those who run in a race all run, but one receives the prize? Run in such a way that you may obtain it" (1 Corinthians 9:24).

Are you running the race of faith in such a way that you may obtain the prize?

The Referee

If you've ever played a sport, you know that referees don't always make the right call. Almost every year, it seems, an undeserving team wins a game because of a blown call. Officials try their best, but they make errors, just like players and coaches.

Jesus doesn't make those errors. Paul calls Him "the righteous Judge," and He always makes the right calls, every time, without exception. No cheating scandals mar the perfection of heaven, no lack of information leads to faulty judgments. Jesus, the righteous Judge, will give out whatever rewards every believing man has earned.

On "that Day"—the time of our Lord's coming when the judgment seat of Christ will take center stage—every one of us will appear before Jesus to receive the things done in the body, whether good or bad. Salvation will not be in view there but rewards for faithful service:

> Now if anyone builds on this foundation with gold, silver, precious stones, wood, hay, straw, each one's work will become clear; for the Day will declare it, because it will be revealed by fire; and the fire will test each one's work, of what sort it is. If anyone's work which he has built on it endures, he will receive a reward. If anyone's work is burned, he will suffer loss; but he himself will be saved, yet so as through fire (1 Corinthians 3:12-15).

Unfortunately, we don't hear much anymore about eternal judgment or rewards for service. Many years ago, in an interview with Billy Graham, David Frost asked, "Dr. Graham, if you had to do it all over again, what would you do differently?"

I don't remember Dr. Graham's exact words, but in essence he replied, "I would preach more on judgment." Today, if you preach on judgment, someone is likely to say, "You should have told them that God loves them." But no preacher loves his congregation if he fails to preach on judgment. Did you know the Lord Jesus Christ spoke of hell three times more often than He did about heaven?

Back in 1741, Jonathan Edwards delivered a famous sermon that God used to change a whole generation. He called it, "Sinners in the Hands of an Angry God." In our own era, I once heard R.G. Lee preach a sermon he called "Payday Someday." Judgment Day is coming—but we don't have to fear it. Paul looked forward to that Day, because he knew he had fought the fight, run the race, and kept the faith. You can have the same confidence.

The Awards Ceremony

The Bible doesn't give us many details about the heavenly award ceremony where Jesus will present us with our rewards, but you know it'll be spectacular. Unlike the modern Olympics, winners won't get just one day or even four years of notoriety, but an eternity to celebrate what God has done through them.

Back in 1992, as the world prepared for the Barcelona Olympic Games, Reebok launched a massive ad campaign to steal some thunder from Nike, the world's largest athletic gear company. It created a series of splashy commercials featuring U.S. decathletes Dan O'Brien and Dave Johnson under the tagline, "Life is short. Play hard." O'Brien and Johnson were essentially the top two decathletes of that day, and Reebok's strategy focused on which one would win the gold and which one the silver. It saw the pair as "battling it out for the title of world's greatest athlete."

Unfortunately for Reebok, O'Brien didn't even make the U.S. Olympic team, and Johnson suffered a stress fracture in his left foot and managed "just" a bronze medal. Reebok had spent twenty-five to thirty million dollars on the campaign, and it didn't rush to re-sign either athlete for further commercial ventures.

That will never happen with Jesus. As the righteous Judge, He longs to present us with awards of "gold, silver, precious stones" as rewards for our faithful service. If we stumble, He won't pull our contracts. He asks us to work hard, by His Spirit, but He doesn't demand that we work perfectly. We need men in God's race who will run with all their might, shooting for the gold, silver, and precious stones.

Remember, Jesus will never forsake you. He's right there with you as you run your race. When things get tough, think of the awards ceremony to come...and keep running.

The Invitation

Jesus has a crown to give, not only to the apostle, "but also to all who have loved His appearing" (2 Timothy 4:8). Literally all over the place in Scripture, God connects Jesus' return with our living in a godly way.

The apostle John, for example, instructs us to "abide in Him [Jesus], that when He appears, we may have confidence and not be ashamed before Him at His coming" (1 John 2:28). To emphasize his point, he wrote that everyone who puts their hope in Christ's return "purifies himself, just as He is pure" (1 John 3:3).

How often do you ponder the Lord's return? If you thought about it more often, would it help you to keep running your race? What do you expect to receive from Jesus when He parcels out His rewards on that day?

How Well Do You Know Him?

We read Paul's farewell address in 2 Timothy, but in Philippians, we hear clearly the passion of his life, what energized him to the very end. His desire was "that I may know Him and the power of His resurrection, and the fellowship of His sufferings, being conformed to His death" (3:10).

Paul saw getting to know Jesus in a deep, intimate way as the reason for his very existence. There's a vast difference between knowing *about* Him and knowing *Him*! Paul wanted his relationship with Christ to massively affect his daily living. The Amplified Bible, Classic Edition, renders the verse like this:

> [For my determined purpose is] that I may know Him [that I may progressively become more deeply and intimately acquainted with Him, perceiving and recognizing and understanding the wonders of His Person more strongly and more clearly], and that I may in that same way come to know the power outflowing from His resurrection [which it exerts over believers], and that I may so share His sufferings as to be continually transformed [in spirit into His likeness even] to His death.

Paul had a fixed, determined purpose to "know Him." And he wanted to know Jesus in at least three major ways.

1. To know Him intimately

The Greek verb *ginosko* (or *epiginosko*) means to know by personal experience. In this verse it appears in the aorist tense, which speaks of an intimate, personal relationship with Jesus Christ, beginning at some point in the past. Paul had come to know Jesus thirty years before on the Damascus Road, but that knowing had present implications—his major passion to that day. When you come to know Christ, you always want to get to know Him better.

When Old Testament writers wrote about the sexual relationship of a husband and wife, they would say that a husband "knew" his wife. The term described the ultimate human relationship of marriage.

In the New Testament, when Matthew says that Joseph "did not know her [Mary]" until after the birth of Jesus, he used the word *ginosko* (Matthew 1:25). He meant that Joseph never became intimate with Mary until after their marriage and after the birth of Jesus. Again, the word describes the deepest possible human union.

Paul wanted to *know* Jesus in the truest biblical sense; not to know merely by intellect but to know by intimacy. Those who know Jesus Christ only in the sense of head knowledge don't know Him like those who know Him in their hearts. When you know Jesus intimately, your life changes, and so you gain enormous influence in God's kingdom. You desire that everybody comes to know Him.

2. To know Him experientially

The apostle had seen Jesus work in his life in amazing ways. It's quite a thrill to be able to say, "God supplied my needs." You and I have that same opportunity.

During our time in college, my wife and I had nothing. I came out of poverty, I hadn't seen my father in about thirteen years, and my mother was on welfare. We were so broke we couldn't pay attention. Still, I sensed God calling me to the ministry, and Gardner-Webb College accepted my application for admission. I had only a GED, however, and the college couldn't let me in on an academic scholarship. I got in only because I received a one-semester government grant.

One Monday night Janet said to me, "Honey, I know God is going to take care of us, but we're out of groceries." We'd just started attending the Bethel Baptist Church in Shelby, North Carolina. That evening the pastor's wife, Mrs. Ezell, came by our place for a visit. She thanked us for coming to Bethel and told us she hoped that while we attended Gardner-Webb College, we would become part of Bethel's ministry.

"I hope y'all don't mind," she continued, "but we sensed yesterday when y'all were here that there was a need in your life. The Lord spoke to us about it, and so if y'all don't mind, we've got some stuff out in the car for you." They went out to the car and brought in a pile of food. They brought in so many goodies, we had enough not only for us, but since we lived in a whole complex of poor preachers, we went around to them and shared with them our surplus.

God was teaching us that we didn't have to preach only in theory that God takes care of His children. We can testify that He not only sent the ravens to feed Elijah, He has ravens today that He still sends out to supply *you*. It is awesome to know Jesus Christ both intimately and experientially!

Did you know that people watch to see how you respond in foul weather? They want to figure out, *Does he really know God? Does God really come? Does God really take care of His children?*

This hurting world desperately needs encouragement, and you can supply it when you know God both intimately and experientially. It will thrill you to hear someone say to you, "There's no explanation for what I just saw happen in your life, apart from the intervention of Almighty God!"

3. To know His power

Paul wanted to know the *power* of Christ's resurrection. At another time he prayed "that you may know what is the hope of His calling, what are the riches of the glory of His inheritance in the saints, and what is the exceeding greatness of His power toward us who believe, according to the working of His mighty power which He worked in Christ when He raised Him from the dead and seated Him at His right hand in the heavenly places" (Ephesians 1:18-20).

Paul did not pray that God's power be *given* to believers, but that they *become aware of* the power they already have in Christ, and then that they *use* it. If you're a Christian, God already has given you His mighty resurrection power as a possession. Now you need to learn how to appropriate it in your daily life.

Some men don't experience this divine power because they have allowed some sin to become a snare in their lives. Even then, though, the resurrection power of Jesus Christ can set them free. Ephesians 3:20 says, "Now to Him who is able to do exceedingly abundantly above all that we ask or think, according to the power that works in us." God's power is unlimited and far beyond our comprehension.

Will you allow God's power to work through you? You *can* walk in victory: "Just as Christ was raised from the dead by the glory of the Father, even so we also should walk in newness of life" (Romans 6:4). Resurrection power alone has the strength to defeat the power of sin.

What a fresh new day it would be in the churches of America if all the men who claim to be saved would bow before Almighty God and say, "Lord, I have all kinds of desires and ambitions, but I want to surrender myself afresh to the sovereign will of God. I belong to You, I'm made by You and for You. Right now, I surrender to Your will for my life."

Do you need to pray that prayer? If so, I urge you to pray right now, and then tell somebody about it, starting with your family. It's time for that fresh new day to begin in the church of Jesus Christ.

Stand Up!

Too many of us stunt our spiritual growth because we never catch sight of a disciple's full potential. Paul wrote, "That if possible I may attain to the [spiritual and moral] resurrection [that lifts me] out from among the dead [even while in the body]" (Philippians 3:11 AMPC). He means, "Whatever it takes, I will be one who lives in the fresh newness of life of those who are alive from the dead." For Paul, this hope had both future and present implications.

Paul wished to become so much like Christ in the way he lived that people would think of him as a resurrected person now, even before his physical death. The word *resurrection* literally means "to stand," and normally highlighted some contrast, as in "to stand out." To the Greek mind, those who had not been born again were lying down. And to experience a resurrection, a man had to stand up.

If you're dead, what are you? A corpse. Paul is saying, "...that I might stand up among the corpses." This is a present tense reference to the resurrection, not a future tense, and it means to "stand up" or to "stand out."

You could translate the verse like this: "I want to know Jesus and the power of His resurrection and the fellowship of His suffering, that I may give the spiritually dead a preview of eternal life in action, as I stand up among those who are spiritually on their backs." Or like this: "As I walk your streets, as I walk into your houses, as I walk into your stores, as I walk into your offices, as I mingle among the sons of men, I want to be so living for Christ, so outstanding for Him, that you can see that I am a living one among the dead ones."

Harold James was a man who stood up. I cried when I heard he'd died. I loved brother Harold. He got saved at my church many years ago, but before then, he was a corpse, dead in his trespasses and sins. The Lord Jesus Christ changed Harold and made him outstanding in the way he stood up for Jesus Christ.

I never came through the back doors of the church on Sunday without him giving me a hug and a word of encouragement. He never wanted just to shake my hand. During a time of prayer one day after his death, I heard someone say, "God, thank You that Tom came to know Jesus Christ because of the way You changed Harold James."

I will miss Harold for many years to come, but I know exactly where he is. He's already with the Lord Jesus Christ, waiting for the awards ceremony when he'll get a pile of rewards.

I want to so stand up for Jesus Christ that I help others to stand up too. I want to have as many men as possible standing up with me when He comes. I want to know Jesus, as Paul did, in a life-changing, world-shaping way.

May God help us all to stand! One day soon, all of us *will* stand before Him. I pray He helps us to stand now that we may count for something on that Day.

Aim at Greatness

Andre Ward went 32-0 as a professional boxer, but he sometimes got knocked down. He got bloodied. He faced some scary situations. The first time he faced light heavyweight Sergey Kovalev, the big Russian had a record of 30-0-1, with twenty-six knockouts. In 2011, Kovalev so pounded an opponent in the ring that the man died shortly after the bell sounded.

Ward, like a lot of boxers, didn't have an easy life. His African-American mother struggled with cocaine addiction and had little role in his growing-up years. His white father reared him but had a heroin addiction, became homeless, and eventually died of a heart attack. "I know what it is to be biracial when both sides won't accept you and you have that confusion of not feeling accepted," Ward said. "You're left asking, 'Who am I?'"[12]

A man named Hunter became almost a surrogate father to Ward during his teen years, and once told him, "I don't know who you are rolling with, but I know this—God's got his hand on you, son. You ain't gonna get away with anything."

Ward eventually came to faith in Jesus Christ and received a lot of help in learning to live right from his pastor, former NFL running back Napoleon Kaufman. Ward's license plate now reads "SOG," which stands for "Son of God."

"The statistics I was faced with?" Ward said. "I shouldn't have made it. With the grace of God, I did."

In his boxing career, Ward aimed at greatness and achieved it. "I know the great ones that have gone before me who said some of the same things I'm saying and didn't finish strong," he said before his final two fights. "I'm trying to avoid those same demons. I'm trying to shake those ghosts."

I think the apostle Paul would have liked watching this guy. Andre Ward gets it. He gave his best to his boxing career, and now, by the grace of God, he wants to give that same dedication and commitment to his community, his family, and his church. For that reason, I expect Andre Ward has a far bigger awards ceremony ahead of him, greater than anything he's experienced until now.

We could do worse than follow his example.

12

DO WHAT YOU WERE CALLED TO DO

My wife and I visited a Cracker Barrel restaurant one morning several years ago to have breakfast. A man approached our table and said, "I don't want to distract you, but can I just have a minute? I need to tell you a story." And then he started crying.

I thought, *Oh, gosh, I'm going to have a counseling appointment during breakfast at Cracker Barrel.*

"One night at church you told us that we needed to expand our facilities," he continued. "I owned a full gym, and as far as I was concerned, that's all I ever needed to do. But God pressed me to do something else." He explained that he wanted to use his gym to host Upward Basketball, an outreach program for kids. Not long afterward, he began the program, it took off, and later I spoke for him at a national Upward Basketball convention.

As a result, over the past twenty years, more than 6.5 million kids have come through Upward Basketball. It hosts between 400,000 and 500,000 kids each year and operates in forty-six states and seventy-two foreign countries. How did that happen? One word at one meeting touched one man, who so far has touched 6.5 million kids and counting.

Your life matters! God wants to use *you* to touch at least one other person who may touch many others. What if this week, when you're full of the Spirit of God and in the flow of Jesus, you touch one person, whose destiny is to reach many others?

How is your life counting so far? Is anybody going to heaven because of you? Have you enriched anybody's life because your life's been enriched? Is anybody encouraged because you have become an encourager? Regardless of your past, God wants to use you to touch your world.

What's Your Purpose?

God has a specific purpose for each man's life, in addition to our highest calling to become like Christ. My specific purpose is not your specific purpose. Neither is your specific purpose mine. For that reason, I don't allow anyone to transfer their vision or burden to my life.

In my early days, I let people intimidate me into trying to fulfill their vision or take up their burden. But I'm no longer so green; I won't allow that to happen anymore. I try to keep in mind what the apostle Paul said in Philippians 3:12-14:

> Not that I have already attained, or am already perfected; but I press on, that I may lay hold of that for which Christ Jesus has also laid hold of me. Brethren, I do not count myself to have apprehended; but one thing I do, forgetting those things which are behind and reaching forward to those things which are ahead, I press toward the goal for the prize of the upward call of God in Christ Jesus.

Paul had a deep desire to press on, to keep moving toward the purpose for which God had laid hold of him. One thing's for sure: None of us will pursue something for which we lack desire, and Paul had a burning desire to fulfill God's purpose for him. When he said he wanted to "lay hold" of God's call on his life, he used a word that means "to capture." Think of a football player who runs down an opposing player to tackle him, to "capture" his opponent. Like that football player, I'd like to capture some things in my own life, and I won't be satisfied until I accomplish what God calls me to do.

What is God calling you to do? What does the Lord want you to pursue at this stage of your life? Has anyone ever challenged you to run your race as hard as you can?

Jimmy Draper, a former president of the Southern Baptist Convention and president emeritus of Lifeway Christian Resources, wrote a book a few years ago titled *Don't Quit Before You Finish*. Jimmy is now in his early eighties. When I was in my thirties, he said to me, "If the Lord continues to use you, would you bring along the generation following you?"

What does that mean? I wondered.

In time, I figured out what he meant. For me, it meant creating the Timothy Barnabas School of Encouragement and Instruction, designed to help the next generation of preachers coming up behind me. God is allowing me to train guys in their twenties, thirties, forties, and fifties. He's allowing me to reach back four decades, and I don't take that privilege lightly.

God wants to do something special with you too. He's no respecter of persons; He's just looking for your availability. The question is, how energetically have you decided to run the specific race the Lord has assigned just to you?

None of Us Has Arrived

Paul realized that the journey toward Christlikeness begins with a sense of honesty and sanctified dissatisfaction. Consider what I journaled one day after I read his words in Philippians:

> Paul's remembering the start of his race. I believe I know what went through his mind: *Damascus road, the day He got hold of me.* He saw Jesus as the starter of the race and the finisher of the race. I love the passage that says, "Wherefore, seeing we are also compassed about with so great a cloud of witnesses, let us lay aside every weight, and the sin which doth so easily beset us, and let us run with patience the race that is set before us, looking unto Jesus, the author and finisher of our faith" (Hebrews 12:1-2 KJV).

Both Paul and the writer of Hebrews used the analogy of a runner to describe a Christian man's spiritual growth. Paul acknowledged that he had not yet arrived at his final goal, nor yet accomplished all in his life that he had been commissioned to do. I'm grateful the apostle spoke like this, because if you know his writings, his life challenges, his commitment, his passion, his transparency, his honesty, and his vulnerability, you also know how greatly the church has always admired him. How many books have been written about Paul and his extraordinary life? It's staggering. And yet we read these verses and we say, "You mean *he* was still growing too?"

Indeed he was. Paul insisted, "I'm not yet perfected." One of the chief marks of Christian maturity is the knowledge that you're not perfect, that you're still in process. Paul gave us an honest evaluation of his own spiritual condition.

Where would you say you are in your walk with Jesus? How would you evaluate your current spiritual condition? Regardless of the results of your evaluation, I'd remind you that Paul admitted to the church, and to us, that he had room in his life for further development. At least four qualities and practices characterized the apostle in his pursuit of spiritual development.

Teachable

Are you teachable? None of us knows all that we need to know, and none of us puts into practice everything that we already know. Just like Paul, we must continue to grow in both areas.

I love Sunday school. I look forward every Lord's Day to attending my Sunday school class at 8:00 a.m. I love sitting under a gifted teacher every week and allowing him to speak God's Word into me. Remaining teachable helps me to keep growing in Christ. Learning from others helps me to keep moving forward.

If you want to accomplish what God called you to do, you have to remain teachable. Anybody who thinks they've arrived is dead on arrival. If you're going to keep helping others, you have to keep growing.

Watchful

Scripture instructs us to be "watchful." The word speaks of a well-balanced and self-controlled life. It more literally refers to someone who abstains from strong drink. Watchfulness gives clarity of mind and sound judgment, which alcohol obliterates. So as long as you live and serve the Lord in some capacity, you must maintain a seriousness of purpose.

Are you taking life seriously? Are you taking God seriously? One day you're going to realize that Randy Alcorn had it right when he said that a moment after you die, you'll know exactly how you should have lived.

Enduring affliction

When things get tough—and they will—don't quit. Endurance forms sound character. You don't quit just because your feelings get hurt. You don't quit your marriage just because of marital disagreements. You don't quit going to church because somebody says something ugly to you. You don't quit obeying God when He disciplines you.

Evangelizing

Paul told Timothy to "do the work of an evangelist" (2 Timothy 4:5). In fact, every Christian man has a call to testify to the work of Jesus in his life. If we don't try to win souls to Christ, who will? God has placed you where He can most use you to reach others. You may be the only Christian some people know.

Don't Get Stuck in Your Past

If you want to move ahead in your journey toward becoming more like Jesus, often you must deal with some issues of your past. Paul wrote, "One thing I do, forgetting those things which are behind."

"That's easier said than done," you might say, and you'd be right. But you don't have a choice if you want to move ahead.

I don't want to spend the rest of my life talking about where I got hurt or who injured me. I don't want to waste hours camping on where I messed up or where I got off track. I don't want to talk incessantly about what's kept me from moving on. Like Paul, I want to forget the things that are behind so that I can move ahead. That doesn't mean I must acquire the capacity to not remember. It means that I have the capacity, with Jesus, to no longer allow the past to negatively influence me.

Do you remember Joseph? Before he became Pharaoh's right-hand man, he endured many years of struggle, hardship, and pain. Do you think he strove to forget those years, to force his memory to fail? He actually did the reverse. He said, "I will name my children after my sorrow." Joseph named his firstborn Manasseh (Genesis 41:50). In Hebrew, *Manasseh* means "making forgetful." What kind of a name is that? Joseph didn't leave us wondering. He explained, "It is because God has made me forget all my trouble and all my father's household" (v. 51 NIV).

Joseph didn't want the facts erased from his memory, but he did want God to take the sting out of them so that no bitterness remained behind. In this way, Joseph conquered the temptation to develop a mean spirit. He didn't lie awake at night, watching mental videos of hurt. Instead he said, "Hey, Manasseh, let me give you a hug."

When a second son came along, Joseph named him Ephraim. In Hebrew, Ephraim means "fruitful." After the boy's birth, Joseph declared, "It is because God has made me fruitful in the land of my suffering" (v. 52 NIV).

If you can't bring your past to the cross—the failures and hurts as well as the successes and the triumphs—then you're grieving the Spirit of God. Joseph felt his past deeply and remembered clearly what had happened to him, but he didn't let any of it cloud his present or his future. Joseph owned it all—the good and the bad, the painful and the joyful—while refusing to permit any of it to limit what God wanted to do in his life *now*. To "forget" the past means to refuse to let it negatively influence or affect you.

Accomplishments can hold you back too. I know many men who have allowed their successes to keep them from becoming all that God calls them to be. Forget *all* that stuff. Cut the chains that keep you bound to the past.

When you allow your past to paralyze you—when you focus on the unsavory things you've done or the good things you failed to do—you continue to let those things dominate you. Why would you want something to control you that you don't even like?

Invite your failures to teach you, but don't ever let them terrorize you. Don't allow your past to distract you. Don't permit your past to debilitate your efforts in the present.

Oswald Chambers wrote, "Leave the irreparable past in God's hands, and step out into an irresistible future with him." What does God want you to do that you haven't yet accomplished? Instead of spending all your time regretting what you have or haven't done, get busy doing something interesting that God has in mind for you today.

Winning in the Fourth Quarter

The average lifespan for a man in the United States is 78.6 years. That means the second quarter of your life ends at age 39. At age 58.5, you've entered the fourth quarter. You've moved into the Hotel California; you can check in, but you can't check out.

Two of my mentors died younger than the national average. Adrian Rogers departed at age 74, Jerry Falwell at age 73. Another friend, Wayne Barber of Precept Ministries, was sitting upright in a chair one night in a hotel bedroom, his wife nearby, when he departed this life at 73 years of age.

Most games are won in the fourth quarter, the ninth inning, the third period. That's true in the Christian life as well. We might run well for years, pursuing all the right things. But as we close in on the end of our life, the enemy tries to get us to relax. At a critical time, whatever has been chasing us can catch us and defeat us. If a man of God ever stops pursuing what is right, the thing behind him will catch him and he'll miss his reward at the end of the race.

Whenever the end comes for me—and none of us knows our time—I want to finish with joy, with energy, and with enthusiasm. I don't want merely to limp across the finish line. I want to keep going and live to my last breath for my life's purpose.

All of us were created in God's image and for God's purposes.

The Lord wants to get glory through us. He wants other people to see our good works and give God glory. When we do what is right, God gets the glory through us.

Paul lived his life with that conviction. By the time he wrote 2 Timothy, he knew he didn't have long to live. He wrote, "I am already being poured out as a drink offering, and the time of my departure is at hand" (2 Timothy 4:6). He saw his impending death as a departure, a leaving.

The word translated "departure" is a prisoner's term. It means "to release." From God's perspective, Paul was facing release, not execution. Emperor Nero said, "I'm putting him to death." Jesus Christ said, "I'm bringing him home."

It's also a term used by farmers. It refers to the unyoking of oxen after a long, hard day at work.

It's also a soldier's word. When the moment came for an army to break camp and take down the tents, this term signaled, "It's time to journey."

It's also a seaman's word. It referred to unmooring a ship so it could weigh anchor and head out to sea. Paul knew he was about to set sail into eternity's ocean.

Last, it's a philosopher's word that meant "an unraveling." How many times have our hearts felt disturbed and our minds paralyzed as we puzzled over this life's mysteries? Paul was about to have all those mysteries fully unraveled.

Paul reminds me of Caleb in the Old Testament. When Caleb got ready to finish his race, he wanted the same thing at the end that he wanted at the beginning. Four and a half decades after God sent the rebellious Israelites into the wilderness, the rebels' children prepared to finally enter the Promised Land. Caleb declared, "Today, I'm eighty-five years old, and I am as strong today as when I started. Now give me this mountain" (see Joshua 14:10-12). Do you know who lived on that mountain? Fierce, scary, hostile giants. Caleb was saying, "I want a giant to kill." He didn't say, "I want to buy a motor home and travel around the Holy Land for a few months."

I doubt I'm as strong today as I was forty-five years ago. These days, it takes me longer to recover. I can still take a six-mile walk one day and feel pretty good the next day, but I could never run those six miles. I still have a lot of energy, but not like when I was twenty. Although I doubt I'm as strong as when I started, I know I'm wiser. And so I'm eager to continue the journey.

How long have you been on your journey? What did you want when you first started on the road with Jesus? Every family member saved? Your town turned upside down for God? Something else? If your God-honoring dreams have changed, what diverted you?

Begin with the End in Mind

One of the top leadership statements is that you should always begin with the end in mind. Your age doesn't matter; begin with the end in mind. Jesus pioneered this approach. What the Lord began with, He stuck with.

Did you know that Jesus began His public ministry by getting baptized? Jesus came from Galilee and went straight to the Jordan River to be baptized by John. Why baptism? John had the same question. "I need to be baptized by You," he said to Jesus, "and are You coming to me?"

"Permit it to be so now," Jesus replied, "for thus it is fitting for us to fulfill all righteousness" (Matthew 3:14-15).

This initial act of Jesus' ministry illustrated both the ultimate purpose of His coming and His last act of earthly ministry. Jesus began with the end in mind. When John put Him under the waters of the Jordan, the event illustrated Christ's death; He was buried through baptism. A few moments later, when Jesus arose out of those waters, He pictured His resurrection from the dead.

What would you like to accomplish for Christ by the end of your journey? What end do you have in mind? How might you increase the chance of your success?

Let Your Last Years Be Your Best

A highly influential church leader said to me one day, "The most important span of your lifetime, if you stay healthy and devoted to God, is your seventies. People in their seventies have a more significant impact on the world than anyone else."

Do you know the second most important season of your life, according to my friend? Your sixties.

A couple of years ago I met with a really cool group of guys, all of them wonderful leaders, including a man who runs a successful national ministry. As I prepared for the meeting, I had dinner with this man, who looked at me and said, "I'm sixty-one years old, and I'm struggling with what's going to happen in the next ten years of my life." This man is a phenomenal golfer, something I'm not. He's even won a Senior Tour event. He can flat out play the game—but in a very emotional tone, he said to me, "Johnny, I'm thinking about throwing my clubs away and not playing anymore."

"What's that all about?" I asked.

"I don't know," he said. "I'm just struggling about the next ten years."

Well, that's something, I thought. *I'm getting ready to host a meeting about "The Next Ten Years" with a dozen of the best leaders Jesus has placed in my life. What's going on here?*

I want to capture the latter years of my life for good. The Bible says, "Listen to counsel and receive instruction, that you may be wise in your latter days" (Proverbs 19:20). Your best days ought to be your latter days.

It's not about whether you have the energy you had "back then." It's not about whether you have the physical strength or the stamina or even the eyesight or hearing. It's all about getting to know Jesus better and becoming more like Him. The outward man perishes, and since the Fall, it always has. But I'm being renewed, day by day, in the inward man. So, if I'm getting stronger in the inward man, then what's the Holy Spirit saying to my inward man about these latter days? What does He want me to do?

Over two decades ago I was sitting in the office of Adrian Rogers when he asked me, "How old are you?"

"Dr. Rogers, I just turned forty," I said.

"You're ready to get started, son," he replied.

By that time, I'd already pastored for seventeen years, and I think he knew it. He spoke with unusual wisdom.

God wants to bless your life in order to use it to foster the growth of others. He wants to use whatever success you've known, whatever experience you've had, as a platform to help others succeed.

The song "Find Us Faithful" reminds me to follow the example of my mentors, that I might leave a heritage of faithfulness to Christ. Oh, that those who follow us find us faithful! May our influence inspire others to believe and obey.

What is the Spirit saying to you? How can you listen to counsel *right now* so that in your latter days you may be wise? What can you do today to make your latter days your best days? What do you need to change to become more like Jesus in the final chapter of your life?

The Judgment Seat of Christ

Martin Luther said, "There are just two days on my calendar. This day and that Day." "That Day" refers to the day when "we must all appear before the judgment seat of Christ, that each one may receive the things done in the body, according to what he has done, whether good or bad" (2 Corinthians 5:10). Luther clearly reflected on his journey's end.

Note that we won't be judged on the things we *know* but on the things we *do*. A man can know it all and do nothing. It's not the truth we know that makes a difference but the truth we obey. Jesus won't render His judgment based on who's on your speed dial or who calls you, but based on what you did with your life.

Some of that doing will cost us. Years before he wrote 2 Timothy, Paul said to the Philippians, "If I am being poured out as a drink offering on the sacrifice and service of your faith, I am glad and rejoice with you all" (Philippians 2:17). Those words sound a lot like the ones in 2 Timothy 4:6, with one major difference: In Philippians, they're conditional, hypothetical. The offering might happen and it might not. But in 2 Timothy, the words are both categorical and actual. Paul had reached his journey's end.

In fact, Paul viewed his entire life as a drink offering, poured out in sacrificial service to God. The drink offering, described in Numbers 15, was the final act in an old covenant sacrificial ceremony. Paul was saying, "Here in this last chapter of my life, I want to pour everything out in sacrificial service for Jesus." This thought actually made the apostle glad. Paul expected this final chapter of his life to be the best.

A friend of mine almost died in Vietnam. Although he knew the Lord, he wasn't where he knew he should be. In a foxhole, he cried out, "God, don't let me die in this condition." That man, Bobby Welch, became one of the leading pastors in this nation, president of our denomination, and a passionate soul-winner. He's never forgotten that wartime incident.

If God called you home today, would you be ready? Or would

you not want to die in your present condition? We used to sing a song that said no one should face Jesus empty-handed.

When I was younger, I was bolder. I remember standing one day on a loading dock for Jacoby Hardware. A truck driver I knew walked up to me while I sang an old song about the Lord's return.

"What are you singing there, Johnny?" he asked.

"'What a beautiful day for the Lord to come again,'" I said.

"Oh no, it's not either," he said.

"I thought you said you were a Christian."

"I am, but I don't want Him to come today. I'm not ready for Him to come today."

All of us ought to live as though Jesus could come today. One day soon, He *is* coming, although none of us knows the time of His arrival. I do know, however, that one day you'll meet Him. Even if He doesn't come for you in the clouds, He's going to call for you to give an account of your life. None of us knows that date or time.

Paul's ministry had begun thirty years prior, on the Damascus Road, and would end in a prison in Rome. The moment he exited the race here, he expected to be with Jesus in heaven. Although he spoke of his "departure," to Timothy he said, "But you be watchful" (2 Timothy 4:5). That's a big contrast! As the apostle prepared to leave, he challenged those coming behind him.

As I write, I'm in my midsixties, which means I have more life behind me than I do in front of me. I want God to continue using me, to keep me energized and serving Him. I want to finish well. If I died in Africa and were given an African funeral, do you know what they'd say about me? When a Christian dies there, the believers say, "He's arrived," not "He's gone."

When I die, wherever that happens, I hope my friends say, "Did you hear about Pastor Johnny? He's arrived."

How can your life help the generation coming along behind

you? How does God want you to pour into their life? How can you get ready to finish well? When you "arrive," what do you hope your friends say about you?

Don't Make It Dull

The Christian life is dynamic and glorious and wonderful, but some of us do our dead-level best to make it dull and boring. My friend, wake up to the reality of who God is. Fall in love with Him! When you do, your life will change for good and for His glory.

Do what you were called to do. Fulfill your ministry. Reach your God-given potential. I love the one-liner by Charles Spurgeon: "We have misjudged our God-given capacity." It's easy to miss everything that God can do with just one man who devotes himself to love and serve God. What could God do with you if you devoted yourself to know and love Him?

Since it's a long way from here to wherever God wants to take you, live obediently. When we train pastors at our Timothy Barnabas School, I teach a lesson about how God wants our final years to be our best years. Dozens of preachers have written me to say, "I'd just about retired on the Lord. And now I'm beginning to see that my best years can be out there in front of me."

Yours too.

PLAY TO WIN

An interviewer once asked fifty people, all in their late nineties, "If you could live your life over again, what would you do differently?" Three answers kept rising to the top:

- I would reflect more.
- I would risk more.
- I would do more things that would live on after I am dead.

Leonardo da Vinci reportedly said, "Shun those studies in which the work that results dies with the workers." All of God's workers die, but we have the privilege while we're alive to do a work that never dies.

Do you want to know why I'm so passionate about living for Jesus? It's because I know that what I'm doing never dies. Dwight L. Moody has been with the Lord for 120 years now. He once said, "I am only one, but I am one. I cannot do everything, but I can do some things, and that which I can do, by the grace of God I will do."

Listen, if you're breathing, your best years can still be ahead of you. Rusty Rustenbach said, "You and I live in an age when only a rare minority of individuals desire to spend their lives in pursuit of objectives which are bigger than they are."

When most men die in our era, it will be as though they had never lived. The average Christian man just goes around, content that he has a fire escape policy: "I'm saved. I'm glad I'm not going to hell." I refuse to let that happen! I refuse to die and let it be as though I'd never lived. I have a whole lot of living to do before I get up there and enjoy His life. I want to play to win. I have no interest in just playing.

I recently read a jarring statement by an older writer: "When you get to my age, you have some long days, but you don't have any more long years." Since I have no more long years out there for me, I want to play to win in the years I have left.

Where are you in your walk with the Lord? Do you know Him and love Him more than you did a year ago, or five years ago, or twenty years ago? The mature Christian man honestly evaluates himself and strives to do better. Stewart Johnson said, "Our business in life is not to get ahead of others but to get ahead of ourselves. To break our own records. To outstrip our yesterday by our today. To do our work with more force than ever before."

What may the Lord be calling you to do with the rest of your life? I have no idea, but I love this one-liner by John Maxwell: "You never find out what you can do until you do all you can to find out." In my own life, I did all I could think of to do in order to lead my best friend to faith in Jesus. That's a story worth sharing, even though it happened many years ago.

A Long, Winding Road

When I got saved, my best friend was Donald Pope. I wanted to see Donald saved, so I witnessed to him. I took him to a Billy Graham crusade. I don't remember what Dr. Graham said, because I prayed the whole time that God would save Donald.

But he didn't get saved.

Donald had never heard me preach, and when as a seminary student I became pastor at Falls Baptist Church in Wake Forest, North Carolina, I called him and said, "Donald, I'm preaching in your community now. You ought to come hear me."

"Sure," he said, "Debbie and I will come hear you on Easter Sunday." I got excited and called lots of Christian friends because I believed that God moves in answer to prayer. I told them, "Pray for Donald and Debbie Pope. Pray that God will save them. They're gonna be here on Easter, so pray that God will save them."

The Popes came on Easter and I preached my heart out. At the end of the service, I gave an invitation. Neither of them came forward. I felt greatly disappointed, but I decided to call him that afternoon.

"Donald," I said, "did you enjoy the service today?"

"Man, I really did," he said.

"Well, Donald, I'll just be honest, man. I was praying for you and I was just wondering—did you sense anything when I gave the invitation? Like, maybe you should have come forward and given your life to Christ? Or maybe that you needed what I preached about?"

I never anticipated his response.

"Yeah," he replied, "to be real honest with you, that did happen. I was really moved. I even thought about stepping out."

I got ready to shout "Hallelujah!" and "Praise Jesus!" So I continued, "Well, how do you feel about it?"

"I got over it," Donald said. "I got over it."

Many months later, when I was supposed to be doing some morning hospital visits, I stayed at home. As my wife stepped in the shower, I told her, "I'm leaving." But by the time she got out of the shower, I hadn't left.

"I thought you were leaving," she said.

"I will in a minute," I said. "I don't know why, but I don't feel as if I'm supposed to go right now." Just then the phone rang. It was Donald. For seven years I'd been trying to live my faith before him and tell him about Jesus. I didn't have to guess why he called.

"I'm sick and tired of living like this," he said. "I want you to come over and share Christ with me."

I practically flew over there and led my best friend to faith in Jesus Christ. It's one thing when God changes your life, but when God also changes the people around you—hellions, just like you— it's something special.

Not long afterwards, Debbie felt so thrilled about Donald's decision that she said, "I want to make the same commitment." I baptized them together.

Who in your life needs you to tell them about Jesus? How may God want to use you to bring that man or woman into His family? Do they see the fruit of the Spirit growing in your life? Have they tasted some of that fruit for themselves? Are you becoming increasingly like Jesus, so that they want what you have?

Not only did God save Donald, but He also called my best friend to preach. He went off to Mid-America Baptist Theological Seminary and began an intern program at Belleview Baptist Church, where Adrian Rogers served. Debbie told me that under Dr. Rogers's ministry she came under deep conviction that she had never really been saved. The sense of conviction grew so heavy that after each service, when the Popes got home, she'd tell Donald she wanted to take a hot shower. She needed someplace to cry without her husband knowing.

"I was fearful what would happen if I admitted that I wasn't saved," she said. "I was a minister's wife, and I thought I would get my husband in trouble. How can a preacher start his ministry when even his wife isn't truly converted?"

Debbie stayed in that hard place for some time. Week in and week out, she continued to do the shower thing, until she just couldn't bear it any longer. Finally, one night she told her husband, "Donald, I've never been saved. I made a decision for Jesus just because you did. You've really been changed, but deep in my heart, I've never really been changed."

That night, Donald led his wife to genuine faith in Christ, and the fruit of the Spirit soon began to bud, blossom, and grow in Debbie's life. Before long, she became a heart-and-soul winner. She'd aggravate you with her soul-winning, she got so strong into evangelism. She became an "altar counselor" at church, and when somebody came forward after a service and said, "I'm just coming to move my membership," she'd reply, "Well, tell me your story."

They'd give a report, but she'd press them: "Are you sure of your salvation?" Debbie wanted to hear, in particular, how God had saved them. Many times it turned out the person didn't really know Jesus as Savior and Lord at all—and Debbie would do her best to lead that individual to faith in Christ.

God calls all of us to be ambassadors for Christ. He instructs us to be ready always to give an answer to anyone who asks us why we have such hope. When we anchor our lives in Jesus, when we abide in Him, bear the Spirit's fruit, and day by day allow God to transform us into the image of Christ, we prepare ourselves to have a major impact on the only game that really matters.

Don't play around.

Play to win.

NOTES

1. "Jesus, Be Jesus in Me," by Eddie Carswell, © 1984, used with permission.

2. "*Messiah* Release Date: December 12, 2019," *Wild About Movies*, https://www.wildaboutmovies.com/netflix/messiah/.

3. Denise Petski, "'Messiah': Netflix Orders Religious Drama Series from Mark Burnett and Roma Downey," *Deadline*, November 16, 2017, https://deadline.com/2017.11messiah-netflix-orders-drama-series-mark-burnett-roma-downey-james-mcteigue-direct-1202208898/.

4. John MacArthur, *Titus* (Chicago: Moody, 1996), 114-15.

5. William Barclay, *The Letter to the Hebrews* (Louisville, KY: Westminster John Knox Press, 1976), 183.

6. John Piper, "The Renewed Mind and How to Have It," https://www.desiringgod.org/messages/the-renewed-mind-and-how-to-have-it.

7. I recall this statement from one of Adrian Rogers's radio messages.

8. J.B. Lightfoot, *Philippians* (Wheaton, IL: Crossway, 1994), 155.

9. Kent Hughes, *Disciplines of a Godly Man* (Wheaton, IL: Crossway, 2001), 73.

10. "The Happy Hour: Ward Reveals Why He Retired, What's Next," *NBC Sports*, www.nbcsports.com/bayarea/video/happy-hour-andre-ward-reveals-why-he-retired-whats-his-next-step.

11. Brin-Jonathan Butler, "Andre Ward Fights to Avoid a Boxer's Bad Ending," *Undefeated*, August 4, 2016, https://theundefeated.com/features/andre-ward-fights-to-avoid-a-boxers-bad-ending/.

12. Ibid., and so throughout the Andre Ward story.

Also by Johnny Hunt

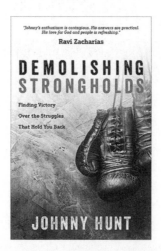

Demolishing Strongholds

Ever wonder how to be a man of God in the trenches of life—in the day-to-day trials and temptations that hound you? It's not impossible! God's promises and strength are real, and you can claim them today.

Whether you feel beaten down by your past failures or trapped in a corner by your current struggles, let hope lift you up. Pastor Johnny Hunt offers the biblical encouragement and guidance that will help you...

- navigate the dangers and discouragements of daily life
- take practical steps toward taming your negative habits
- use your blessings to influence others for God's glory

It's time to learn how to break spiritual strongholds so you can move forward in God's will and become the kind of man you've always wanted to be.

The Verse
by the Side
of the Road

The Story of the Burma-Shave Signs and Jingles

By Frank Rowsome, Jr.

Drawings by Carl Rose

A Dutton Paperback

NEW YORK
E. P. DUTTON

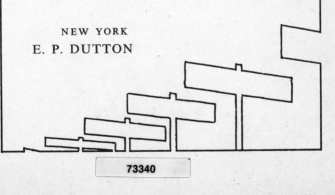

Contents

1:

Remember, Remember

LIKE SO MUCH ELSE, the cars too were different in those days. The last of the spidery but agile Model T Fords had scurried off the production line in May 1927, having been overtaken in the national preference by the disk-wheeled Chevy. Its replacement, the Model A Ford— a nifty vehicle equipped with such elegances as windshield wings, four-wheel brakes, and an authentic gearshift lever sprouting from the floor—was now offered in colors other than black. It was unveiled nationally, in a masterly flurry of exploitation, on December 2, 1927, when thousands queued patiently outside showrooms for their first glimpse of the new wonder.

There were, in those springtime days of America's love affair with its automobiles, many other beloveds. There was the doughty Dodge, as reliable as an Airedale despite its willfully mixed-up gearshift pattern; the substantial Reo and Buick; the sprightly Pontiac and Overland; the Willys- and Stearns-Knights with their exotic sleeve valves; and the radical, warily regarded, air-cooled Franklin. For owners who disdained the commonplace there were ponderous Lincolns and Cadillacs; long-hooded Packards, special favorites with prospering bootleggers; and the lordly, spacious Pierce-Arrow, its wide-apart headlights staring with hauteur. For sportier tastes there were Kissels and Jordans, Auburns and Dusenbergs, Marmons and Templars, as well as the celebrated Stutz, a potent chariot that Cannonball Baker drove from city to city (making his runs in the after-midnight hours when traffic was lightest) at awesome averages of 55 and even 60 mph.

This was not, of course, the way most of us drove. Instead we climbed up—a two-stage ascent—into Old Betsy (very possibly a Studebaker or Nash, an Essex or Peerless) and set forth on our family Sunday-afternoon drive. We were perhaps headed for Nantasket Beach, or all the way around the lake, or out beyond Fort Loudon to

2

Mr. Welch's roadside stand where, among the brightly painted windmills, there would be an opportunity to buy some freshly picked corn or cucumbers. Because this trip might, with variation and caprice, amount to as much as sixty or sixty-five miles, we prudently stopped at Snow's Garage down on Village Avenue for gasoline, oil, and, if need be, free air and water.

Snow's had by now largely outworn its livery-stable origin. The red gasoline pump stood near the door, topped by a glass cylinder into which the fuel was pumped, thence to descend by gravity into the tank between the half-elliptic springs by Betsy's spare tire. Snow's also had a portable gasoline pump, a wheeled rectangular cart with a cranked pump, and this could be trundled out in the event that two cars needed fuel at the same time. If Betsy should need some oil, it was dispensed from a barrel into a quart measure and funneled into her engine. (Snow's newest and most formidable competitor, an oil-company gas station across the street, had already begun to serve up its beautiful dark-green oil in prefilled glass bottles, each with a screwed-on spout and carried out in a compartmented wire basket, like milk bottles.)

At the end of town, just before the sharp turn and the striped wooden barriers that guarded the railroad crossing, there was a red-and-green traffic light hung out over the intersection. Everyone in town was very pleased with that traffic light. Not for us the primitive pipe-and-painted-tin semaphores, dutifully swiveled by the policeman on duty. The red-and-green light symbolized the town's growth and importance, and the increasing flow of traffic coming through on State Route 31. We admitted, to be sure, that State 31 really wasn't at all like the celebrated Lincoln Highway, an awesome transcontinental artery, two lanes wide and with red-white-and-blue markers painted on its adjoining telegraph poles. It was said that along the Lincoln Highway you could often glimpse dusty,

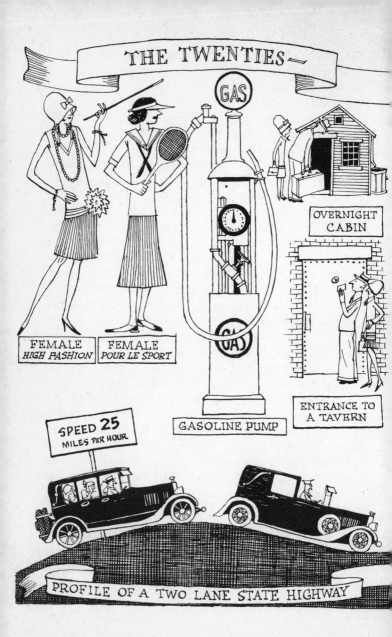

A PARTIAL PANORAMA

POPULAR BALLROOM DANCE

DEALER IN WINE & SPIRITS

MALE COUNTRY CLUB ATTIRE

MALE WINTER PLUMAGE

A PRESIDENT OF THE UNITED STATES

INCLUDING POPULAR CARS OF THE TIME

powerful cars with extra containers of fuel, oil, and water affixed to their running boards, and even with rope and axes for possible use during difficult passages coast to coast.

The highways, as well as the cars, were different and changing in the Twenties. Once out of town they still narrowed down to two lanes, narrow enough so that you warily surveyed each oncoming car for any tendencies toward road-hogging. Even when a two-lane road wasn't awkwardly narrow, drivers had to practice a routine now in relative disuse: the complex art of overtaking and passing another car. This was tricky, calling for skill, patience, resolution, and a knowledge of just how briskly Betsy could get out and around. Sometimes a driver misjudged and had to break off and tuck in behind, his face darkening with embarrassment and anger.

Curves there were in abundance in those days. Some rose naturally from the pre-automobile perambulations of roads. Even in the section-line Midwestern states, where curves were far less common, a sudden T-shaped corner (perhaps originating from property lines) could bring to a somnolent driver the humiliation of having to back out of an alfalfa field. Some curves were purely man made, arising from the parsimonious calculations of highway departments which held that the shortest bridge was the cheapest, even if it did mean a turn at each end. And curves occurred abundantly in the vertical plane as well, for this was long before earthmovers had developed their prodigious ability to cut and fill. Many small tads, perched back in the tonneau of the family touring car, would beseech a parent to drive *faster, faster* on the "roller-coaster road," sometimes called shoot-the-chutes or bump-the-bumps.

Often a picnic lunch was taken, with the food packed in advance, according to the custom of the Twenties, rather than, as now, with oddments flung into an alu-

6

minum ice chest. There were hard-boiled eggs (with a pinch of salt folded in a square of waxed paper); a shoebox of sandwiches, perhaps peanut butter and jam, or slices of corned beef, or ham and cheese. There'd also be soda crackers, a tin of deviled ham (with wonderful forked-tail red imps on the wrapper), and a jar of stuffed olives. There'd be a bag of potato chips, some cold roast chicken that had been located at the extreme back of the icebox, a supply of grapes or oranges and tangerines, cold milk in the Thermos, and bottles of ginger ale or grape juice for those grown up, or almost so. All this would be neatly stowed in a wicker hamper. When opened by the side of the road thirty miles from home, the hamper would be found to lack an opener for the deviled ham or the bottles. This lack would, among cries of recrimination, be ultimately remedied by use of the pliers and screwdriver from Betsy's toolbox, at the cost of no more than a spilled and fuzzing mouthful of ginger ale, and an injured expression on the face of the mother or aunt who had packed the lunch.

Those years of the Twenties were ones of continuous change. The roads grew steadily better, as did the cars. It was no longer necessary to carry elaborate kits for roadside tire repairs. And where the old car had had a natural cruising speed of about 35 mph and became excited at speeds above 45, displaying a disquieting tendency to lunge, the new Model A Fords or Chevys or Overlands were perfectly willing to lope all day long at 50, and had the brakes to suit. As the driving radius extended, it was no longer feasible to brag about a 225-mile day. More and more we took highway vacation trips. Roadside cabins began to appear—one- or two-room dollhouses arranged in an arc, with whitewashed stones outlining the curve of the driveway. They could be rented for two dollars or three dollars a night and were noticeably more convenient than tourist rooms, as well as cheaper than the Hotel Majestic downtown, where it was necessary to put on a necktie to confront the room clerk. Social historians should record the effect of cabins on, among other things, sports clothes, the practice of traveling with pets, and the growth of an additional meaning for the word "vacancy."

In times of continuous change it is difficult to recognize small beginnings. But in the fall of 1925, and again during the following year, one small beginning took place that would later catch the fancy of, and amuse, whole generations of highway-faring Americans.

2:

On the Road
to Red Wing

"MY GRANDFATHER was an attorney in the early days of Minneapolis. In those times lawyers were short on education and long on enterprise, and Grandfather had each of these attributes. For a time he was the U.S. marshal here, with the duty of apprehending men who sold liquor to the Indians. In his law office he also manufactured a liniment—lawyers were into all kinds of things then, because in those days law practice wasn't as fruitful as it is now."

The speaker was Leonard Odell, a husky, broad-shouldered man in his late fifties, the president of the Burma-Vita Company, a division of Philip Morris, Inc. Odell was recounting the early beginnings of Burma-Shave to a recent visitor to the firm's plant on the western outskirts of Minneapolis. Beyond the executive-office walls, mixing and packaging machinery occasionally made staccato and profitable noises. Outside the window and beyond the freight siding Bassett's Creek and a city park could be glimpsed.

"He claimed he'd procured the liniment recipe from an old sea captain, and perhaps he did. Of course most all of those liniments came from sea captains; they traveled the world and encountered witch doctors and collected secret potions. Anyhow, Grandfather made it in his office up in the old Globe Building. It was a potent liniment both in action and smell. You could smell it on the ground floor when he was mixing it on the fifth floor, which probably didn't endear him to his fellow tenants. But he made it there for many years, selling it through a couple of drugstores in lower Minneapolis.

"His son, Clinton, was educated in law at the University of Minnesota, and he was a practicing attorney. Dad was also in the insurance business, and he was a very successful man. He founded the White-Odell agency, which, at one time, had more insurance on its books than

10

any other single agency in the United States. Dad was a *whale* of a salesman. He worked hard, probably too hard, because in 1920 he took sick—sciatic rheumatism, nerve disorders, couldn't walk. He was miserable. Took him pretty near three years to get the thing cured so he could walk again. He climbed out of his illness about 1923, when I was in high school and my brother Allan was at the University. The doctors told him he shouldn't try anything hard-driving again if he wanted to keep his health.

"Well, the family all had this liniment in their homes. I had an aunt who was burned severely on the hand about then with hot fat. In desperation she stuck her hand into this liniment, and in spite of what you might think, the pain stopped immediately. She had no blisters and no scars. It was a marvelous thing.

"So Dad, casting around for something to do, said maybe we can market this. My grandfather had had a stroke by then, and was confined to the house, and Dad was taking care of him. Dad made a royalty arrangement with him and we set out to sell it. We called it Burma-Vita. *Burma* because most of the essential oils in the liniment came from the Malay peninsula and Burma, and *Vita* from the Latin for life and vigor—the whole name meaning Life from Burma.

"Well, we sure starved to death on that product for a couple of years. With a liniment you have to catch a customer who isn't feeling well, and even when you do you only sell him once in a while. The wholesale drug company in town, the people that we got the ingredients from, kept reminding Dad that it would be better if we could find something we could sell everybody, all the time, instead of just hunting for people who were sick. They gave Dad some Lloyd's Euxesis to see what he thought of it.

"Now Lloyd's Euxesis, made in England, was the original brushless shaving cream on the world market. It was a sticky, gummy substance. Still, as an old traveling man, Dad could see the advantage of a brushless shaving cream. You didn't have to pack that wet brush in your grip, where it would mildew and get foul-smelling before you got home. (Remember how they used to get green at the base?)

"Some time before, Dad had heard about a chemist in town who had taken seriously sick, perhaps fatally, and had pulled up stakes for Arizona to see if he could recover. Dad was touched by the story, and in December he wrote him a note with a check for twenty-five dollars, and wished him a merry Christmas. Well, it was about a year later, in 1925, when we were close to the low ebb of all time with the liniment, when the door opened and in walked this chemist, Carl Noren. He said 'Here I am, and I'm well, and what can I do for you?'

"Dad said 'What do you know about a brushless shaving cream?' Carl said 'I never heard of one.' Dad tossed him a tube of Lloyd's Euxesis and said 'Can you make a better one than this?' Carl took a look at it and said 'Well, I can sure try—I used to be chief cosmetic chemist for the old Minneapolis Drug Company.' Then Carl picked up the phone and ordered the ingredients that he thought he'd need, and about three o'clock that afternoon batch number one of Burma-Shave came off the fire. It was, frankly, terrible stuff. We had formulations on and off the market about three times. It wasn't until we got to Formula One Forty-three that we came up with a good, stable product. Actually we'd gone by it and were up close to Formula Three Hundred, and then Dad discovered some of old One Forty-three left in a jar and got a real fine shave from it. That's how we discovered that, if you *aged* old One Forty-three for two or three months, you got a fine shave with it.

"All of us went out and tried to market it. My brother Allan was down in Joliet, Illinois, working with a program that we called Jars on Approval. You'd just walk into a man's office and say 'Here's a jar of Burma-Shave.' 'What's *that*?' he'd ask. You'd explain and tell him how to use it. You'd say 'Take it home and try it and if you like it, give me fifty cents when I come back next week. If you don't, just give me back what's left then and we'll still be friends.'

"Jars on Approval—if you want to starve to death fast, that's one way to do it. I guess Al was pretty discouraged. One day on the road between Aurora and Joliet he saw a set of small serial signs advertising a gas station: Gas, Oil, Restrooms, things like that—maybe a dozen of them—and then at the end a sign would point in to the gas station. Al thought 'Every time I see one of these setups, I read every one of the signs. So why can' you sell a product that way?'

"Well, it sounded good to me, and to everyone else. Except when he came home to tell Dad about his idea, Dad said 'The trouble with you is that you're homesick.' But Dad talked to some of the big advertising men here, and in Chicago—and they said that, year in and year out, it would never work. But Allan sold Dad on giving him two hundred dollars to try out his idea. I think Dad did it more to shut him up than anything else.

"We bought secondhand boards over at the Rose Brothers Wrecking Company. They had plenty of nail-holes in them and some were burned on one side. We sawed them up into thirty-six-inch lengths and painted them up, using a thin brass stencil and brush. They were pretty crude. These signs didn't have rhymes or jingles— just what you might call prose: SHAVE THE MODERN WAY / FINE FOR THE SKIN / DRUGGISTS HAVE IT / BURMA-SHAVE. It was getting on into the fall of 1925, and we had to hurry like the dickens to get them into the ground before it froze solid. We put them on two roads out of Minneapolis. One was Route Sixty-five to Albert Lea, and the other was the road to Red Wing. Maybe we had ten or twelve sets of signs on those two highways.

"By the start of the year we were getting the first repeat orders we'd ever had in the history of the company— all from druggists serving people who traveled those roads. As he watched those repeat orders rolling in, Dad began to feel that maybe the boys were thinking all right, after all. He called us in and said 'Allan, I believe you've got a real great idea here. It's tremendous. The only trouble is, we're broke.'

"With this, Dad did one of the greatest sales jobs I've ever heard of. He had a busted company, he had a product that most people had never heard of, much less believed in, and he had an advertising idea that ad men said wouldn't work. With these three things going for him, he incorporated and then went out and sold forty-nine percent of the stock in less than three weeks. This testified not only to his sales ability but also to the fact that he was a highly respected man that a lot of people had confidence in.

"So early in 1926 we set up our first sign shop. Using slogans and selling lines that Dad and Al thought up, we made a pile of silk-screen signs that weren't *quite* as crude as those first stenciled ones. And Al went out ahead and bought the locations, and I came along behind and dug the holes and tamped in the posts. Boy, did I learn this business starting from three feet under ground."

Leonard Odell walked over to the window, looking out over Bassett's Creek to the parkland beyond. "If you watch for a moment, you can almost always see a pheasant," he told his visitor. "There are thousands of them now. You know, Dad helped import the first pheasants into this state. He was a great conservationist. Made a hobby out of wildflowers, too. He was active in civic affairs and good politics. A hard-driving and conscientious man, with a lot of friends. After that spring we were on our way, and we had a lot of fun over the years. Boy, was Dad enthusiastic! He was a real stem-winder."

3:

And Oh Louise

THE ESSENTIAL SPIRIT of Burma-Shave—what made America first notice and later cherish the jaunty little signs—was of course their light-heartedness. Humor has always been infrequent in advertising, and in the years of the Depression it was so scarce as to be virtually a trace element. If one examines the newspapers and magazines of the period the nearest in the way of intentional humor one is likely to find is an occasional spasm of jocosity, as when an artist would depict a chubby, golden-ringleted female toddler, so busy holding her ice-cream cone above the leaps of a frisky puppy that her defective suspenders threaten to disclose her infant buttocks.

They were days when many advertisers preferred long blocks of copy, composed around the "reason why" principle. In drugstore products in particular, with business poor and competition fierce, many advertisers were aiming single-mindedly for the jugular. Listerine and Lifebuoy were instilling the thought that each citizen was needlessly malodorous; Absorbine Jr. was developing the concept that many apparently beautiful women had cracked and scabby toes; and numerous national advertisers, from Fleischmann's Yeast to Feenamint, were preaching the doctrine that infrequent and faulty bowel movements were both a national disgrace and a grievous personal failure.

It was upon this advertising scene—a lapel-grabbing, intensely serious hard sell—that the Odells arrived with their distinctive, often ironic humor: HE PLAYED / A SAX / HAD NO B. O. / BUT HIS WHISKERS SCRATCHED / SO SHE LET HIM GO. There was even an occasional note of irreverence toward other advertising: IT'S NOT TOASTED / IT'S NOT DATED / BUT LOOK OUT / IT'S IMITATED. The little signs first startled, then delighted, the highway traveler. Their unwillingness to be portentous, their amiable iconoclasm,

18

pleased people in the same way that *Ballyhoo* magazine briefly caught the national fancy, or that *Mad* magazine has recently charmed the young. The signs did not shout, and the only odors mentioned were pleasing ones: HIS FACE WAS SMOOTH / AND COOL AS ICE / AND OH LOUISE! / HE SMELLED / SO NICE. There was also an impious absurdity that was captivating, for no advertisers had ever spoken to us this way before: DOES YOUR HUSBAND / MISBEHAVE / GRUNT AND GRUMBLE / RANT AND RAVE / SHOOT THE BRUTE SOME / BURMA-SHAVE. There was unexpectedness about these flippant new signs; one would cruise a familiar highway and come upon, newly installed, a series such as: THE ANSWER TO / A MAIDEN'S / PRAYER / IS NOT A CHIN / OF STUBBY HAIR.

One aspect to the signs not evident at first was that several special advantages were concealed in an arrangement of six small messages planted one hundred paces apart. At 35 miles an hour it took almost three seconds to proceed from sign to sign, or eighteen seconds to march through the whole series. This was far more time and attention than a newspaper or magazine advertiser could realistically expect to win from casual viewers. Yet Burma-Shave almost automatically exacted this attention from virtually every literate passerby; as Alexander Woollcott once observed, it was as difficult to read just one Burma-Shave sign as it was to eat one salted peanut. Once the Odells had taught us that their signs were constructed with a jingling cadence, and were frosted with a topping of folk humor, we grew addicted to a degree that few advertisers have ever achieved for their copy.

Another advantage lay hidden in the spaced-out signs: they established a controlled reading pace, and even added an element of suspense. The eye could not race ahead and anticipate or spoil the effect, as it could on a printed page. Instead the arrangement, like the bouncing ball

19

in a movie group-singing short, concentrated attention on one sign at a time, building effects for the pay-off line, which was usually the fifth. The result was to deliver the message in much the style of a practiced raconteur who sets the stage for his snapper: PITY ALL / THE MIGHTY CAESARS / THEY PULLED / EACH WHISKER OUT / WITH TWEEZERS. Concentrating the effect in the fifth line was not simply a story-telling device; it also had echoes from childhood and even infancy when, perhaps to avert the threatened approach of bedtime, we begged (just once more) for a favorite rhyme or song: THE BEARDED LADY / TRIED A JAR / SHE'S NOW / A FAMOUS / MOVIE STAR.

Curious and wonderful results, unprecedented in the history of advertising, developed from these hidden characteristics of the six-line highway jingle. One was that people soon developed favorites, reading them aloud with even more savor than the first time they were encountered. The entire carload would chant as if a litany: BENEATH THIS STONE / LIES ELMER GUSH / TICKLED TO DEATH / BY HIS / SHAVING BRUSH. With many families the privilege of reading Burma-Shave signs aloud was a rotated honor, leading inevitably to sharp contention ("It is *so* my turn!"). There was also often someone assigned the duty of peering backward to capture and unscramble the signs that faced in the other direction, a task that required quick wit and a good memory: OF THEM FOR SEED / TO LEAVE ONE HALF / YOU DON'T NEED / WHISKERS / WHEN CUTTING.

Certain themes recurred through all the Burma-Shave jingles, like a motif for a French horn echoing through a symphony. One was the accept-no-substitutes theme. Substitution is an idea that eats corrosively into the mind of advertisers, most particularly those whose products are retailed in groceries and drugstores. The idea is embittering, like a plot from Greek tragedy: one has spent

20

money in building up a demand, and a customer wanders in off the street, maybe not having the name of The Product just right, and then a wretched clerk foists off on him a jar of The Competition, and all that fine money has gone to waste, and, worse, The Competition has rung up a sale, and is even started down the road of earning Product Loyalty for the stuff. It is a nightmare that can make advertisers writhe, and the Odells were no exception. But where conventional, printed-media advertisers would exhort Accept No Substitutes, making virtually no effect whatever on the glazed or unseeing eyes of their readers, the Odells contrived even here a note of gaiety: GIVE THE GUY / THE TOE OF YOUR BOOT / WHO TRIES / TO HAND YOU / A SUBSTITUTE. The intensity of hostility felt toward errant clerks is reflected in another jingle: THE GAME LAWS / OUGHT TO / LET YOU SHOOT / THE BIRD WHO HANDS YOU / A SUBSTITUTE. Occasionally one could detect a resolute effort to take a calm and rational view toward the matter: LET'S GIVE THE / CLERK A HAND / WHO NEVER / PALMS OFF / ANOTHER BRAND. A goaded-beyond-endurance patience was reflected this way: SUBSTITUTES / WOULD IRK A SAINT / YOU HOPE THEY ARE / WHAT YOU KNOW / THEY AIN'T.

The selling of a brushless shaving cream required the changing of settled habits. Gramps and Father had both used a badger-hair brush and perhaps a specially marked shaving mug; why should one change a time-honored and, indeed, traditionally masculine rite? Allan Odell approached the problem from a variety of ways: convenience, modernity, speed, improved results, and the elimination of a need, when traveling, to pack a wet brush. Sometimes the competitive arguments were graphic. Noting the growing acceptance of electric shavers, Clinton Odell himself tossed off a humdinger: A SILKY CHEEK /

21

SHAVED SMOOTH / AND CLEAN / IS NOT OB-
TAINED / WITH A MOWING MACHINE.

It was almost inevitable that competitive arguments
inched close to the edge of propriety. For years Clinton
recalled with wry amusement what happened when he,
perhaps nodding for an instant, had approved a slightly
distasteful jingle. As luck would have it, the jingle was
installed directly across from a fashionable and dignified
church in suburban Minneapolis. Bright new signs chanted
the message SHAVING BRUSH / ALL WET / AND
HAIRY / I'VE PASSED YOU UP / FOR SANITARY
/ BURMA-SHAVE. On the Sunday following the appearance of these unfortunate words, a party of stony-
faced deacons assembled, marched across the street in
their formal garb, and bodily plucked the motes from
their eye.

Hairy brushes were by no means the sole competitors.
Also striving for the favor of whiskery U.S. males were
three other major brushless preparations, Mollé, Krank's
Shave Cream, and Barbasol. Further, as soon as it grew

apparent that the creams were making inroads into the overall market, what the trade called the Big Soapers—Colgate, Palmolive, Williams, and the rest—promptly began to sell brushless creams of their own. And in the depression years, dozens of private brands appeared in the drug chains and the "pine board" (discount) stores. Being manufactured by regional cosmetic companies and bearing higher profit margins for retailers, these private brands added special meaning to Allan's preoccupation with substitution. In the heat of competition there would sometimes be a flash of tooth at the breezy little upstart. At one point Barbasol brandished its lawyers ominously over the jingle lines NO BRUSH / NO LATHER / NO RUB-IN. It was alleged that these words were the exclusive property of Barbasol, as evidenced by the nightly caroling over the American airwaves of the theme song of Singin' Sam, the Barbasol Man. Sam's song was "Barbasol, Barbasol—no brush, no lather, no rub-in—wet your razor and begin." "I don't think they really had a case," said Leonard Odell, "but we didn't bother to

fight them over it. By that time we were jingling so much we didn't need the line."

Procuring an adequate supply of jingles threatened for a time to be a serious problem. (At first they weren't even verses, just advertising admonitions. But as the Odell high spirits took over, and the advantages of rhyme became evident, the basic format was established.) Allan and Clinton composed all copy for the first few years. They gave birth to a few classics, notably EVERY SHAVER / NOW CAN SNORE / SIX MORE MINUTES / THAN BEFORE, and another of the early great ones: HALF A POUND / FOR / HALF A DOLLAR / SPREAD ON THIN / ABOVE THE COLLAR. Yet by the end of the Twenties it was painfully evident that their muse was growing haggard and scrawny. After a brief and unpromising dalliance with staff "jingle artists," Allan turned to the idea of an annual contest, with $100 paid for each verse accepted. When entries poured in by the thousands, it became excitingly clear that, thanks to industrious versifiers all over the country, the Burma-Shave muse was not only rejuvenated but, indeed, more fetching than ever.

Leonard Odell explained the contest mechanisms this way: "We were out for the best jingles we could get. Each year we advertised the contest over the radio, in magazines and newspapers, and in syndicated Sunday comic sections. We also made sure that people who had previously submitted winners were reminded of the new contest. At the beginning Dad was the principal screener. He'd go up to our summer camp with thousands of entries—we'd send more up to him each day—and for three or four weeks he'd scratch out the ones that had no possibilities, or that might have offended people. Then all of us would whittle away at his preliminary selection.

"After a while it got to be too much for Dad; some of the contests drew more than fifty thousand entries. We hired a couple of experts, women who worked as ad-

24

agency copywriters, to come in for a few weeks and filter out the best ones. They were darned good at it, too, once they got the hang of it. Not all of the entries were clean; it was hard to believe that people would sit down and write the things they did. Anyhow, after they'd picked the top thousand, we'd make copies of them for the company officers and the board of directors. Each of us would pick the twenty or twenty-five best, and we'd meet and find out that we'd picked different ones, and then the arguments began. We had a whale of a lot of fun—much more than in most directors' meetings. But we also took them very seriously, because jingles were our bread and butter. We'd just keep thinning them down, going back for more readings, trading favorites with each other, and meeting again. Sometimes it took us several weeks to agree on the next crop."

Quite naturally the disputations often turned on matters of taste. THE OTHER WOMAN / IN HIS LIFE / SAID "GO BACK HOME / AND SCRATCH YOUR WIFE" was regretfully vetoed for highway use, as was another on a reciprocal theme: MY MAN / WON'T SHAVE / SEZ HAZEL HUZ / BUT I SHOULD WORRY / DORA'S DOES. As senior officer, Clinton Odell served as a kind of Horatius at the bridge, vigilantly defending the American highway against anything off-color or scatological. LISTEN, BIRDS / THESE SIGNS COST / MONEY / SO ROOST A WHILE / BUT DON'T GET FUNNY had strong advocacy in committee, although it was never used. Another near miss: THE WIFE OF BRISTLY / BRUSHMUG ZAYMER / BOUGHT TWIN BEDS / WHO CAN BLAME HER?

Possibly one reason why these disputations arose was an awareness in the boardroom that the certified clean, boy-girl jingles were near the core of the most memorable Burma-Shave verse: SAID JULIET / TO ROMEO / IF YOU WON'T SHAVE / GO HOMEO. Often it was amiably suggested that Burma-Shave could facilitate courtship: WITH / A SLEEK CHEEK / PRESSED TO HERS / JEEPERS! CREEPERS! / HOW SHE PURRS. The same remedy was also prescribed for luckless males who didn't know any girls: HIS FACE / WAS LOVED / BY JUST HIS MOTHER / HE BURMA-SHAVED / AND NOW—— / OH, BROTHER! The grim possibility of a loveless life was sketched in one cautionary lyric: BACHELOR'S QUARTERS / DOG ON THE RUG / WHISKERS TO BLAME / NO ONE / TO HUG. A record of persistent failure with females might be accounted for this way: TO GET / AWAY FROM / HAIRY APES / LADIES JUMP / FROM FIRE ES-CAPES.

Perhaps the all-time classic among boy-girl jingles, however, was a compact and metrically memorable verse from 1934. For reasons beyond easy analysis, it appears to have become engraved on the collective American memory: HE HAD THE RING / HE HAD THE FLAT / BUT SHE FELT HIS CHIN / AND THAT / WAS THAT.

4:

Don't Stick
Your Elbow
Out so Far

FOR PAINTING   COWSHED   BARN OR FENCE

LEAFING THROUGH a list of old Burma-Shave jingles is
also to leaf through almost unrecalled memories and as-
sociations. Suddenly you are driving to Maine again in that
hot summer of 1932 and your companion, a radiant girl
who is now a grandmother, is delighted north of Portland
to come upon FOR PAINTING / COW-SHED / BARN
OR FENCE / THAT SHAVING BRUSH / IS JUST
IMMENSE. Or the half-recollected fact that the Burma-
Shave people devoted many signs to the cause of highway
safety comes back with a rush at the sight of REMEMBER
THIS / IF YOU'D / BE SPARED / TRAINS DON'T
WHISTLE / BECAUSE THEY'RE SCARED.

Public service, as it happened, was one of the major
themes recurring in the complete canon. Two other
themes, Allan Odell once told an advertising trade journal,
are "straight advertising and exaggerated humor." Another
way of putting it would be to classify the jingles as being
either product advertising or public-service advertising,
each category being served up in tones that ranged from
the reasonably serious to the wildly rib-poking. And no
matter how much the first five signs devoted themselves
to the public weal, that sixth one always mentioned the

THAT SHAVING BRUSH / IS JUST IMMENSE / Burma-Shave

product. It was notable, in fact, that we were nationally conditioned to put it in even if it wasn't there, as various other advertisers who attempted to imitate the serial format ruefully discovered.

The first public-service jingle appeared in 1935, written by Allan. It managed deftly to combine a safety admonition with a plug for the product: KEEP WELL / TO THE RIGHT / OF THE ONCOMING CAR / GET YOUR CLOSE SHAVES / FROM THE HALF-POUND JAR. In 1937 a woman in Nebraska contributed a tersely macabre thought: DRIVE / WITH CARE / BE ALIVE / WHEN YOU / ARRIVE. In 1938 a man in Wichita received $100 for a lyric that would later recur in variant forms: DON'T TAKE / A CURVE / AT 60 PER / WE HATE TO LOSE / A CUSTOMER. The following year the safety theme came on strong, used in six of the twenty-one new jingles planted along the highways for 1939.

The moving force behind this trend was Clinton Odell. "Dad felt that we'd grown to be a part of the U.S. roadside," Leonard explained, "and had a duty to do what we could about the mounting accident rate. He figured that if people would remember our humorous messages, they just might have more effect than routine do-this, don't-do-that safety advice. And of course we always had our name at the end of each set." It was a shrewd policy also in that it established the firm as being public-spirited, an attitude that could only be an asset in confronting the ominously growing anti-billboard forces. Throughout the country, regulation, special taxes, and outright prohibition of road signs were spreading; and it befitted Burma-Shave, which almost alone among businesses was solely dependent on road signs, to cultivate the reputation of being helpful as well as cheerful.

Several of that first large crop in 1939 managed to effect a jaunty tone with what could scarcely have been described as a droll theme. Wrote a woman from Illinois: HARDLY A DRIVER / IS NOW ALIVE / WHO PASSED / ON HILLS / AT 75. From Michigan came a variation on the hate-to-lose-a-customer concept: PAST / SCHOOLHOUSES / TAKE IT SLOW / LET THE LITTLE / SHAVERS GROW. (A decade later the idea was retooled this way: AT SCHOOL ZONES / HEED INSTRUCTIONS! / PROTECT / OUR LITTLE / TAX DEDUCTIONS.) Sardonic advice arrived from a New Jerseyite: AT CROSSROADS / DON'T JUST / TRUST TO LUCK / THE OTHER CAR / MAY BE A TRUCK.

The following year the number of highway-safety jingles had risen to seven out of twenty-two. The feat of linking shaving cream and highway safety was managed, at slight metric cost, by a Philadelphian who composed: ALWAYS REMEMBER / ON ANY TRIP / KEEP TWO THINGS / WITHIN YOUR GRIP / YOUR STEERING WHEEL AND / BURMA-SHAVE. As was perhaps inevitable, the boundary between the catchy and the grim was not easily established. Observed one plain-speaking lady: WHEN YOU DRIVE / IF CAUTION CEASES / YOU ARE APT / TO REST / IN PIECES. A distinctly gloomy prediction came from Indiana: DON'T PASS CARS /

PAST

SCHOOLHOUSES

TAKE IT SLOW

LET THE LITTLE

SHAVERS GROW

Burma-Shave

ON CURVE OR HILL / IF THE COPS / DON'T GET YOU / MORTICIANS WILL. A lady from Shamrock, Texas, won her $100 with a Cassandra-like forecast: DON'T STICK / YOUR ELBOW / OUT SO FAR / IT MIGHT GO HOME / IN ANOTHER CAR.

The basic problem was beautifully stated in a 1942 jingle: DROVE TOO LONG / DRIVER SNOOZING / WHAT HAPPENED NEXT / IS NOT / AMUSING. In time a variety of devices were used to adapt the somber aspects of safety to the genial Burma-Shave format. One such device was to employ the boy-girl theme so successful with other jingles: IF HUGGING / ON HIGHWAYS / IS YOUR SPORT / TRADE IN YOUR CAR / FOR A DAVENPORT. Or as a poet from the Southwest noted: TRAINS DON'T WANDER / ALL OVER THE MAP / FOR NO ONE / SITS ON / THE ENGINEER'S LAP. A matron of Birmingham, Alabama, evidently a spiritual daughter of La Rochefoucauld, composed what was clearly more an epigram than a jingle: A GIRL / SHOULD HOLD ON / TO HER YOUTH / BUT NOT / WHEN HE'S DRIVING.

A second adaptive device was to use Pearly-Gates imagery, for here familiarity from long use by humorists and cartoonists had leached away the grimness: AT INTERSECTIONS / LOOK EACH WAY / A HARP SOUNDS NICE / BUT IT'S HARD TO PLAY. From a lady of Issaqua, Washington, came this thought: GUYS WHOSE EYES / ARE IN THEIR BACKS / GET HALOS CROSSING / RAILROAD TRACKS.

Puns and wordplay, another Burma-Shave staple, also helped: HE SAW / THE TRAIN / AND TRIED TO DUCK IT / KICKED FIRST THE GAS / AND THEN THE BUCKET. Yet puns proved as unreliable for the Burma-Shave versifiers as they have been for the rest of mankind, being sometimes fine and sometimes ghastly: HER CHARIOT / RACED AT 80 PER / THEY

HAULED AWAY / WHAT HAD / BEN HUR. It was in fact with puns that the Burma-Shave editorial taste, ordinarily so finely attuned to the highway readership, proved sometimes uncertain: TRAIN APPROACHING / WHISTLE SQUEALING / PAUSE! / AVOID THAT / RUNDOWN FEELING!

It would be inaccurate, however, to suggest that the overtones of highway safety gave serious problems to most jinglers. Often they selected naturally undistressing hazards: TWINKLE, TWINKLE / ONE-EYED CAR / WE ALL WONDER / *WHERE* / YOU ARE. A woman of Illinois earned $100 with her blithe inquiry: IS HE / LONESOME / OR JUST BLIND / THIS GUY WHO DRIVES / SO CLOSE BEHIND? Drunken driving came in for full attention, once with an intricate multiple pun: DRINKING DRIVERS / NOTHING WORSE / THEY PUT THE QUART / BEFORE THE HEARSE.

But trouble can lie in wait for the unwary, however well intentioned. In 1948 a jingle announced: THE MIDNIGHT RIDE / OF PAUL / FOR BEER / LED TO A / WARMER HEMISPHERE. No sooner was this rather undistinguished lyric erected about the country than a scorching letter arrived on the desk of the Burma-Shave board chairman. It was from a national association of beer haulers, and its gist, as the Odells recall, was "Doggone it, we've got about forty-one jillion members, and if you don't get that set of signs off the road pronto you're going to start losing a lot of customers, because beer-haulers shave just like everybody else." Since Clinton's policy was never to give offense, the midnight ride of Paul for beer disappeared as rapidly as the crews could replace it. Safety was furthered equally well by jingles that mentioned no commercial products: AROUND / THE CURVE / LICKETY-SPLIT / IT'S A BEAUTIFUL CAR / WASN'T IT?

The actual value of the highway-safety jingles was inherently unmeasurable, although it must have been substantial. A sheaf of praising letters and testimonials from safety officials and highway commissioners collected in the office, pleasing Clinton Odell greatly. He was also delighted to hear of a study on average highway speeds conducted by the University of Pennsylvania; it reported parenthetically that no phenomenon more reliably slowed down speeders than a set of Burma-Shave signs. This behavior was reflected in a 1955 jingle: SLOW DOWN, PA / SAKES ALIVE / MA MISSED SIGNS / FOUR / AND FIVE.

As Clinton interpreted it, public service extended beyond highway safety. A number of jingles on the prevention of forest fires were erected during the Fifties, spotted in locations where they could do the most good. Although of surely commendable intent, it was interesting and perhaps significant that they lacked the expected Burma-Shave zest: MANY A FOREST / USED TO STAND / WHERE A / LIGHTED MATCH / GOT OUT OF HAND. Something of this slightly devitalized quality had been evident earlier. In the months following Pearl Harbor, a number of sequences exhorting citizens to purchase bonds were quickly tooled up, and it was notable that they were marked more by laudable patriotism than by memorable concept and phrase: LET'S MAKE HITLER / AND HIROHITO / LOOK AS SICK AS / OLD BENITO / BUY DEFENSE BONDS. However, by evoking boot camps, basic training, and weekend passes, the main-line jingles quickly captured the essential Burma-Shave spirit: "AT EASE," SHE SAID / "MANEUVERS BEGIN / WHEN YOU GET / THOSE WHISKERS / OFF YOUR CHIN."

5:

The Way
It Worked

Fidelia M. Dearlove, for thirty-three years Allan Odell's secretary, did most of the paperwork on the road signs, and it was considerable. From her route lists, files, and pin-bristling maps, she could almost always tell what jingle was located where, when it had been inspected last, when the agreement with the farmer or landholder would expire, and when the crew in a truck would be along to change copy to a sprightly new verse. With nearly seven thousand sets amounting to forty thousand individual signs scattered from Maine to Texas, and with twenty to twenty-five new jingles being installed regularly to replace an equal number already out, Miss Dearlove had a complex, ever changing situation to keep track of. What made it especially difficult was its dynamic quality: each day there would be mail or phoned reports from an advance man or the crews of installers on the road— they began in the south in winter and fanned out north as the weather bettered—reporting on departures from the original plan, or on new local sign taxes or other circumstances. It was no wonder that when some question about signs came up, almost everyone in the home office had the instinctive reaction of "ask Fidelia."

In the decade following the appearance of those first primitive signs on the roads to Albert Lea and Red Wing, Burma-Shave verses began to sprout like wildflowers. By the fall of 1926, with $25,000 spent on signs, they were dotted through Minnesota, Wisconsin, and Iowa; and sales had grown from virtually zero to about $68,000. In 1927, with an advertising appropriation of $45,000, signs had spread through most of the rest of the Midwest, and sales doubled. By 1929, with $65,000 spent on signs, the first exploratory tongues had reached both the Atlantic and Pacific coasts, with sales doubling once again. In 1930 the signs diffused through the South and New England. Carl Noren, risen to serving as a director of the Burma-Vita Company, was able to say with comfortable precision that "we never knew that there was a depression." During its peak times the company grossed more than $3,000,000 a year, demonstrating the greater effectiveness of cheerful jingles over the door-to-door appeal of Jars on Approval.

The only states that the roadside signs never formally appeared in were Arizona, Nevada, and New Mexico—deemed to have insufficient traffic density—and Massachusetts, deemed to present such obstacles as winding roads, excessive and obscuring foliage, and insufficient numbers of reasonably priced locations.

The first portent of a Burma-Shave invasion into new territory was the sight of the advance man, assigned to buy locations. He'd cruise along main, through highways, watching for spots that met his requirements: a straight and fairly level stretch, at road height, or no more than three or four feet lower, never higher. A place bearing other signs was to be avoided, particularly big billboards that could eclipse part of a series. The site should be visible for a considerable distance, it having been found that, if the set began just after a curve, some people would miss the first sign or two, an annoyance sufficient, in some cases, to generate testy letters of complaint.

Once a likely spot was identified, the advance man (who, like so many others connected with Burma-Shave, was likely to have a hearty, friendly personality) would approach the farmer owning the land, present him with a jar of the product, show him a sign, and begin negotiations: "How'd you like to have a set of these signs put up along the fence there?" This may not always have been the ideal opener, for it was recorded that exceptionally rustic farmers were known to counter warily: "How much is it going to cost me?" But in general a mutually agreeable deal could be concluded without difficulty, a year's lease of rights to install and maintain the signs

39

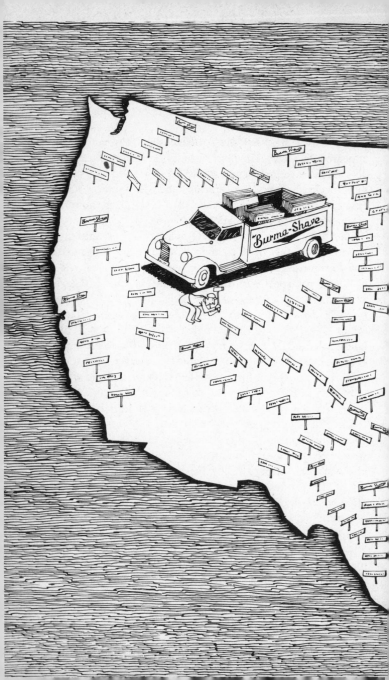

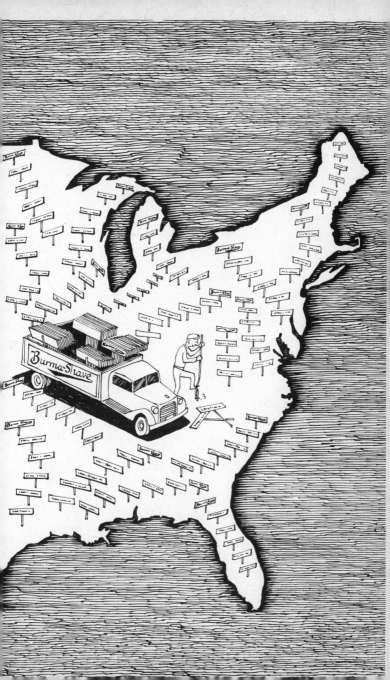

bringing the farmer from five to twenty-five dollars, depending on the desirability of the location. Occasionally a David Harum who owned a particularly choice spot, and who was resistant to the marked friendliness of the advance man, might get fifty dollars or even more a year, although such cases were rare.

Renewals were handled by mail; Fidelia worked out a system of sending out new contracts well in advance of expiration. If a farmer balked at signing, displaying inflated ideas of the site's value, she simply instructed a truck crew to remove the signs at their next passage. Mostly the relationship between farmers and Burma-Shave was an amiable one, with many leases extending for decades. "Oh, occasionally we'd get a man who'd pull down some signs to patch up his barn," noted John Kammerer, head of the company sign shop, "but it was mainly all the other way. The farmers were kind of proud of those signs. They'd often write us if a sign had become damaged, asking us to ship a replacement that they'd put up themselves. In the years when we brought old signs back here to the plant, when lumber was short, I'd sometimes see where they had repaired or repainted signs on their own hook, often doing a fine job of it, too."

Once the advance man had signed up the farmer, the two would pace off the location, tying bright strips of red or orange cloth to the fence to signal the spot for the installation crew following along behind. The crew, traveling in a 1½-ton truck jauntily painted with such admonitions as Cheer Up, Face, the War Is Over, would typically be manned by several husky Minnesota youngsters, appropriately muscled for the assignment of digging thirty-six postholes per day, each one no less than three feet deep. According to carefully fostered rumor, any indolent lad who found that digging to this depth through stubborn shale or past heavy boulders was excessively fatiguing, and who therefore covertly sawed off a foot or eighteen inches from the *bottom* of the post, was liable to summary discharge.

The company displayed a characteristic old-shoe informality in its sign operations. Periodic attempts to systematize it—special regional crews, a complex pattern of leaving trucks and gear in storage in remote parts of the country—were tried and discarded. Instead, the firm settled in to an informal but effective pattern. The dozen or so people in the sign shop, having pitched in during the cruelest part of the Minnesota winter to start production on the new crop of signs and having shipped off the first few hundred sets to regional warehouses, would then divide up in part to set out on the highways. They would be subdivided into several advance men, traveling solo, and three or four truck-borne pairs of installers, laden with signs and equipment, and all bearing Fidelia's latest route maps. With almost the dedication of Crusaders or seekers of the Holy Grail, they would often set out at the end of February and not return home to Minnesota until the ground froze around Thanksgiving. Each truck bore about forty sets of signs, perhaps six or seven working days' supply, after which it was necessary to put in at a regional warehouse and load up again.

There was much informal doubling of duties. The advance man would circle back after signs had been up in a new territory for a few weeks, paying sales calls on drugstores and wholesalers, and usually discovering that a pleasing demand had been generated. The muscular young installers—whom the Odells were accustomed to describe as qualified PhDs, the letters standing for Posthole Diggers—were also often pressed into service as the nucleus of a crew of "samplers," busily handing out small free tubes or jars at ball games, wrestling matches, and other convocations of males.

"We made a few mistakes," noted Burdette Booth, a shyly friendly man who has worked for Burma-Shave

43

all his life. "Once in Los Angeles I had a crew giving out sample jars to men as they filed in to a wrestling match. Then everybody got mad at one of the wrestlers, and they started pitching those jars into the ring—they were just like *rocks,* perfect for throwing—and it was a wonder no one got klonked. After that I learned to sample as people were coming out of a gathering, not as they went in." In New York Leonard Odell learned the same lesson when a crew of his passed out sample tubes of Burma-Shave to baseball fans entering Ebbets Field. After the plate umpire made a call unfavorable to the Dodgers, much of the infield became so densely carpeted with tubes of brushless shaving cream that it was necessary to suspend play until the groundskeepers could tidy up.

Booth, who has served as installer, advance man, salesman, sampler, and plant engineer during his thirty-four years with the company, remembers each assignment as being a lot of fun, in different ways. "Of course you were away from home for long stretches. If I knew I'd be in an area for a while my wife would join me and we'd get a furnished room somewhere. Ohio was one state that I worked over real hard; I put up more than seven hundred sets of signs there. That could be real work—digging postholes all day long. Sometimes when you came back to the cabin or motel after work, people would see the truck painted Cheer Up, Face, and they'd say 'So *you're* the Burma-Shave man!' They sort of thought of you as the Good Humor man, and expected you to be comical on the spot, which was not always easy with an aching back."

The signs themselves underwent continuous evolution. For the first five years they were one-inch pine boards, ten inches high and a yard long, dip-painted twice with the background color mixed with preservative. The lettering, a standard sign painter's Gothic, was applied by silk screen. Letters were four inches high unless the line doubled, when they were squeezed to three and one-fourth inches. To emphasize the new crop of jingles, signs alternated by years between red with white lettering and orange with black lettering. Signs were bolted to steel posts nine feet long. Depending on the length of the location, they were installed ten to twenty yards apart, usually inside the farmer's fence or stone wall. Since highway rights-of-way were narrow in the late Twenties, the signs were usually set back only fifteen or twenty feet from the road's edge.

But times have a way of changing. In 1931 the Odells hired John Kammerer, a young Minneapolis sign and silk-screen expert, to look into a little problem they were having in the paint shop with "bleeding, weeping, and running." The little problem was soon licked, but Kam stayed on for thirty-four years, absorbed in experimenting with and improving the signs. Learning that the steel posts rusted out prematurely in wet ground and near the coasts, Kam had them replaced with pressure-treated wood posts that did fine. Then it was noted that signs had a way of disappearing completely on dark nights if they were located near college towns. These depredations were greatly reduced after Kam had the boltholes counter-bored so that the nuts could be unscrewed only with a special wrench, and after he had crosspieces fitted to the bottoms of the posts as anchors. It was still quite possible for an energetic and larcenous lad to decorate his quarters with a Burma-Shave sign, but he now needed more tools and effort than would normally be brought to an impulse theft.

As roads grew wider and cars went faster, Kam and his crew worked steadily to keep up. In stages over the years the signs grew to twelve and then eighteen inches high and to forty inches in width, with corresponding increase of letter height. Posts were located farther back from the highway, as much as forty or fifty feet from the center line. And the distance between signs steadily lengthened until they were planted, the location permitting, as much as fifty yards apart.

Yearly alterations of color had seemed a good way to call attention to the new signs, but it was noticed that whenever people spoke of Burma-Shave signs, they invariably described them as red and white. Orange-and-black ones seem to have made no impression whatever on the public's retina, or at least on its memory. At this the company gave up, going almost exclusively to red and white. It made things simpler, especially as the early pattern of an annual change became increasingly difficult and expensive with thousands of sets of signs scattered around the country. So the company settled into a custom of inspecting each set each year, but replacing it only every other year.

Simplification was an excellent goal because, the company noted, things tended in general to get steadily more complicated. Several states passed laws taxing each working side of a sign, and since the words *Burma-Shave* normally appeared on the reverse of every sign, the tax load in these states abruptly doubled. The response was a special series of "bareback" signs. Again, South Dakota had a law reserving the color red for danger signs; another special series of white-on-blue signs was created for Fidelia's South Dakota route list, which also included part of Minnesota. And again, high taxes on signs and the growing scarcity of good locations, especially on the close-in approaches to such potentially lucrative concentrations of shavers as New York City, San Francisco, and Los Angeles, made the standard six-sign highway set relatively inefficient. For these troublesome roads the response was a special crop of bobtailed signs. They used three, two, or only one board, and the copy usually settled for a single rhyme or pun:

GOOD TO THE LAST STROP

COVERS A MULTITUDE OF CHINS
PAYS DIVIDENDS IN LADY FRIENDS

Still the basic six-sign set, freighted with puns and outrageous humor, remained spread over the American heartland. Experience accumulated for the sign shop and the installers. It was found, for example, that skunks, beavers, and woodchucks were generally less of a nuisance than college boys, although infrequently some rodent with an atypical taste for creosoted wood would gnaw down a sign. Cows as a rule made good neighbors, except that crews would sometimes find where cows had ruminatively rubbed the posts to a bright shine, tilting the set slightly askew in the process. Hunters, who appear to have an uncontrollable tendency to bag all highway signs, perforated many a Burma-Shave set, although usually with small effect. "One nice thing about a pine board," observed Kam recently, "is its ability to absorb gunfire. A drawback to the aluminum signs that we experimented with for a time was that bullet holes were much more conspicuous than with wood. Of course if a youngster with a twelve-gauge shotgun blasted away from a distance of ten feet, it wouldn't do any sign much good."

In the first decades the strangest natural enemies of Burma-Shave signs were horses. Signs in fields where horses were pastured would be found broken off forcibly at the attachment point. Although several jingles referred pejoratively to horses (e.g., OLD DOBBIN / READS THESE SIGNS / EACH DAY / YOU SEE, HE GETS / HIS CORN THAT WAY), the broken signs did not represent literary criticism. Study by Kam and his crew revealed that the signs were being installed at a perfect height to serve as horse back-scratchers. Throughout the country enterprising horses were discovering that, by sidling under an overhanging sign and humping slightly,

47

a richly sensuous scratching could be achieved; and often, in some transport of equine ecstasy, the sign would snap. A partial remedy, quickly instituted, was to use ten-foot posts in place of nine-footers. It is not recorded how horses felt about this deprivation, although the damage was substantially decreased. A combination of uneven ground and tall, enterprising horses allowed it still to happen on occasion, but, as Kam noted a little sadly, "Our horse problem disappeared as, in fact, horses themselves disappeared from American farms. Tractors don't itch."

6:

Free—Free
A Trip to Mars

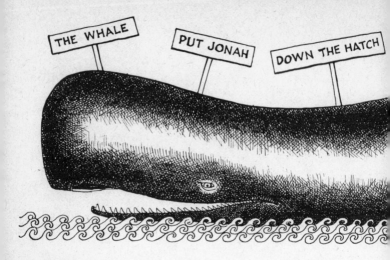

THE WHALE

PUT JONAH

DOWN THE HATCH

Selling shaving cream by jingle may have been an odd way to make a living, but it had its compensations. For one thing, the mail was full of surprises, and Clinton Odell's don't-offend-people dictum meant that all complaints, however odd, had to be judiciously considered. Not all complaints were acted on, though. THE WHALE / PUT JONAH / DOWN THE HATCH / BUT COUGHED HIM UP / BECAUSE HE SCRATCHED drew criticism for irreverence as well as indelicacy, but the signs stayed up. On the other hand, to ease problems of lettering space for Kam's signs, a little simplified spelling was employed experimentally—e.g., *tonite, thot, sez*—but it took only a few reprimands in the mail from English teachers to bring that to a speedy end. And a minor classic of the Thirties, NO LADY LIKES / TO DANCE / OR DINE / ACCOMPANIED BY / A PORCUPINE, although it seemed wholly innocuous, drew an inflamed reproof composed on the letterhead of the Porcupine Club of Boston. We'll have you *know,* the executive secretary wrote in thin-lipped indignation, that

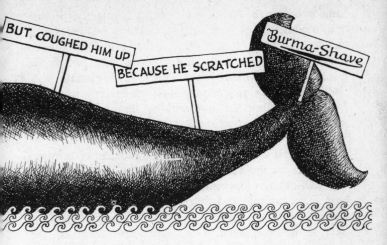

BUT COUGHED HIM UP

BECAUSE HE SCRATCHED

Burma-Shave

our fraternal organization gives *frequent* dances, attended by ladies who give *every* evidence of *enjoying* themselves. To Leonard Odell fell the task of sending a soothing response. After assurances of exceptional respect by the Burma-Vita Company for porcupines everywhere, he explained that in the New York Advertising Club he was personally a member of a subgroup called the Exalted Order of Goats, and that, speaking as an ex-Grand Odor, he had never felt badly about unfortunate references to namesakes. It was a repy that appeared to mollify the Porcupines.

The mail was unpredictable. WITH GLAMOR GIRLS / YOU'LL NEVER CLICK / BEWHISKERED / LIKE A / BOLSHEVIK, appearing in 1940, brought an especially testy complaint. It was postmarked from New York City, with an address from a locality near Union Square. Keep up this sort of thing, it rasped in Humphrey Bogart manner, and the old red herring will *really* get you. Allan held this letter for some days, eyeing it uneasily. It was evidently still on his mind a week later when, returning from lunch, he found a parcel on his desk bearing a

51

similar postmark. As he was opening it gingerly, peering into a corner of its wrapping, he suddenly realized that it ticked ominously. It took only a few strides for him to race to the mixing room down the hall and plunge the package into a tank of water. This reaction virtually convulsed the office and factory staff, all covertly watching, who had collaborated in assembling the package, and in choosing an old alarm clock for the dangerous implications of its tick.

Burdette Booth also remembered a moment of surprise. "We were on the Texas route, changing copy and giving out half-ounce tubes as samples. In Austin we noticed that some cartons of samples were leaking—poor crimping on the tubes, maybe. I phoned Minneapolis and Al said to destroy them. 'Don't just leave them on the dump where someone might find them' he said. So early next morning, in a misty dawn, we stopped the truck on a bridge over a fair-sized river and pitched over the eight or ten leaky boxes. I knew the cartons would come apart and the tubes would sink.

"That afternoon in a town a hundred miles away I was parking the truck when I saw a Texas Ranger in the left-hand mirror. Then I saw another one in the right-hand mirror, and they both had their guns drawn. 'All right' they said, just like Gary Cooper. 'Get out slowly, with your hands high.' They made us unload the whole truck while they inspected the contents. What happened, I found out, was that a housewife had reported seeing two men on the bridge heaving a dismembered body into the river. So the authorities dragged the river but all they found was a piece of carton with *Burma-Shave* on it, and then they radioed out to pick us up. I explained what we'd done. 'All right, but don't do it again' the captain said, and we sure didn't. It's sweaty work unloading the whole truck while hard-eyed guys hold guns on you."

Something about the road-sign operation seemed to invite the unexpected. Leonard recalls a time in the Thirties, posthole-digging his way across New England, when he had just completed the laborious installation of OLD MC DONALD / ON THE FARM / SHAVED SO HARD / HE BROKE HIS ARM / THEN HE BOUGHT / BURMA-SHAVE. He was driving slowly past the signs to check them when he noticed from the mailbox, and verified from Fidelia's route list, that the farmer's name was in fact McDonald. "I didn't know what to do. I figured that we probably ought to take down the whole set, even though it was getting on toward dark. Finally we nervously hunted him up. He was a big man, kind of solemn. When I explained, he just looked at me for a long moment. Then he burst out laughing. Turned out that he got a big kick out of it, and of course the whole neighborhood did too."

In another case a young sailor sent in a long letter. His ship had just returned from an extended training cruise off Alaska, and he wished to relate a most remarkable occurrence, memorable to the several hundred young trainees aboard. They had been steaming above the Aleutians and, the weather being favorable, had passed through the Bering Strait into the Bering Sea. Those off duty had gathered on deck during the passage through the Strait, with Big Diomede Island on the portside and beyond it the mainland of Asia. Ice floes dotted the dark waters. As the ship nosed past a large floe, those on deck were flabbergasted to see a familiar row of small red signs strung along the ice. Binoculars revealed that all but the last sign—which clearly said *Burma-Shave*—were lettered eerily in the Russian alphabet. One sailor with a smattering of Russian announced that the jingle appeared to make some Cyrillic witticism about polar bears. The ship steamed slowly on, bearing several hundred baffled trainees. It was only later that the explanation circulated

53

through the ship's company: the signs had been planted, as an elaborate but thoroughly rewarding practical joke, by the crew of a helicopter flying ahead on ice reconnaissance.

The friendly relationship between Burma-Shave and the U.S. Navy was reflected later, during Operation Deepfreeze in Antarctica. Would the company care to contribute some signs, the Navy asked gravely, to sustain the morale of the men stationed on that remote subcontinent? Gosh, yes, Allan replied, enclosing a list of the sign sets then available. The three jingles chosen mirrored nicely the circumstances near the South Pole. One set was a public-service admonition on forest fires, and was erected on a road from the airbase at McMurdo Sound some thousand miles from the nearest combustible tree. A second set reflected the generally whiskery state prevailing: DEAR LOVER BOY / YOUR PHOTO CAME / BUT YOUR DOGGONE BEARD / WON'T FIT / THE FRAME.

MANY A FOREST   USED TO STAND   WHERE A

The third jingle chosen recalled, perhaps wistfully, the fact that human females were not permitted in Antarctica: USE OUR CREAM / AND WE BETCHA / GIRLS WON'T WAIT / THEY'LL COME / AND GETCHA.

It was characteristic of the luck of the Odells that photographs of the last series—erected in a howling wilderness with a snow tractor in the background and five politely interested penguins gracing the foreground—were picked up by United Press International and distributed to scores of U.S. newspapers. Even after allowing for the fact that Burma-Shave had become a sort of national institution, it was evident that Allan and Leonard had a knack for unpaid publicity that Barnum would have envied.

During the great days of radio, hundreds of "mention permissions" were granted to everyone from Amos 'n Andy to Jimmy Durante and Bob Hope. When television bloomed, it was not unnoticed that the signs could be as

visual as the jingles had been oral. Many of the mentions on network air were brief (e.g., said Fibber McGee scornfully, "I've read better poetry than that on Burma-Shave signs with the last two posts missing"), but some were not, as in 1941 when Bob Hope devoted almost fifteen minutes to a Burma-Shave episode. Fred Allen had a particular fondness for gags built around the signs. One night on the Texaco Hour he devoted so much time to a skit titled "The Murder of the Burma-Shave Poet" that the Odells concluded that "we probably got more out of that network broadcast than Texaco did." Requests for permission to mention usually arrived by phone or telegram, with a note of urgency, and everyone in the office, down to the newest secretary, was authorized to issue permission "just so it was clean and wouldn't offend people."

Sometimes it was even possible to exploit a slightly misfiring jingle. In a time when retailing was being deviled by a fad for coupons, Allan wrote a satirical jingle: FREE OFFER! FREE OFFER! ! / RIP A FENDER / OFF YOUR CAR / MAIL IT IN FOR / A HALF-POUND JAR. While some 99 percent of those seeing this jingle interpreted it as satire, or at least as the light-hearted lunacy to be expected from Burma-Shave, the remaining 1 percent constituted a problem in cleanliness and rubbish disposal. Scores of fenders of notable decrepitude arrived at the plant by parcel post and express. Many enterprising people scavenged Minnesota junkyards, triumphantly bearing off rusty horrors that they lugged to the Burma-Shave offices. Others shipped in fenders forcibly detached from toy cars, which at least had the merit of depositing less dirt and rust. Each donor was greeted with simulated polite surprise, and courteously presented with a jar of Burma-Shave. As Leonard observed, it was one of those delightful little things that happen occasionally. Perhaps more to the point, by later relating the anecdote to the press, the Odells reaped far more value in publicity than the worth of the jars given out.

Once, however, the Odells met their match as amateur Barnums. Again the initiating jingle had been written by Allan, in this case the repeat of an earlier spoof: FREE—FREE / A TRIP / TO MARS / FOR 900 / EMPTY JARS. Although this offer seemed safe, the Odells had not reckoned on Arliss French, manager of a supermarket in Appleton, Wisconsin, one of a chain of Red Owl stores. Mr. French, widely known as Frenchy and no mean exploiter himself, took up the challenge with enthusiasm. He wired Burma-Shave that he was accepting their offer and where should the jars be shipped? After a bit of pencil-chewing, Allan wired back: If a trip to Mars you'd earn, remember, friend, there's no return.

But Frenchy was not easily put off; and besides, business in his store was being stirred up gratifyingly. He countered with a second publicized telegram: Let's not quibble, let's not fret, gather your forces, I'm all set. To this the Odells sent an almost obligatory response: Our rockets are ready; we ain't splitting hairs; just send us the jars—and arrange your affairs. They also sent Ralph Getchman, the general manager of Burma-Shave, to Appleton to see just what was going on.

As Leonard remembers it, "Ralph telephoned me soon: 'This boy's serious! He's got big reproductions of our signs running the full length of his store. He's putting full-page ads in the local paper saying Send Frenchy to Mars! In the store he's got jars heaped up in a huge pile. Any time people buy Burma-Shave he empties the cream into an ice-cream carton and keeps the jar. He's got some kind of rocket plane in the store that kids are swarming all over, and he's got little green men on the roof firing toy rocket gliders out over the parking lot.' I told Ralph the best I could think of for the moment was to send him

57

to the Mars Candy Company down in Chicago for a weekend on the town, which was just barely good enough of an idea to get me off the phone.

"Meantime, though, the Red Owl chain was getting a big kick out of it, especially with the way the volume in the store was up. To help Frenchy they hired a publicity man named Moran, a fellow with a big red beard. He came to see us and said that we had a *great* idea going here. He'd discovered that there was a little town in Germany called Mars—spelled Moers actually, but pronounced Mars—population about a hundred and twenty-two, near Düsseldorf. He said that if we'd pay the plane fare, he'd take care of the rest, and that's how we did it. We decided to send Mrs. French along too, figuring that since she had eleven or twelve children maybe she could use a little vacation.

"So Frenchy showed up here with a bubble on his head, dressed in a silvery space suit with a big red owl on the front. They rented a Brink's armored truck to deliver the jars; it had a big sign on it, Sending Frenchy to Mars. We gave him some full jars that he could use in Mars to barter for goods and services. It made quite an affair for the TV and news photographers. The Frenches spent the night in Al's house, and he drove them to the airport in the morning. In Mars there was a three-day festival that was a dilly, with dancing in the streets and people coming in for miles around. The Frenches had a marvelous time, and when they got home they wrote us a wonderful letter. We still get Christmas cards from them.

"It was a real fun kind of thing," Leonard Odell concluded. "And syndicated right across the country."

7:

An End
to the
Road Signs

THE LITERARY QUALITY of the Burma-Shave verse was highly variable, not surprising, perhaps, considering that even Shakespeare did not attempt seven hundred sonnets. A minority of the jingles were—there is no other word for it—appalling: PEDRO / WALKED / BACK HOME BY GOLLY / HIS BRISTLY CHIN / WAS HOT-TO-MOLLY. Every now and then one moved beyond gaiety toward agitation: HE ASKED / HIS KITTEN / TO PET AND PURR / SHE EYED HIS PUSS / AND SCREAMED "WHAT FUR!" A few skirted the limits of felicity: HE LIT A MATCH / TO CHECK GAS TANK / THAT'S WHY / THEY CALL HIM / SKIN-LESS FRANK. There was, finally, a taste for the kind of whimsy that can sweep like a breeze across a grammar-school playground: HIS BRUSH IS GONE / SO WHAT'LL WE DO / SAID MIKE ROBE I / TO MIKE ROBE II.

At times numerous observers (including the Odells themselves) have dismissed the jingles as corny. This is an easy if not notably discerning assessment. Disregarding an occasional deviation, the jingles were in total a remarkable potpourri of folk humor, wit, and skillfully offbeat merchandising. While to dissect is sometimes to destroy, it is nevertheless possible to isolate certain of the elements that produced such generally pleasing and popular effects.

One characteristic, partly enforced by the format, was conciseness—an attribute that has been broadly popular from Aesop through Poor Richard to the fad for Confucius Say. The shortest full-sized jingle of record needed only seven words for its safety admonition: FROM / BAR / TO CAR / TO / GATES AJAR. Another notable compaction was: BROKEN ROMANCE / STATED FULLY / SHE WENT WILD / WHEN HE / WENT WOOLY.

Humor was, obviously, the second important characteristic. Those who undertake to analyze the complete canon will find that at least seven different strains of humor were employed. One was punning and wordplay, often enhanced by the serial effect: MY JOB IS / KEEPING FACES CLEAN / AND NOBODY KNOWS / DE STUBBLE / I'VE SEEN. Another was pure slapstick, in the mainstream of Buster Keaton and Red Skelton: SHE KISSED / THE HAIRBRUSH / BY MISTAKE / SHE THOUGHT IT WAS / HER HUSBAND JAKE. A pseudo-proverb was a favorite device, effective because the sententiousness associated with apothegms set up a nice contrast: WITHIN THIS VALE / OF TOIL / AND SIN / YOUR HEAD GROWS BALD / BUT NOT YOUR CHIN. (This jingle, incidentally, was a special favorite of the Odells'.) An irritable if not waspish wit was often used with telling effect, as in this highway-safety note: DON'T LOSE / YOUR HEAD / TO GAIN A MINUTE / YOU NEED YOUR HEAD / YOUR BRAINS ARE IN IT. The flirty-but-clean sex theme mentioned earlier was good for many a giggle, as was the use (rare among road signs) of topical themes: WE DON'T / KNOW HOW / TO SPLIT AN ATOM / BUT AS TO WHISKERS / LET US AT 'EM. Lastly, the sardonic and quietly sharp tongue often heard in country stores was basic: EVERY DAY / WE DO / OUR PART / TO MAKE YOUR FACE / A WORK OF ART.

A graduate-school dissertation recently prepared by George Odell, Allan's son, *The Burma-Vita Company and Its Relationship to Twentieth Century America,* makes a number of subtle observations about the corpus of the jingles. Their humor, George Odell notes, was often based on the image of the whisker, a concept faintly ludicrous to begin with, and certainly not as repulsive as many other drugstore advertising images. There was also the typically Western humor of exaggeration: WE'VE MADE / GRANDPA / LOOK SO TRIM / THE LOCAL / DRAFT BOARD'S AFTER HIM. This wide-swinging extravagance, traceable back past Mark Twain, Josh Billings, and Bret Harte, found sympathetic responses everywhere west of the Mississippi. The consistent use of slang and colloquialism, George Odell wrote, was comforting to viewers; it was reassuring to find a chatty, familiar jingle on a road many miles from home. Almost inevitably the impression was given that the company sure must be made up of friendly plain folks, very different from those other advertisers of drugstore products, who noisily threatened malodorousness, disease, and decay.

* * *

The commercial fortunes of the Burma-Vita Company can be read like tea leaves in the jingles themselves. For most of the first twenty years the company had at least one jingle per crop that engagingly bragged about the increased number of users. In 1947 came this spirited cock-a-doodle-doo: ALTHO / WE'VE SOLD / SIX MILLION OTHERS / WE STILL CAN'T SELL / THOSE COUGHDROP BROTHERS. But from then on there were notes of strain. In 1948, writing in a house organ called *The Burma Sign Post,* Allan reported slightly decreasing sales and greatly increasing costs, with company officers taking cuts in salary. Other omens followed. The bragging jingle of 1955 showed no increase: 6 MILLION HOUSEWIVES / CAN'T BE WRONG / WHO KEEP / THEIR HUSBANDS / RIGHT ALONG IN / BURMA-SHAVE.

This seven-year plateau was hardly promising in a time of national expansion. Other evidences piled up: increased re-use of existing, bought-and-paid-for rhymes; a tendency to choose the more hard-selling among these; a sharp drop in the ratio of public-service jingles; and then, most ominous of all, a four-year hiatus in which no new jingles whatever were erected. Although it was not visible from the texts of the verses, these were years in which the company was experimenting with alternative methods of advertising, such as radio and TV, as well as with economies of sign manufacture and maintenance.

Clearly the sales magic was slowly draining out of the sprightly little red signs. There were as many explanations as explainers. People were driving too fast to read small signs. Or the fun had gone out of the jingles themselves. Or it was all the fault of the superhighways with their sprawling rights-of-way and frequent exclusion of all commercial signs. Or it was urban growth and associated suburban spraddle. (Despite huge sampling drives, bus and car cards, and special signs on the feeder routes, large cities were a continuing problem that the Burma-Shave strategists never solved satisfactorily. This failure was serious because important marketing areas of the country were turning into supercities, accreting together more each year, like globules and curds on a slowly spreading puddle.)

Some mandarins of advertising had, quite naturally, a lucid if self-serving explanation: homemade, corny little signs, produced without benefit of agency commission, were no longer enough; now it was vital to portray graphic-ally why the product was superior to its competitors, as by TV demonstrations. An opinion-polling marketing analyst made a depth study that was festooned with im-pressive garlands of statistical theory; the corporate image and possible future of Burma-Shave that emerged dimly from the welter of decimal places was, as is the custom with such studies, made up of equal parts of encourage-ment, discouragement, and enigma. Allan himself had a terser verdict: "Times change. If we were starting over now, I'm not sure the idea would work today."

It should not be thought that the Burma-Vita Company

had any intention of lurching blindly into bankruptcy. Impressive numbers of males were still purchasing jars, tubes, and their new aerosol siblings. Modest sidelines of after-shave and pre-electric lotions, deodorants, and even a tooth powder were adding to the gross. There was the memory of a mosquito repellent that had been discontinued only after a singularly mosquito-free summer, and a line of razor blades that had done just fine until the war had cut off supplies of adequate steel. Instead, the difficulty lay in the managerial implications of the situation: there were clear evidences that the road signs were not only growing costlier (some $200,000 a year by the 1960s) but also steadily less effective. Plainly it was expedient to divert more and more of this money into such standard advertising media as print, radio, and TV; and less of it into the fine goofy old road signs that had built and nourished the business.

This dreary if prudent course was already in effect when, on February 7, 1963, it was announced publicly that the Burma-Vita Company had been sold to Philip Morris, Inc. It would become an operating division of a subsidiary, American Safety Razor Products. Allan Odell, for fifteen years president and treasurer of Burma-Vita and in a sense its major creator, chose to enter semi-retirement although he would serve the new entity as a consultant; his younger brother Leonard would act as president of the new division. The two brothers were no longer young; and their father, Clinton, had died in 1958 at the age of eighty. "We were the last of the original Big Four to sell out," Leonard noted recently. The sale was a major milestone on the route that had begun, thirty-eight years before, on the road to Red Wing.

The Odells' decision to reduce gradually the number of road signs, replacing them with other advertising media, was ratified by the new owners. The action was, in fact, accelerated. It was determined that all signs were to be taken down as soon as practicable. One couldn't simply leave them up to fade into picturesque decay; and besides, counsel were of the opinion that if the signs stayed up, one might be held to continue to owe farmers rent money. So the trucks—still painted Cheer Up, Face—were sent out for the last time, fanning across the country on Fidelia Dearlove's routes. Crews unbolted the anti-college-boy attachment points and uprooted the posts, so that nothing visible remained of what had been. Only where the posts were so firmly embedded that extraction was virtually impossible did the crews saw them off flush with the ground, leaving the prescribed three feet of depth buried like an invisible marker. Farmers often seemed sad at the removal, and not just because of the cessation of rent checks. "It's sort of like losing an old friend," crews were told.

Characteristically, Allan and Leonard made the most of the elegiac spirit implied in such comment. Scores of newspaper feature writers and columnists proved eager to do pieces about the demise of Burma-Shave road signs; editorial writers fell into a mood of *Eheu! fugaces;* and the *Saturday Evening Post* ran a beautifully crafted article by William K. Zinsser that was later re-used in the *Reader's Digest.* At the Advertising Club of New York, a well-touted luncheon (with a jingle briefly erected outside along the dignified center mall of Park Avenue) was held for the joint purposes of saying farewell to the signs and of introducing Miss Nobu McCarthy, a Eurasian actress of exceptional charm hired to make Burma-Shave TV commercials. In general, farewells to the signs grew into a promotion that quite dwarfed such earlier triumphs as torn-off fenders and Frenchy's weekend in Mars.

It was also evident that all this was eyed with a certain tart envy within advertising and promotion circles; comment in the trade press noted that the Odells had "set off a wave of nostalgia" and that the "signs were having

as many retirements as an aging opera star." Probably the prevailingly wary attitude toward the Odells was most nicely expressed in 1964 by a man from the Washington *Star.* He described Leonard as a "genial, talkative man of fifty-seven with a highly suspect hayseed air. 'I'm just a country boy,' he will say disarmingly, but there is something about him that makes a city slicker count his fingers after a handshake."

On this occasion Leonard was in Washington to give a set of signs to the Smithsonian. The cultural-history section of that institution, alerted and possibly alarmed by all the publicity about the disappearance of the signs, had requested a typical set. After some thought the Odells chose their favorite about your-head-grows-bald-but-not-your-chin for permanent preservation. (There was, needless to say, no hesitancy about passing over hot-to-Molly or skinless Frank.) The presentation made a fine news story, and was comforting to all connected with the company. It remained for George Odell, Allan's son, to point out the special irony of preserving in the Smithsonian the advertising device of a firm that, in an earlier day, had plastered the country with: SHAVING BRUSHES / YOU'LL SOON SEE 'EM / ON THE SHELF / IN SOME / MUSEUM.

A question is often raised today as to whether the Burma-Shave road signs are actually all gone. Perhaps it is a quirk of memory or some persistence of vision, but many people will assure an inquirer that a set was noticed just a few weeks ago on the road to Chambersburg, or maybe it was that straight stretch just south of Winthrop. So far as is known, this is an illusion, a memory in masquerade. (Yet with some thirty-five thousand individual signs once planted about the nation, it is certainly not impossible for a few to have evaded the dismantling crews; so the chance of a few spectral sets, picked up in the headlights of certain older cars on misty nights, should perhaps not be wholly discounted.) But to the knowledge of the Burma-Vita Company, the only signs in existence today outside the factory are those donated to museums, or given to friends and gracing winding private driveways, and a few that have turned up, bearing outrageous price tags, in enterprising antique shops.

The question of the physical existence of a possible handful of remaining signs is scarcely worth a search program. Unlike the annual count of whooping cranes, this census would in the end be like one conducted to count the passenger pigeon or the great auk. More meaningful, perhaps, is the fact that the little red signs still exist, very much alive, in thousands of memories. The setting in each case is individual, although the memories have much in common. It may be that you are en route to Shady Grove by Pine Lake, driving a spunky Ford V-8 or a delightful Packard with bright red hexagons on its hubcaps. The sun is high, the sky blue, and drifting into the open car there is the warm tar smell from the road, blended with new honeysuckle. Then along the roadside this cadenced message unfolds:

> IF YOU
> DON'T KNOW
> WHOSE SIGNS
> THESE ARE
> YOU CAN'T HAVE
> DRIVEN VERY FAR.

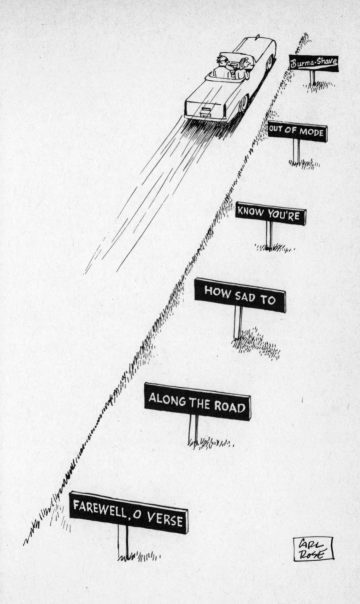

Appendix:

Texts of All
Burma-Shave
Signs

Iᴛ ʜᴀs ʙᴇᴇɴ sᴀɪᴅ that the most carefully perfected plan for the cataloging of a heterogeneous body of objects can never be more than partially satisfactory, and this is eminently true of the Burma-Shave jingles. The listing below, prepared from the company's own records and thus as complete and exact as is possible today, nevertheless presents various technical difficulties to a compiler. The Burma-Vita Company, although expert in the manufacture and sale of shaving cream, had neither a trained historian nor an archivist, and their records present several problems:

1. Texts of the very first sets of homemade signs, placed experimentally on the roads to Red Wing and Albert Lea, are lost. Testimony of participants indicates, however, that the texts used in 1927 were slight elaborations of the originals—i.e., that the earliest texts are contained within the 1927 series.

2. Variant forms of a number of jingles occurred when they were subsequently re-used. The commonest change was to revise the division of words among signs, but textual revision was not unknown. Note for example that in the "museum" jingle of 1930 the line *Way down East* recurs later as *On the shelf*.

3. Records on special jingles for regional tests or for such regionally marketed products as tooth powder, blades, or lotion were not always detailed. The special bobtailed jingles employed on the approaches to certain cities in 1939 and later are not identified by year of use, and were not always changed in annual or biennial cycles.

Finally, a note about editing. The texts here presented are precisely those in company records, shown unaltered. Changes made have been limited to the elimination of authors' names and addresses, of incomplete notations of sign colors used, and of identifying code numbers.   F.H.R. Jʀ.

71

SHAVE THE
    MODERN WAY
NO BRUSH
NO LATHER
NO RUB-IN
BIG TUBE 35¢
    DRUG STORES
BURMA-SHAVE

GOODBYE!
    SHAVING BRUSH
HALF A POUND
    FOR
HALF A DOLLAR
VERY FINE
    FOR THE SKIN
DRUGGISTS HAVE IT
CHEER UP FACE
    THE WAR IS OVER
BURMA-SHAVE

1928

HOLLER
HALF A POUND
    FOR
HALF A DOLLAR
OH BOY!
SHAVING JOY
COMPLEXION SAVE
BURMA-SHAVE

SHAVE THE MODERN WAY
WASH THE FACE
APPLY WITH FINGERS
SHAVE
BIG TUBE 35¢
BURMA-SHAVE

TAKES THE "H"
    OUT OF SHAVE
MAKES IT
    SAVE
SAVES COMPLEXION
SAVES TIME & MONEY
NO BRUSH
    NO LATHER
BURMA-SHAVE

ONE OF THE
    GREAT DISCOVERIES
GOODBYE! SHAVING
    BRUSH
OLD MEN LOOK YOUNGER
YOUNG MEN LOOK
    HANDSOMER
VERY FINE FOR THE SKIN
BURMA-SHAVE

1929

EVERY SHAVER
NOW CAN SNORE
SIX MORE MINUTES
THAN BEFORE
BY USING
BURMA-SHAVE

YOUR SHAVING BRUSH
HAS HAD ITS DAY
SO WHY NOT
SHAVE THE MODERN WAY
WITH
BURMA-SHAVE

TWO
HUNDRED
THOUSAND
MEN
USE
BURMA-SHAVE

HALF A POUND
FOR
HALF A DOLLAR
SPREAD ON THIN
ABOVE THE COLLAR
BURMA-SHAVE

1930

ONE POUND	85¢
HALF POUND	50¢
BIG TUBE	35¢

DON'T PUT IT OFF
PUT IT ON
BURMA-SHAVE

DOES YOUR HUSBAND
MISBEHAVE
GRUNT AND GRUMBLE
RANT AND RAVE
SHOOT THE BRUTE SOME
BURMA-SHAVE

SHAVING BRUSHES
SUCH A BOTHER
BURMA-SHAVE
LOOKS GOOD
TO
FATHER

EARLY TO BED
EARLY TO RISE
WAS MEANT FOR THOSE
OLD FASHIONED GUYS
WHO DON'T USE
BURMA-SHAVE

BE
NO
LONGER
LATHER'S SLAVE
TREAT YOURSELF TO
BURMA-SHAVE

UNCLE RUBE
BUYS TUBE
ONE WEEK
LOOKS SLEEK
LIKE SHEIK
BURMA-SHAVE

THO STIFF
THE BEARD
THAT NATURE GAVE
IT SHAVES LIKE DOWN
WITH
BURMA-SHAVE

SHAVING BRUSHES
YOU'LL SOON SEE 'EM
WAY DOWN EAST
IN SOME
MUSEUM
BURMA-SHAVE

FIVE
HUNDRED
THOUSAND
MEN
USE
BURMA-SHAVE

CHEER UP FACE
THE WAR IS PAST
THE "H" IS OUT
OF SHAVE
AT LAST
BURMA-SHAVE

HALF A POUND
FOR
HALF A DOLLAR
AT THE DRUG STORE
SIMPLY HOLLER
BURMA-SHAVE

SHAVING BRUSHES
YOU'LL SOON SEE 'EM
ON THE SHELF
IN SOME
MUSEUM
BURMA-SHAVE

SIX
HUNDRED
THOUSAND
MEN
USE
BURMA-SHAVE

1880 A.D.
STRAIGHT RAZOR AND
SHAVING SOAP
1930 A.D.
SAFETY RAZOR AND
BURMA-SHAVE

THE 50¢ JAR
SO LARGE
BY HECK
EVEN THE SCOTCH
NOW SHAVE THE NECK
BURMA-SHAVE

ARE YOUR WHISKERS
WHEN YOU WAKE
TOUGHER THAN
A TWO-BIT STEAK?
TRY
BURMA-SHAVE

MODERN MAN
SPREADS IT ON
PATS IT IN
SHAVES IT OFF
SEE HIM GRIN
BURMA-SHAVE

BUY A TUBE
USE IT ONE WEEK
IF YOU THEN WANT
YOUR MONEY BACK
SEND US THE TUBE
BURMA-SHAVE

HINKY DINKY
PARLEY VOO
CHEER UP FACE
THE WAR
IS THRU
BURMA-SHAVE

1931

EIGHT
HUNDRED
THOUSAND
MEN
USE
BURMA-SHAVE

TAKE A TIP
FOR YOUR TRIP
NO WET BRUSH
TO SOAK
YOUR GRIP
BURMA-SHAVE

74

FILM PROTECTS
YOUR NECK
AND CHIN
SO YOUR RAZOR
WON'T DIG IN
BURMA-SHAVE

IT'S A GOOD
OLD SPANISH CUSTOM
TAKE YOUR MUG
AND BRUSH
AND BUST 'EM
BURMA-SHAVE

HELLO DRUGGIST
I DON'T MEAN MAYBE
YES
SIR!
THAT'S THE BABY
BURMA-SHAVE

GOLFERS!
IF FEWER STROKES
ARE WHAT YOU CRAVE
YOU'RE OUT OF THE
    ROUGH
WITH
BURMA-SHAVE

SHAVING BRUSH
ALL WET
AND HAIRY
I'VE PASSED YOU UP
FOR SANITARY
BURMA-SHAVE

THE ONE HORSE SHAY
HAS HAD ITS DAY
SO HAS THE BRUSH
AND LATHER WAY
USE
BURMA-SHAVE

NO MATTER HOW
YOU SLICE IT
IT'S STILL YOUR FACE
BE HUMANE
USE
BURMA-SHAVE

HALF A POUND
FOR
HALF A BUCK
COME ON SHAVERS
YOU'RE IN LUCK
BURMA-SHAVE

THO TOUGH
AND ROUGH
FROM WIND AND WAVE
YOUR CHEEK GROWS
    SLEEK
WITH
BURMA-SHAVE

MAKES SHAVING
A
GRIN GAME
NOT
A SKIN GAME
BURMA-SHAVE

1932

POLITICAL PULL
MAY BE
OF USE
FOR RAZOR PULL
THERE'S NO EXCUSE
BURMA-SHAVE

LISTEN SHAVERS
KNOCK ON WOOD
WHEN OFFERED
SOMETHING
"JUST AS GOOD"
BURMA-SHAVE

_____(HEBREW)
_____(CHINESE)
_____(GREEK)
THE BEST SHAVE
IN ANY LANGUAGE
BURMA-SHAVE

A SHAVE
THAT'S REAL
NO CUTS TO HEAL
A SOOTHING
VELVET AFTER-FEEL
BURMA-SHAVE

THE CANNONEERS
WITH HAIRY EARS
ON WIRY WHISKERS
USED TIN SHEARS
UNTIL THEY FOUND
BURMA-SHAVE

THE TUBE'S
A WHOPPER
35 CENTS
EASY SHAVING
LOW EXPENSE
BURMA-SHAVE

BARGAIN HUNTERS
GATHER 'ROUND
FIFTY CENTS
BUYS
HALF A POUND
BURMA-SHAVE

FROM NEW YORK TOWN
TO PUMPKIN HOLLER
IT'S HALF A POUND
FOR
HALF A DOLLAR
BURMA-SHAVE

FREE
ILLUSTRATED
JINGLE BOOK
IN EVERY
PACKAGE
BURMA-SHAVE

YOU'LL LOVE YOUR WIFE
YOU'LL LOVE HER PAW
YOU'LL EVEN LOVE
YOUR MOTHER-IN-LAW
IF YOU USE
BURMA-SHAVE

FOR PAINTING
COW-SHED
BARN OR FENCE
THAT SHAVING BRUSH
IS JUST IMMENSE
BURMA-SHAVE

GIVE THE GUY
THE TOE OF YOUR BOOT
WHO TRIES
TO HAND YOU
A SUBSTITUTE FOR
BURMA-SHAVE

WHEN THE JAR
IS EMPTY
WIFE BEGINS
    TO SING
"FOR SPICES, JAM & JELLY
THAT JAR IS JUST
    THE THING"
BURMA-SHAVE

LAWYERS, DOCTORS
SHEIKS AND BAKERS
MOUNTAINEERS AND
    UNDERTAKERS
MAKE THEIR BRISTLY
    BEARDS BEHAVE
BY USING BRUSHLESS
BURMA-SHAVE

SEVERAL MILLION
MODERN MEN
WILL NEVER
GO BACK
TO THE BRUSH AGAIN
BURMA-SHAVE

1933

MOONLIGHT
AND ROSES
WHISKERS
LIKE MOSES
JUST DON'T GO TOGETHER
BURMA-SHAVE

THE MILLIONTH MAN
HAS JOINED
OUR RANKS
OF HAPPY SHAVERS
MANY THANKS!
BURMA-SHAVE

TRAVELERS!
ALL
YOU NEED IS
A RAZOR
AND
BURMA-SHAVE

LATE RISERS!
SHAVE IN JUST
2 MINUTES FLAT
KISS YOUR WIFE
GRAB YOUR HAT
BURMA-SHAVE

LITTLE SHAVERS
DON'T OVERLOOK
ILLUSTRATED
JINGLE BOOK
IN EVERY PACKAGE
BURMA-SHAVE

IT'S NOT TOASTED
IT'S NOT DATED
BUT LOOK OUT—
IT'S IMITATED
INSIST ON
BURMA-SHAVE

SHAVING BRUSH
WAS LIKE
OLD ROVER
WHEN HE DIED
HE DIED ALL OVER
BURMA-SHAVE

WISE OLD SANDY
SHOPPED AROUND
THIS IS WHAT
OLD SANDY FOUND
50¢ BUYS HALF A POUND
BURMA-SHAVE

THE ANSWER TO
A MAIDEN'S
PRAYER
IS NOT A CHIN
OF STUBBY HAIR
BURMA-SHAVE

SHAVING BRUSH
DON'T YOU CRY
YOU'LL BE A
SHOE DAUBER
BY AND BY
BURMA-SHAVE

WITHIN THIS VALE
OF TOIL
AND SIN
YOUR HEAD GROWS BALD
BUT NOT YOUR CHIN—USE
BURMA-SHAVE

EVERYTHING
IN IT
IS FINE
FOR THE
SKIN
BURMA-SHAVE

BRIDGE PRIZE
FOR MEN
JUST HALF A BUCK
TRY IT, HOSTESS
CHANGE YOUR LUCK
BURMA-SHAVE

RUDDY CHEEKS
AND FACE
OF TAN
NEATLY SHAVEN
WHAT A MAN!
BURMA-SHAVE

MUG AND BRUSH
OLD ADAM
HAD 'EM
IS YOUR HUSBAND
LIKE ADAM, MADAM?
BURMA-SHAVE

TO SHAVING BRUSH
I NEED
NOT CLING
I WILL NOT HUSH
OF THEE I SING
BURMA-SHAVE

FREE OFFER!
    FREE OFFER! !
RIP A FENDER
OFF YOUR CAR
MAIL IT IN FOR
A HALF-POUND JAR
BURMA-SHAVE

HE PLAYED
A SAX
HAD NO B.O.
BUT HIS WHISKERS
    SCRATCHED
SO SHE LET HIM GO
BURMA-SHAVE

THRIFTY SHAVERS
NOW ARE FOUND
BUYING SHAVES
BY THE POUND
ONE LB. JAR 85¢
BURMA-SHAVE

IF YOUR HUBBY
TRUMPS YOUR ACE
HERE'S SOMETHING
THAT WILL
SAVE HIS FACE
BURMA-SHAVE

(Regional Contest, 1933)

25 PRIZES
EVERY WEEK
THRUOUT THE FOOTBALL
    SEASON
YOU'LL FIND YOU'D
    RATHER
USE NO LATHER
B'GOLLY THERE'S A
    REASON
BURMA-SHAVE

PRIZE CONTEST DETAILS
MAY BE OBTAINED
AT FOOTBALL BROADCAST
EVERY SATURDAY
OVER WCCO
BURMA-SHAVE

HIT 'EM HIGH
HIT 'EM LOW
FOLLOW YOUR TEAM
OVER WCCO
AND WIN A PRIZE
BURMA-SHAVE

HIT 'EM HIGH
HIT 'EM LOW
IT'S ACTION ROOTERS
   CRAVE
MILLIONS BOAST—
   MILLIONS TOAST
THE ALL-AMERICAN
   SHAVE
BURMA-SHAVE

THERE'S FOOTBALL IN
   THE AIR
AND PRIZES FOR ALL TO
   SHARE
ACCEPT OUR INVITATION
WCCO'S THE STATION
(MANY PRIZES
GET YOUR SHARE)

1934

HE HAD THE RING
HE HAD THE FLAT
BUT SHE FELT HIS CHIN
AND THAT
WAS THAT
BURMA-SHAVE

YOUR BEAUTY, BOYS
IS JUST
SKIN DEEP
WHAT SKIN YOU'VE GOT
YOU OUGHT TO KEEP
BURMA-SHAVE

THE ANSWER TO
A SHAVER'S DREAM
A GREASELESS
NO BRUSH
SHAVING CREAM
BURMA-SHAVE

WHEN CUTTING
WHISKERS
YOU DON'T NEED
TO LEAVE ONE HALF
OF THEM FOR SEED
BURMA-SHAVE

EVERY DAY
WE DO
OUR PART
TO MAKE YOUR FACE
A WORK OF ART
BURMA-SHAVE

THE BEARDED LADY
TRIED A JAR
SHE'S NOW
A FAMOUS
MOVIE STAR
BURMA-SHAVE

JONAH TOOK
NO BRUSH
TO MOP HIS FACE
WHERE JONAH WENT
HE NEEDED SPACE
BURMA-SHAVE

THE GAME LAWS
OUGHT TO
LET YOU SHOOT
THE BIRD WHO HANDS
   YOU
A SUBSTITUTE
BURMA-SHAVE

79

BACHELOR'S QUARTERS
DOG ON THE RUG
WHISKERS TO BLAME
NO ONE
TO HUG
BURMA-SHAVE

THO LIVING COSTS
ARE UPWARD BOUND
FOUR BITS
STILL BUYS
HALF A POUND
BURMA-SHAVE

LATHER WAS USED
BY DANIEL BOONE
HE LIVED
A 100 YEARS
TOO SOON
BURMA-SHAVE

COLLEGE BOYS!
YOUR COURAGE MUSTER
SHAVE OFF
THAT FUZZY
COOKIE DUSTER
BURMA-SHAVE

THAT "PINK TOOTH-
  BRUSH"
IS A CURSE
BUT THAT PINK RAZOR'S
A DARN SIGHT WORSE
USE
BURMA-SHAVE

BRISTLY BEARD
OR SILKY FUZZ
JUST SHAVE 'EM BACK
TO WHERE
THEY WAS
BURMA-SHAVE

PITY ALL
THE MIGHTY CAESARS
THEY PULLED
EACH WHISKER OUT
WITH TWEEZERS
BURMA-SHAVE

BENEATH THIS STONE
LIES ELMER GUSH
TICKLED TO DEATH
BY HIS
SHAVING BRUSH
BURMA-SHAVE

EVERY SECOND
WITHOUT FAIL
SOME STORE
RINGS UP
ANOTHER SALE
BURMA-SHAVE

NOAH HAD WHISKERS
IN THE ARK
BUT HE WOULDN'T GET
  BY
ON A BENCH
IN THE PARK
BURMA-SHAVE

1935

HIS FACE WAS SMOOTH
AND COOL AS ICE
AND OH LOUISE!
HE SMELLED
SO NICE
BURMA-SHAVE

WATER HEATER
OUT OF KILTER
TRY THE BRUSHLESS
WHISKER
WILTER
BURMA-SHAVE

80

HELPS
YOUR BUDGET
HOLD ITS GROUND
HALF A DOLLAR
HALF A POUND
BURMA-SHAVE

CUTIE INVITED
VARSITY HOP
GUY FULL
OF WHISKERS
PARTY A FLOP
BURMA-SHAVE

DEWHISKERED
KISSES
DEFROST
THE
MISSES
BURMA-SHAVE

IT TOOK YEARS
TO PERFECT
FOR YOU
A BRUSHLESS CREAM
THAT'S GREASELESS TOO
BURMA-SHAVE

WITH 200 KINDS
FROM WHICH TO CHOOSE
2 MILLION MEN
PREFER
TO USE
BURMA-SHAVE

I JUST JOINED
THE YOUNG MAN SAID
A NUDIST CAMP
IS MY FACE RED?
NO! I USE
BURMA-SHAVE

AVOID THE STORE
WHICH CLAIMS
YOU SHOULD
BUY SOMETHING ELSE
THAT'S JUST AS GOOD
BURMA-SHAVE

20 MILES PER GAL.
SAYS WELL-KNOWN CAR
TO GO 10,000
MILES PER GAL
BUY HALF-POUND JAR
BURMA-SHAVE

IF YOU THINK
SHE LIKES
YOUR BRISTLES
WALK BARE-FOOTED
THROUGH SOME THISTLES
BURMA-SHAVE

YOU KNOW
YOUR ONIONS
LETTUCE SUPPOSE
THIS BEETS 'EM ALL
DON'T TURNIP YOUR NOSE
BURMA-SHAVE

GRANDPA'S BEARD
WAS STIFF AND COARSE
AND THAT'S WHAT
CAUSED HIS
FIFTH DIVORCE
BURMA-SHAVE

TUBE
IMMENSE
35 CENTS
EASY SHAVING
LOW EXPENSE
BURMA-SHAVE

KEEP WELL
TO THE RIGHT
OF THE ONCOMING CAR
GET YOUR CLOSE SHAVES
FROM THE HALF-POUND
    JAR
BURMA-SHAVE

ENTHUSIASTIC USER
HENRY J. MC LASS
SPREADS OUR PRODUCT
ON THE LAWN
WHEN HE CUTS THE
    GRASS
BURMA-SHAVE

BE A MODERN
PAUL REVERE
SPREAD THE NEWS
FROM EAR
TO EAR
BURMA-SHAVE

THE HAPPY GOLFER
FINDS WITH GLEE
THE SHAVE
THAT SUITS HIM
TO A TEE
BURMA-SHAVE

WHISKERS LONG
MADE SAMSON STRONG
BUT SAMSON'S GAL
SHE DONE
HIM WRONG
BURMA-SHAVE

EENY-MEENY
MINY-MO
SAVE YOUR SKIN
YOUR TIME
YOUR DOUGH
BURMA-SHAVE

AT XMAS TIME
AND BIRTHDAYS TOO
WE SOLVE
YOUR PROBLEMS RIGHT
FOR YOU—GIVE
BURMA-SHAVE

SHAVING BRUSH
IS OUT OF DATE
USE THE
RAZOR'S
PERFECT MATE
BURMA-SHAVE

HALF A BUCK
HALF A POUND
NO SUBSTITUTE
IS EVER FOUND
FOR
BURMA-SHAVE

IF SUBSTITUTION
HE SHOULD TRY
JUST LOOK THAT CLERK
RIGHT IN THE EYE
AND BELLOW:
BURMA-SHAVE

1936

RIOT AT
DRUG STORE
CALLING ALL CARS
100 CUSTOMERS
99 JARS
BURMA-SHAVE

TO GET
AWAY FROM
HAIRY APES
LADIES JUMP
FROM FIRE ESCAPES
BURMA-SHAVE

SPECIAL TREATMENT
EVERY HAIR
HOLDS IT UP
AND CUTS
IT SQUARE
BURMA-SHAVE

YOUR RAZOR
FLOATS THRU
THE HAIR
WITH THE
GREATEST OF EASE
BURMA-SHAVE

ED'S FACE
IS ROUGH
AND RUGGED
ED'S WIFE
DOESN'T HUG ED
BURMA-SHAVE

SHAVING BRUSH
& SOAPY SMEAR
WENT OUT OF
STYLE WITH
HOOPS MY DEAR
BURMA-SHAVE

TO EVERY MAN
HIS SHAVE
IS BEST
UNTIL HE MAKES
THE FINAL TEST
BURMA-SHAVE

GOLFERS!
HOLE IN ONE
IS QUITE A FEAT
UNLESS THAT HOLE
IS IN YOUR MEAT
BURMA-SHAVE

IF YOU
AND WHISKERS
DO HOBNOB
SOME SAILOR GOB
WILL STEAL YOUR SQUAB
BURMA-SHAVE

IF YOU'RE JUST
AN AVERAGE MAN
WANTING TO LOOK
THE BEST YOU CAN
USE
BURMA-SHAVE

THE CREAM
PRESERVES
PA'S RAZOR BLADE
THE JAR PRESERVES
MA'S MARMALADE
BURMA-SHAVE

FISHERMAN!
FOR A LUCKY STRIKE
SHOW THE PIKE
A FACE
THEY'LL LIKE
BURMA-SHAVE

SMITH BROTHERS
WOULD LOOK IMMENSE
IF THEY'D JUST
COUGH UP 50 CENTS
FOR HALF POUND JAR
BURMA-SHAVE

JIMMIE SAID A
NAUGHTY WORD
JIMMIE'S MOTHER OVER-
    HEARD
SOAPSUDS? NO!
HE PREFERRED
BURMA-SHAVE

CONGRESSMAN PIPP
LOST THE ELECTION
BABIES HE KISSED
HAD NO PROTECTION
TO WIN—USE
BURMA-SHAVE

LET'S GIVE THE
CLERK A HAND
WHO NEVER
PALMS OFF
ANOTHER BRAND
BURMA-SHAVE

HIS TENOR VOICE
SHE THOUGHT DIVINE
TILL WHISKERS
SCRATCHED
SWEET ADELINE
BURMA-SHAVE

OLD MC DONALD
ON THE FARM
SHAVED SO HARD
HE BROKE HIS ARM
THEN HE BOUGHT
BURMA-SHAVE

AS YOU JOURNEY
DOWN THE YEARS
YOUR MIRROR IS
THE GLASS THAT CHEERS
IF YOU USE
BURMA-SHAVE

CHEER CHEER
THE GANG'S
ALL HERE
RIDING ALONG
THREE MILLION STRONG
FOR
BURMA-SHAVE

HEAR ABOUT
THE JOLLY TAR
IT SMELLED SO GOOD
HE ATE
A JAR
BURMA-SHAVE

COOTIES LOVE
BEWHISKERED PLACES
CUTIES LOVE THE
SMOOTHEST FACES
SHAVED BY
BURMA-SHAVE

FREE! FREE! !
A TRIP
TO MARS
FOR 900
EMPTY JARS
BURMA-SHAVE

ALL THESE YEARS
YOUR SKIN
HAS DRIED
WHY NOT MOISTEN
UP YOUR HIDE
BURMA-SHAVE

1937

HOLLER!
HALF A POUND
FOR HALF A DOLLAR
ISN'T THAT
A CHEERFUL EARFUL
BURMA-SHAVE

DRIVE
WITH CARE
BE ALIVE
WHEN YOU
ARRIVE
BURMA-SHAVE

84

WEEK-OLD BEARD
SO MASKED HIS FACE
HIS BULL DOG
CHASED HIM
OFF THE PLACE
BURMA-SHAVE

LITTLE WILLIE
MODERN SOUL
BUSTED PAPA'S
BRUSH AND BOWL
NICE WORK WILLIE
BURMA-SHAVE

'MID RISING
TAXES
SOARING RENTS
STILL HALF A POUND
FOR FIFTY CENTS
BURMA-SHAVE

SUBSTITUTES!
SMOOTH GUYS SELL 'EM
EASY MARKS USE 'EM
WELL GROOMED MEN
ALWAYS REFUSE 'EM
BURMA-SHAVE

EVERY
SHEBA
WANTS A SHEIK
STRONG OF MUSCLE
SMOOTH OF CHEEK
BURMA-SHAVE

IF *HER* WHISKERS
SCRATCHED *YOUR* CHEEK
YOU WOULD
SEND HER OUT
TO SEEK
BURMA-SHAVE

THE CANNIBALS
TOOK JUST ONE VIEW
AND SAID
HE LOOKS TOO NICE
TO STEW
BURMA-SHAVE

YOU'VE LAUGHED
AT OUR SIGNS
FOR MANY A MILE
BE A SPORT
GIVE US A TRIAL
BURMA-SHAVE

IF HARMONY
IS WHAT
YOU CRAVE
THEN GET
A TUBA
BURMA-SHAVE

THE BURMA GIRLS
IN MANDALAY
DUNK BEARDED LOVERS
IN THE BAY
WHO DON'T USE
BURMA-SHAVE

KIDS! ATTENTION!
44 BEST JINGLES
USED SO FAR
IN JINGLE BOOK
WITH TUBE OR JAR
BURMA-SHAVE

MEN
WHO'VE TESTED
EVERY BRAND
ARE JUST THE ONES
WHO NOW DEMAND
BURMA-SHAVE

IT'S IN
THE BAG
OF EVERY MAN
WHO TRAVELS
LIGHTLY AS HE CAN
BURMA-SHAVE

FROM SASKATOON
TO ALABAM'
YOU HEAR MEN PRAISE
THE SHAVE
WHAT AM
BURMA-SHAVE

MY NECK WAS SORE
IN FRONT BEFORE
AND ALSO
SORE BEHIND
BEFORE
BURMA-SHAVE

STOMACH ACHE!
DOCTOR—
TOOTHACHE!
DENTIST—
WHISKERS!
BURMA-SHAVE

THE CROWD
YOU SEE
AROUND THAT STORE
ARE BURMA-SHAVERS
BUYING MORE
BURMA-SHAVE

BATHROOM SHELF
SURPRISES ME
FROM SHAVING CLUTTER
IT'S NOW FREE
I'M USING
BURMA-SHAVE

FINGERS WERE MADE
BEFORE BRUSHES—
USE 'EM
THEY'RE MUCH SAFER
YOU CAN'T LOSE 'EM
BURMA-SHAVE

SALESMEN, TOURISTS
CAMPER-OUTERS
ALL YOU OTHER
WHISKER-SPROUTERS
DON'T FORGET YOUR
BURMA-SHAVE

NO PULLING
AT THE WHISKER BASE
A SOOTHING FILM
PROTECTS
YOUR FACE
BURMA-SHAVE

PAPER HANGERS
WITH THE HIVES
NOW CAN
SHAVE WITH
CARVING KNIVES
BURMA-SHAVE

ROMANCES ARE
WRECKED
BEFORE THEY BEGIN
BY A HAIR
ON THE COAT
OR A LOT ON THE CHIN
BURMA-SHAVE

"THEY'RE OFF"
HE CRIED
AND FELT HIS CHIN
'TWAS JUST ANOTHER
EASY WIN FOR
BURMA-SHAVE

FIRE! FIRE!
KEEP COOL
BE BRAVE
JUST GRAB
YOUR PANTS AND
BURMA-SHAVE

A SILKY CHEEK
SHAVED SMOOTH
AND CLEAN
IS NOT OBTAINED
WITH A MOWING
      MACHINE
BURMA-SHAVE

CHEEK TO CHEEK
THEY MEANT TO BE
THE LIGHTS WENT OUT
AND SO DID HE
HE NEEDED
BURMA-SHAVE

HENRY THE EIGHTH
PRINCE OF FRISKERS
LOST FIVE WIVES
BUT KEPT
HIS WHISKERS
BURMA-SHAVE

DON'T TAKE
A CURVE
AT 60 PER
WE HATE TO LOSE
A CUSTOMER
BURMA-SHAVE

IF YOU HAVE
A DOUBLE CHIN
YOU'VE TWO
GOOD REASONS
TO BEGIN USING
BURMA-SHAVE

ON A HIGHWAY AD
HE SPIED IT
BOUGHT A JAR
NOW GLAD HE
TRIED IT
BURMA-SHAVE

RING OUT THE OLD
RING IN THE NEW
WHAT GOOD CAN
SHAVING
BRUSHES DO?
BURMA-SHAVE

SAY, BIG BOY
TO GO
THRU LIFE
HOW'D YOU LIKE
A WHISKERED WIFE?
BURMA-SHAVE

ARE YOU
AN EVEN-TEMPERED GUY
MAD ALL
THE TIME
BETTER TRY
BURMA-SHAVE

THE CREAM
ONE HEARS
THE MOST OF NOW
COMES FROM A JAR
NOT FROM A COW
BURMA-SHAVE

THE TIME
TO START
A REAL DISPUTE
IS WHEN YOU'RE
OFFERED A SUBSTITUTE
BURMA-SHAVE

OTHER THINGS HAVE
GONE SKY HIGH
HALF A DOLLAR
STILL WILL BUY
HALF POUND JAR
BURMA-SHAVE

BEFORE I TRIED IT
THE KISSES
I MISSED
BUT AFTERWARD—BOY!
THE MISSES I KISSED
BURMA-SHAVE

NO LADY LIKES
TO DANCE
OR DINE
ACCOMPANIED BY
A PORCUPINE
BURMA-SHAVE

IN EVERY
HALF A POUND
MY BOY
YOU GET A TON
OF SHAVING JOY
BURMA-SHAVE

HERE'S SOMETHING
THAT COULD
EVEN SOAK
THE WHISKERS OFF
A RADIO JOKE
BURMA-SHAVE

RIP VAN WINKLE
SAID HE'D RATHER
SNOOZE FOR YEARS
THAN SHAVE
WITH LATHER
BURMA-SHAVE

TRAILER FOLK
HAVE LITTLE SPACE
FOR TOTIN' THINGS
TO FIX THE FACE
THEY USE
BURMA-SHAVE

(Special Razor Blade
Promotion, 1938)

AFTER ONE TRIAL
YOU'LL WANT MORE
AT THE NEXT
GOOD DRUG STORE
15 FOR 25¢
BURMA-SHAVE
    BLADES

HERE'S THE WINNING
SHAVING TEAM
THE PERFECT BLADE
THE PERFECT CREAM
BURMA-SHAVE BLADES
BURMA-SHAVE

SHARPEST BLADE
EVER MADE
COMFORT SPEED
GUARANTEED
15 FOR 25¢
BURMA-SHAVE
    BLADES

HARDLY A DRIVER
IS NOW ALIVE
WHO PASSED
ON HILLS
AT 75
BURMA-SHAVE

DARLING I AM
GROWING OLD
NONSENSE!
DO AS YOU
ARE TOLD—GET
BURMA-SHAVE

A WHISKERED GENT
AT A BAZAAR
PAID FOR
A KISS
BUT GOT A JAR
BURMA-SHAVE

DRIVE LIKE
A RAILROAD ENGINEER
TAKE IT EASY
WHEN THE ROAD'S
NOT CLEAR
BURMA-SHAVE

MIRROR ON
THE BATHROOM WALL
WHAT'S THE
SMOOTHEST SHAVE
OF ALL?
BURMA-SHAVE

TRY A TUBE
THE CREAM
THAT'S IN IT
IS MAKING FRIENDS
A MAN A MINUTE
BURMA-SHAVE

SOAPS
THAT IRRITATE
THEIR MUGS
TURN JOLLY GENTS
TO JITTERBUGS
BURMA-SHAVE

PAST
SCHOOLHOUSES
TAKE IT SLOW
LET THE LITTLE
SHAVERS GROW
BURMA-SHAVE

MOM AND POP
ARE FEELING GAY
BABY SAID
AS PLAIN
AS DAY
BURMA-SHAVE

IF YOU DISLIKE
BIG TRAFFIC FINES
SLOW DOWN
'TILL YOU
CAN READ THESE SIGNS
BURMA-SHAVE

SHIVER MY TIMBERS
SAID CAPTAIN MACK
WE'RE TEN KNOTS OUT
BUT WE'RE TURNING
    BACK
I FORGOT MY
BURMA-SHAVE

SPECIAL SEATS
RESERVED IN HADES
FOR WHISKERED GUYS
WHO SCRATCH
THE LADIES
BURMA-SHAVE

A PEACH
LOOKS GOOD
WITH LOTS OF FUZZ
BUT MAN'S NO PEACH
AND NEVER WUZ
BURMA-SHAVE

SPREAD IT ON
AND LIGHTLY TOO
SHAVE IT OFF
THAT'S ALL
YOU'RE THROUGH
BURMA-SHAVE

SHAVING BRUSHES
SOON WILL
BE TRIMMIN'
THOSE SCREWY HATS
WE SEE ON WIMMIN
BURMA-SHAVE

I PROPOSED
TO IDA
IDA REFUSED
IDA WON MY IDA
IF IDA USED
BURMA-SHAVE

THE QUEEN
OF HEARTS
NOW LOVES THE KNAVE
THE KING
RAN OUT OF
BURMA-SHAVE

AT CROSSROADS
DON'T JUST
TRUST TO LUCK
THE OTHER CAR
MAY BE A TRUCK
BURMA-SHAVE

CHRISTMAS COMES
BUT ONCE
A YEAR
ONE SWELL GIFT
THAT'S ALWAYS HERE
BURMA-SHAVE

CARELESS DRIVING
SOON WE HOPE
WILL GO
THE WAY
OF BRUSH AND SOAP
BURMA-SHAVE

CARELESS
BRIDEGROOM
DAINTY BRIDE
SCRATCHY WHISKERS
HOMICIDE
BURMA-SHAVE

(These special bobtailed jingles were employed in 1939 and later
on the approach routes to a number of large cities, where locat-
tions for full-length jingles were difficult to obtain. Each ended,
of course, with the words *Burma-Shave*. They were displayed
variously on two or three signs, sometimes even on a single
extra-tall board.)

GOOD TO THE LAST STROP

COVERS A MULTITUDE OF CHINS

NIX ON NICKS

FOR FACES THAT GO PLACES

DON'T PUT IT OFF—PUT IT ON

SHAVE FASTER WITHOUT DISASTER

MAKES GOOD BECAUSE IT'S MADE GOOD

TAKES THE "H" OUT OF SHAVE

NO DIGGING IN ON TENDER SKIN

MAKES MISSES MRS.

BRUSH? NO! TOO SLOW

EQUIP YOUR GRIP

NO PUSHEE NO PULLY SMOOTH SHAVY
FEEL BULLY

BEARD UNRULY—MEET YOURS TRULY

AID THE BLADE

THOSE WHO CLICK—PICK

BETTER SHAVING AT A SAVING

START THE DAY THE MODERN WAY

50% QUICKER 100% SLICKER

YOU'LL ENTHUSE AS YOU USE

LOOK "SPIFFY" IN A "JIFFY"

NO SOONER SPREAD THAN DONE

SAVES YOUR JACK—HOLDS YOUR JILL

ROMANCE NEVER STARTS FROM SCRATCH

TRY OUR WHISKER LICKER

JOIN THE MILLIONS USING SOOTHING

A WORD TO THE WIVES IS SUFFICIENT

JUST SPREAD, THEN PAT—NOW SHAVE,
THAT'S THAT!

HOT TIP, PAL—MORE SMILES PER GAL

WON BY A HAIR THAT WASN'T THERE

PAYS DIVIDENDS IN LADY FRIENDS

IS YOUR FACE HER MISFORTUNE? TRY

IF GETTING UP GETS YOU DOWN—USE

WHEN YOU SHOP FOR YOUR POP

ONCE A DAY THE EASY WAY

NO TRICK TO CLICK IF QUICK TO PICK

OTHER DAYS—OTHER WAYS. NOWADAYS

DELUXE DE LOOKS WITH

HE'S NIFTY AND THRIFTY—LOOKS 30 AT 50

BEST REFERENCE—PUBLIC PREFERENCE

ECONOMIZE WITH THIS SIZE

A BETTER BUY—WHY NOT TRY

RIGHT ABOUT FACE

1940

SAID JULIET
TO ROMEO
IF YOU
WON'T SHAVE
GO HOMEO
BURMA-SHAVE

SUBSTITUTES AND
IMITATIONS
SEND 'EM TO
YOUR WIFE'S
RELATIONS
BURMA-SHAVE

WHEN YOU DRIVE
IF CAUTION CEASES
YOU ARE APT
TO REST
IN PIECES
BURMA-SHAVE

HE MARRIED GRACE
WITH SCRATCHY FACE
HE ONLY
GOT ONE DAY
OF GRACE!
BURMA-SHAVE

ALL LITTLE RHYMING
JOKES ASIDE
DON'T BE CONTENT
UNTIL YOU'VE
TRIED
BURMA-SHAVE

COLLEGE CUTIE
PIGSKIN HERO
BRISTLY KISS
HERO
ZERO
BURMA-SHAVE

YOU CAN'T REACH 80
HALE AND HEARTY
BY DRIVING 80
HOME FROM
THE PARTY
BURMA-SHAVE

BUY A JAR
TAKE IT FROM ME
THERE'S SO
MUCH IN IT
THE LAST HALF'S FREE
BURMA-SHAVE

HE'S THE BOY
THE GALS FORGOT
HIS LINE
WAS SMOOTH
HIS CHIN WAS NOT
BURMA-SHAVE

PUT YOUR BRUSH
BACK ON THE SHELF
THE DARN THING
NEEDS A
SHAVE ITSELF
BURMA-SHAVE

IT'S BEST FOR
ONE WHO HITS
THE BOTTLE
TO LET ANOTHER
USE THE THROTTLE
BURMA-SHAVE

DON'T PASS CARS
ON CURVE OR HILL
IF THE COPS
DON'T GET YOU
MORTICIANS WILL
BURMA-SHAVE

WITH GLAMOUR GIRLS
YOU'LL NEVER CLICK
BEWHISKERED
LIKE A
BOLSHEVIK
BURMA-SHAVE

A SCRATCHY CHIN
LIKE BRIGHT
PINK SOCKS
PUTS ANY ROMANCE
ON THE ROCKS
BURMA-SHAVE

ALWAYS REMEMBER
ON ANY TRIP
KEEP TWO THINGS
WITHIN YOUR GRIP
YOUR STEERING WHEEL
    AND
BURMA-SHAVE

GIVE HAND SIGNALS
TO THOSE BEHIND
THEY DON'T KNOW
WHAT'S IN
YOUR MIND
BURMA-SHAVE

THE BEARDED DEVIL
IS FORCED
TO DWELL
IN THE ONLY PLACE
WHERE THEY DON'T SELL
BURMA-SHAVE

SUBSTITUTES
WOULD IRK A SAINT
YOU HOPE THEY ARE
WHAT YOU KNOW
THEY AIN'T
BURMA-SHAVE

PRICKLY PEARS
ARE PICKED
FOR PICKLES
NO PEACH PICKS
A FACE THAT PRICKLES
BURMA-SHAVE

GUYS WHOSE EYES
ARE IN
THEIR BACKS
GET HALOS CROSSING
RAILROAD TRACKS
BURMA-SHAVE

A CHRISTMAS HUG
A BIRTHDAY KISS
AWAITS
THE WOMAN
WHO GIVES THIS
BURMA-SHAVE

JUST SPREAD
THEN PAT
NOW SHAVE
THAT'S
THAT
BURMA-SHAVE

1941

HERE'S
A GOOD DEED
FOR A SCOUT
TELL YOUR DAD
ALL ABOUT
BURMA-SHAVE

DON'T STICK
YOUR ELBOW
OUT SO FAR
IT MIGHT GO HOME
IN ANOTHER CAR
BURMA-SHAVE

THEY MISSED
THE TURN
CAR WAS WHIZZ'N
FAULT WAS HER'N
FUNERAL HIS'N
BURMA-SHAVE

SOLDIER
SAILOR
AND MARINE
NOW GET A SHAVE
THAT'S QUICK AND CLEAN
BURMA-SHAVE

TELL
THE DEAR
WHO SHOPS AROUND
THAT HALF A BUCK
BUYS HALF A POUND
BURMA-SHAVE

REMEMBER THIS
IF YOU'D
BE SPARED
TRAINS DON'T WHISTLE
BECAUSE THEY'RE
    SCARED
BURMA-SHAVE

SHE KISSED
THE HAIRBRUSH
BY MISTAKE
SHE THOUGHT IT WAS
HER HUSBAND JAKE
BURMA-SHAVE

WHEN BETTER
SHAVING BRUSHES
ARE MADE
WE'LL STILL SHAVE
WITHOUT THEIR AID
BURMA-SHAVE

HE USED
UMBRELLA
FOR PARACHUTE
NOW REJECTS
EVERY SUBSTITUTE
BURMA-SHAVE

WHEN JUNIOR TAKES
YOUR TIES
AND CAR
IT'S TIME TO BUY
AN EXTRA JAR
BURMA-SHAVE

94

GETS EACH
WHISKER
AT THE BASE
NO INGROWN HAIR
ON NECK OR FACE
BURMA-SHAVE

THE ANSWER TO
A MAIDEN'S PRAYER
IS A MAN
MOST ANYWHERE
USING
BURMA-SHAVE

IF MAN BITES DOGGIE
THAT IS NEWS
IF FACE
SCARES DOGGIE
BETTER USE
BURMA-SHAVE

RHYME AND REASON
EVERY SEASON
YOU'VE READ
THE RHYME
NOW TRY THE REASON
BURMA-SHAVE

AT INTERSECTIONS
LOOK EACH WAY
A HARP SOUNDS NICE
BUT IT'S
HARD TO PLAY
BURMA-SHAVE

WILD
DASHES
FROM BY-WAYS
CAUSE CRASHES
ON HIGHWAYS
BURMA-SHAVE

LIFE IS SWEET
BUT OH HOW BITTER!
TO LOVE A GAL
AND THEN
NOT GIT 'ER
BURMA-SHAVE

SUBSTITUTES
RESEMBLE
TAIL-CHASING PUP
FOLLOW AND FOLLOW
BUT NEVER CATCH UP
BURMA-SHAVE

TRAINS DON'T WANDER
ALL OVER THE MAP
FOR NO ONE
SITS ON
THE ENGINEER'S LAP
BURMA-SHAVE

FROM
BAR
TO CAR
TO
GATES AJAR
BURMA-SHAVE

WHEN PETER PIPER
PICKLE PICKER
KISSED HIS GAL
HIS BEARD
WOULD PRICK 'ER
BURMA-SHAVE

IF EVERY SIP
FILLS YOU
WITH ZIP
THEN YOUR SIPPER
NEEDS A ZIPPER
BURMA-SHAVE

95

BROKEN ROMANCE
STATED FULLY
SHE WENT WILD
WHEN HE
WENT WOOLY
BURMA-SHAVE

1942

PA LIKES THE CREAM
MA LIKES THE JAR
BOTH LIKE
THE PRICE
SO THERE YOU ARE
BURMA-SHAVE

STORES ARE FULL
OF SHAVING AIDS
BUT ALL YOU NEED
IS THIS
AND BLADES
BURMA-SHAVE

BROTHER SPEEDERS
LET'S
REHEARSE
ALL TOGETHER
"GOOD MORNING, NURSE!"
BURMA-SHAVE

PA ACTED
SO TICKLED
MA THOT
HE WAS PICKLED
HE'D JUST TRIED
BURMA-SHAVE

'MID RISING
TAXES
SOARING RENTS
STILL HALF A POUND
FOR FIFTY CENTS
BURMA-SHAVE

ICEMAN'S GRANDSON
NOW FULL GROWN
HAS COOLING SYSTEM
ALL HIS OWN
HE USES
BURMA-SHAVE

APPROACHED
A CROSSING
WITHOUT LOOKING
WHO WILL EAT
HIS WIDOW'S COOKING?
BURMA-SHAVE

IF YOU
DON'T KNOW
WHOSE SIGNS
THESE ARE
YOU CAN'T HAVE
DRIVEN VERY FAR

DROVE TOO LONG
DRIVER SNOOZING
WHAT HAPPENED NEXT
IS NOT
AMUSING
BURMA-SHAVE

LET'S MAKE HITLER
AND HIROHITO
LOOK AS SICK AS
OLD BENITO
BUY DEFENSE BONDS
BURMA-SHAVE

CAN'T SHAVE DAILY?
TENDER HIDE?
NOW BE HONEST
HAVE YOU
TRIED
BURMA-SHAVE

THERE'S NO WHISKER
IT WON'T SOFTEN
SHAVE 'EM CLOSE
AND NOT
SO OFTEN
BURMA-SHAVE

IF HUGGING
ON HIGHWAYS
IS YOUR SPORT
TRADE IN YOUR CAR
FOR A DAVENPORT
BURMA-SHAVE

SHAVING BRUSH
IN ARMY PACK
WAS STRAW THAT BROKE
THE ROOKIE'S BACK
USE BRUSHLESS
BURMA-SHAVE

A GIRL
SHOULD HOLD ON
TO HER YOUTH
BUT NOT
WHEN HE'S DRIVING
BURMA-SHAVE

MAYBE YOU CAN'T
SHOULDER A GUN
BUT YOU CAN SHOULDER
THE COST OF ONE
BUY DEFENSE BONDS
BURMA-SHAVE

OF ALL
THE DRUNKS
WHO DRIVE ON SUNDAY
SOME ARE STILL
ALIVE ON MONDAY
BURMA-SHAVE

"AT EASE," SHE SAID
"MANEUVERS BEGIN
WHEN YOU GET
THOSE WHISKERS
OFF YOUR CHIN"
BURMA-SHAVE

SUBSTITUTES
LIKE UNSEEN BARTER
OFTEN MAKE ONE
SAD
BUT SMARTER
BURMA-SHAVE

TRAVELING MEN
KNOW EASE
AND SPEED
THEIR SHAVING KITS
HOLD WHAT THEY NEED
BURMA-SHAVE

WHAT YOU SHOUTED
MAY BE TRUE,
BUT
DID YOU HEAR
WHAT HE CALLED YOU?
BURMA-SHAVE

BUYING DEFENSE BONDS
MEANS MONEY LENT
SO THEY
DON'T COST YOU
ONE RED CENT
BURMA-SHAVE

97

TO MOST BRUSH SHAVERS
IT'S QUITE CLEAR
THE YANKS AREN'T
     COMING
THE YANKS ARE HERE
USE BRUSHLESS
BURMA-SHAVE

1943

EVERY SHAVER
NOW CAN SNORE
SIX MORE MINUTES
THAN BEFORE
BY USING
BURMA-SHAVE

ONE POUND JAR   85¢
HALF POUND JAR   50¢
BIG TUBE   35¢
DON'T PUT IT OFF
PUT IN ON
BURMA-SHAVE

HALF A POUND
FOR
HALF A DOLLAR
SPREAD ON THIN
ABOVE THE COLLAR
BURMA-SHAVE

SHAVING BRUSHES
YOU'LL SOON SEE 'EM
ON THE SHELF
IN SOME
MUSEUM
BURMA-SHAVE

DOES YOUR HUSBAND
MISBEHAVE
GRUNT AND GRUMBLE
RANT AND RAVE
SHOOT THE BRUTE SOME
BURMA-SHAVE

IT'S A GOOD
OLD SPANISH CUSTOM
TAKE YOUR MUG
AND BRUSH
AND BUST 'EM
BURMA-SHAVE

EARLY TO BED
EARLY TO RISE
WAS MEANT FOR THOSE
OLD FASHIONED GUYS
WHO DON'T USE
BURMA-SHAVE

WITHIN THIS VALE
OF TOIL
AND SIN
YOUR HEAD GROWS BALD
BUT NOT YOUR CHIN—USE
BURMA-SHAVE

SLAP
THE JAP
WITH
IRON
SCRAP
BURMA-SHAVE

THE CANNONEERS
WITH HAIRY EARS
ON WIRY WHISKERS
USED TIN SHEARS
UNTIL THEY FOUND
BURMA-SHAVE

FILM PROTECTS
YOUR NECK
AND CHIN
SO YOUR RAZOR
WON'T DIG IN
BURMA-SHAVE

THO TOUGH
AND ROUGH
FROM WIND AND WAVE
YOUR CHEEK GROWS
    SLEEK
WITH
BURMA-SHAVE

1945

MANY A WOLF
IS NEVER LET IN
BECAUSE OF THE HAIR
ON HIS
CHINNY-CHIN-CHIN
BURMA-SHAVE

SHE RAISED CAIN
WHEN HE RAISED
    STUBBLE
GUESS WHAT
SMOOTHED AWAY
THEIR TROUBLE?
BURMA-SHAVE

BIG MISTAKE
MANY MAKE
RELY ON HORN
INSTEAD OF
BRAKE
BURMA-SHAVE

FROM STATISTICS
THAT WE GATHER
THE SWING IS TO
NO BRUSH
NO LATHER
BURMA-SHAVE

NO MAN CAN REALLY
DO HIS STUFF
WITH A FACE THAT'S
    SORE
OR A CHIN
THAT'S ROUGH
BURMA-SHAVE

FIRST MEN BUY IT
THEN APPLY IT
THEN ADVISE
THEIR FRIENDS
TO TRY IT
BURMA-SHAVE

IF THESE
SIGNS BLUR
AND BOUNCE AROUND
YOU'D BETTER PARK
AND WALK TO TOWN
BURMA-SHAVE

THIS IS NOT
A CLEVER VERSE
I TRIED
AND TRIED
BUT JUST
GOT WORSE

YOU CAN BEAT
A MILE A MINUTE
BUT THERE AIN'T
NO FUTURE
IN IT
BURMA-SHAVE

SLEEP IN A CHAIR
NOTHING TO LOSE
BUT A NAP
AT THE WHEEL
IS A PERMANENT SNOOZE
BURMA-SHAVE

LIFE WITH FATHER
IS MORE PLEASANT
SINCE
HE GOT THIS
BIRTHDAY PRESENT
BURMA-SHAVE

TO A SUBSTITUTE
HE GAVE A TRIAL
IT TOOK OFF
NOTHING
BUT HIS SMILE
BURMA-SHAVE

IT SPREADS SO SMOOTH
IT SHAVES SO SLICK
IT FEELS
LIKE VELVET
AND IT'S QUICK
BURMA-SHAVE

'TWOULD BE
MORE FUN
TO GO BY AIR
IF WE COULD PUT
THESE SIGNS UP THERE
BURMA-SHAVE

HIS LINE WAS SMOOTH
BUT NOT HIS CHIN
HE TOOK HER OUT
SHE TOOK HIM IN
TO BUY SOME
BURMA-SHAVE

DRINKING DRIVERS
ENHANCE THEIR
CHANCE
TO HIGHBALL HOME
IN AN AMBULANCE
BURMA-SHAVE

WHY DOES A CHICKEN
CROSS THE STREET?
SHE SEES A GUY
SHE'D LIKE TO MEET
HE USES
BURMA-SHAVE

THE CHICK
HE WED
LET OUT A WHOOP
FELT HIS CHIN AND
FLEW THE COOP
BURMA-SHAVE

TESTED
IN PEACE
PROVEN IN WAR
BETTER NOW
THAN EVER BEFORE
BURMA-SHAVE

BOTH HANDS
ON WHEEL
EYES ON ROAD
THAT'S THE SKILLFUL
DRIVER'S CODE
BURMA-SHAVE

1947

YOU'VE USED
OUR CREAM
NOW TRY OUR BLADES
PAIR UP THE BEST
IN SHAVING AIDS
BURMA-SHAVE

DON'T LOSE
YOUR HEAD
TO GAIN A MINUTE
YOU NEED YOUR HEAD
YOUR BRAINS ARE IN IT
BURMA-SHAVE

THAT SHE
COULD COOK
HE HAD HIS DOUBTS
UNTIL SHE CREAMED
HIS BRISTLE SPROUTS
    WITH
BURMA-SHAVE

THE WOLF
WHO LONGS
TO ROAM AND PROWL
SHOULD SHAVE BEFORE
HE STARTS TO HOWL
BURMA-SHAVE

AS YOU DRIVE
PLAY THIS GAME
CONSTRUCT
A JINGLE
WITH THIS NAME
BURMA-SHAVE

IF A GIFT
YOU MUST CHOOSE
GIVE HIM
ONE THAT
HE CAN USE
BURMA-SHAVE

WHEN THE STORK
DELIVERS A BOY
OUR WHOLE
DARN FACTORY
JUMPS FOR JOY
BURMA-SHAVE

JOIN
OUR HAPPY
BRUSHLESS THRONG
SIX MILLION USERS
CAN'T BE WRONG
BURMA-SHAVE

FAMOUS LAST WORDS
"IF HE WON'T
DIM HIS
I WON'T
DIM MINE"
BURMA-SHAVE

CAR IN DITCH
DRIVER IN TREE
MOON WAS FULL
AND SO
WAS HE
BURMA-SHAVE

SUBSTITUTES
THAT PROMISE
    PERFECTION
ARE LIKE
SOME CANDIDATES
AFTER ELECTION
BURMA-SHAVE

SANTA'S
WHISKERS
NEED NO TRIMMIN'
HE KISSES KIDS
NOT THE WIMMIN
BURMA-SHAVE

ALTHO
WE'VE SOLD
SIX MILLION OTHERS
WE STILL CAN'T SELL
THOSE COUGHDROP
    BROTHERS
BURMA-SHAVE

WE KNOW
HOW MUCH
YOU LOVE THAT GAL
BUT USE BOTH HANDS
FOR DRIVING, PAL
BURMA-SHAVE

IN CUPID'S LITTLE
BAG OF TRIX
HERE'S THE ONE
THAT CLIX
WITH CHIX
BURMA-SHAVE

THRIFTY JARS FOR
STAY AT HOMES
HANDY TUBES
FOR HIM
WHO ROAMS
BURMA-SHAVE

I USE IT TOO
THE BALD MAN SAID
IT KEEPS MY FACE
JUST LIKE
MY HEAD
BURMA-SHAVE

GRANDPA'S
OUT WITH
JUNIOR'S DATE
OLD TECHNIQUE
WITH BRAND NEW BAIT
BURMA-SHAVE

NO SOGGY BRUSHES
IN YOUR GRIP
YOU'VE ALWAYS
GOT A
FINGER TIP
BURMA-SHAVE

IF YOU WANT
A HEARTY SQUEEZE
GET OUR
FEMALE
ANTI-FREEZE
BURMA-SHAVE

SUBSTITUTES WOULD
HAVE THEIR PLACE
IF YOU COULD
SUBSTITUTE
YOUR FACE
BURMA-SHAVE

MAN PASSES
DOG HOUSE
DOG SEES CHIN
DOG GETS OUT
MAN GETS IN
BURMA-SHAVE

A GUY
WHO WANTS
TO MIDDLE-AISLE IT
MUST NEVER SCRATCH
HIS LITTLE VIOLET
BURMA-SHAVE

PRICES RISING
O'ER THE NATION
HERE IS ONE
THAT MISSED
INFLATION
BURMA-SHAVE

(Burma-Vita Tooth Powder Jingles)

THE FIRST
IMPROVEMENT
IN MANY A YEAR
FOR CLEANING TEETH
IS FINALLY HERE
BURMA-VITA TOOTH
  POWDER

SPEAKING OF
GREAT EVENTS
BURMA-SHAVE
PROUDLY PRESENTS
ANOTHER FINE PRODUCT
BURMA-VITA TOOTH
  POWDER

102

JUST MOISTEN
YOUR TOOTH BRUSH
DIP IN JAR
AND YOU'LL ENJOY
CLEANER TEETH BY FAR
BURMA-VITA TOOTH
    POWDER

DON'T WASTE POWDER
DOWN THE DRAIN
BY MISSING BRUSH
WITH FAULTY AIM
A DIP DOES IT
BURMA-VITA TOOTH
    POWDER

BETTER TOOTH CLEANSER
LOW EXPENSE
YOUR DRUGGIST
SELLS IT
40 CENTS
BURMA-VITA TOOTH
    POWDER

TOBACCO STAINS
AND STALE BREATH TOO
ARE TWO
OF THE THINGS
IT TAKES FROM YOU
BURMA-VITA TOOTH
    POWDER

1948

ROAD
WAS SLIPPERY
CURVE WAS SHARP
WHITE ROBE, HALO
WINGS AND HARP
BURMA-SHAVE

SPEED
WAS HIGH
WEATHER WAS NOT
TIRES WERE THIN
X MARKS THE SPOT
BURMA-SHAVE

HAT AND TIE
SMART AND CLEAN
SPACE BETWEEN
SPOILED THE SCENE
HE SHOULD USE
BURMA-SHAVE

WHY WORK UP
A DAILY LATHER
ONCE YOU'VE TRIED
WE'RE SURE
YOU'D RATHER
BURMA-SHAVE

THE BOY WHO GETS
HIS GIRL'S APPLAUSE
MUST ACT
NOT LOOK
LIKE SANTA CLAUS
BURMA-SHAVE

IF YOU THINK
SHE LIKES
YOUR BRISTLES
WALK BARE-FOOTED
THROUGH SOME THISTLES
BURMA-SHAVE

WITHIN THIS VALE
OF TOIL
AND SIN
YOUR HEAD GROWS BALD
BUT NOT YOUR CHIN—USE
BURMA-SHAVE

THE MORE
YOU SHAVE
THE BRUSHLESS WAY
THE MORE YOU'LL BE
INCLINED TO SAY—
BURMA-SHAVE

SUBSTITUTES AND
IMITATIONS
SEND 'EM TO
YOUR WIFE'S
RELATIONS
BURMA-SHAVE

IT'S NOT
HOW FAST OR SLOW
YOU DRIVE
THE QUESTION IS
HOW YOU ARRIVE
BURMA-SHAVE

HIGHWAYS ARE
NO PLACE
TO SLEEP
STOP YOUR CAR
TO COUNT YOUR SHEEP
BURMA-SHAVE

A MAN WHO PASSES
ON HILLS AND CURVES
IS NOT A MAN
OF IRON NERVES—
HE'S CRAZY!
BURMA-SHAVE

THE MINUTES
SOME FOLKS
SAVE THROUGH SPEED
THEY NEVER EVEN
LIVE TO NEED
BURMA-SHAVE

I'VE READ
THESE SIGNS
SINCE JUST A KID
NOW THAT I SHAVE
I'M GLAD I DID
BURMA-SHAVE

AT SCHOOL ZONES
HEED INSTRUCTIONS!
PROTECT
OUR LITTLE
TAX DEDUCTIONS
BURMA-SHAVE

WE DON'T
KNOW HOW
TO SPLIT AN ATOM
BUT AS TO WHISKERS
LET US AT 'EM
BURMA-SHAVE

REGARDLESS OF
POLITICAL VIEWS
ALL GOOD PARTIES
ALWAYS
CHOOSE
BURMA-SHAVE

PAPER HANGERS
WITH THE HIVES
NOW CAN
SHAVE WITH
CARVING KNIVES
BURMA-SHAVE

THE MIDNIGHT RIDE
OF PAUL
FOR BEER
LED TO A
WARMER HEMISPHERE
BURMA-SHAVE

WILD MEN PULLED
THEIR WHISKERS OUT
THAT'S WHAT MADE
THEM WILD
NO DOUBT—
BURMA-SHAVE

LOOK
DON'T LISTEN
POP IS TRYING
A SUBSTITUTE
INSTEAD OF BUYING
BURMA-SHAVE

A MAN
A MISS
A CAR—A CURVE
HE KISSED THE MISS
AND MISSED THE CURVE
BURMA-SHAVE

LITTLE BO-PEEP
HAS LOST HER JEEP
IT STRUCK
A TRUCK
WHEN SHE WENT TO
    SLEEP
BURMA-SHAVE

WHISKERS
EASY COME,
YOU KNOW
WHY NOT MAKE THEM
EASY GO?
BURMA-SHAVE

(Special Anti-inflation Signs, 1948)

BARGAIN HUNTERS
GATHER 'ROUND
FOR FIFTY CENTS
STILL
HALF A POUND
BURMA-SHAVE
NO PRICE INCREASE

FROM NEW YORK TOWN
TO PUMPKIN HOLLER
STILL
HALF A POUND
FOR HALF A DOLLAR
BURMA-SHAVE
NO PRICE INCREASE

OTHER THINGS HAVE
GONE SKY HIGH
HALF A DOLLAR
STILL WILL BUY
HALF POUND JAR
BURMA-SHAVE
NO PRICE INCREASE

A BIG
IMPROVEMENT
SINCE THE WAR
IS NOW ON SALE
IN YOUR DRUG STORE
BURMA-SHAVE
NO PRICE INCREASE

TUBE IMMENSE
STILL
35 CENTS
EASY SHAVING
LOW EXPENSE
BURMA-SHAVE
NO PRICE INCREASE

LEAP YEAR'S OVER
YOU'RE SAFE, MEN
ALL YOU COWARDS
CAN SHAVE AGAIN
WITH BRUSHLESS
BURMA-SHAVE

JUST THIS ONCE
AND JUST FOR FUN
WE'LL LET YOU
FINISH
WHAT WE'VE BEGUN
? ? ?

HE SAW
THE TRAIN
AND TRIED TO DUCK IT
KICKED FIRST THE GAS
AND THEN THE BUCKET
BURMA-SHAVE

WITH TELEVISION
ON THE SET
STARS ARE
RUNNING OUT
TO GET
BURMA-SHAVE

HEADLINE NEWS
FOR FACE
AND CHIN
NOW IMPROVED
WITH LANOLIN
BURMA-SHAVE

WITH
A SLEEK CHEEK
PRESSED TO HERS
JEEPERS! CREEPERS!
HOW SHE PURRS
BURMA-SHAVE

HIS FACE
WAS LOVED
BY JUST HIS MOTHER
HE BURMA-SHAVED
AND NOW—
OH, BROTHER

MEN
WHO HAVE TO
TRAVEL LIGHT
FIND THE HANDY TUBE
JUST RIGHT
BURMA-SHAVE

WHEN FRISKY
WITH WHISKEY
DON'T DRIVE
'CAUSE IT'S
RISKY
BURMA-SHAVE

SINCE HUBBY
TRIED
THAT SUBSTITUTE
HE'S 1/3 MAN
AND 2/3 BRUTE
BURMA-SHAVE

HIS BEARD
WAS LONG
AND STRONG AND TOUGH
HE LOST HIS
CHICKEN IN THE ROUGH
BURMA-SHAVE

HE ALWAYS USED
A STEAMING TOWEL
AND MUG AND BRUSH
AND LANGUAGE FOUL
'TIL HE TRIED
BURMA-SHAVE

IF YOU
MUST SAMPLE
HER "PUCKER PAINT"
BETTER DRIVE
WHERE TRAFFIC AIN'T
BURMA-SHAVE

IT GAVE
SWELL SHAVES BEFORE
NOW YOU'LL LIKE IT
EVEN MORE
THE NEW—IMPROVED
BURMA-SHAVE

PULL OFF
THE ROAD
TO CHANGE A FLAT
PROTECT YOUR LIFE—
NO SPARE FOR THAT!
BURMA-SHAVE

THO TOUGH
AND ROUGH
FROM WIND AND WAVE
YOUR CHEEK
GROWS SLEEK WITH
BURMA-SHAVE

IN SEVENTY YEARS
OF BRUSHIN' SOAP ON
GRAMPS COULDA
    PAINTED
THE PENTAGON
USE BRUSHLESS
BURMA-SHAVE

THESE THREE
PREVENT MOST
    ACCIDENTS
COURTESY
CAUTION
COMMON SENSE
BURMA-SHAVE

SAID ONE WHISKER
TO ANOTHER
CAN'T GET TOUGH
WITH THIS STUFF
BROTHER
BURMA-SHAVE

OLD DOBBIN
READS THESE SIGNS
EACH DAY
YOU SEE, HE GETS
HIS CORN THAT WAY
BURMA-SHAVE

TO SOOTHE
AND SMOOTH
YOUR TENDER SKIN
IT'S NOW IMPROVED
WITH LANOLIN
BURMA-SHAVE

ONE BURMA-SHAVE
THE SCHOOL BOY CRIED
AT LEAST
I'LL SMELL
AS IF I TRIED
BURMA-SHAVE

(Minnesota and
Wisconsin, 1949)

ASHES TO ASHES
FORESTS TO DUST
KEEP MINNESOTA
    GREEN
OR WE'LL
ALL GO BUST
BURMA-SHAVE

ASHES TO ASHES
FORESTS TO DUST
KEEP WISCONSIN GREEN
OR WE'LL
ALL GO BUST
BURMA-SHAVE

HIS CHEEK
WAS ROUGH
HIS CHICK VAMOOSED
AND NOW SHE WON'T
COME HOME TO ROOST
BURMA-SHAVE

TWINKLE, TWINKLE
ONE-EYED CAR
WE ALL WONDER
WHERE
YOU ARE
BURMA-SHAVE

ON CURVES AHEAD
REMEMBER, SONNY
THAT RABBIT'S FOOT
DIDN'T SAVE
THE BUNNY
BURMA-SHAVE

WHEN
SUPER-SHAVED
REMEMBER, PARD
YOU'LL STILL GET
    SLAPPED
BUT NOT SO HARD
BURMA-SHAVE

HIS BRUSH IS GONE
SO WHAT'LL WE DO
SAID
MIKE ROBE I
TO MIKE ROBE II
BURMA-SHAVE

THE PLACE TO PASS
ON CURVES
YOU KNOW
IS ONLY AT
A BEAUTY SHOW
BURMA-SHAVE

A WHISKERY KISS
FOR THE ONE
YOU ADORE
MAY NOT MAKE HER MAD
BUT HER FACE WILL BE
    SORE
BURMA-SHAVE

BURMA-SHAVE
WAS SUCH A BOOM
THEY PASSED
THE BRIDE
AND KISSED
THE GROOM

THESE SIGNS
WE GLADLY
DEDICATE
TO MEN WHO'VE HAD
NO DATE OF LATE
BURMA-SHAVE

IF YOUR PEACH
KEEPS OUT
OF REACH
BETTER PRACTICE
WHAT WE PREACH
BURMA-SHAVE

A GUY
WHO DRIVES
A CAR WIDE OPEN
IS NOT THINKIN'
HE'S JUST HOPIN'
BURMA-SHAVE

TO KISS
A MUG
THAT'S LIKE A CACTUS
TAKES MORE NERVE
THAN IT DOES PRACTICE
BURMA-SHAVE

THE WHALE
PUT JONAH
DOWN THE HATCH
BUT COUGHED HIM UP
BECAUSE HE SCRATCHED
BURMA-SHAVE

DOESN'T
KISS YOU
LIKE SHE USETER?
PERHAPS SHE'S SEEN
A SMOOTHER ROOSTER! !
BURMA-SHAVE

VIOLETS ARE BLUE
ROSES ARE PINK
ON GRAVES
OF THOSE
WHO DRIVE AND DRINK
BURMA-SHAVE

NO USE
KNOWING
HOW TO PICK 'EM
IF YOUR HALF-SHAVED
WHISKERS STICK 'EM
BURMA-SHAVE

CANDIDATE SAYS
CAMPAIGN
CONFUSING
BABIES KISS ME
SINCE I'VE BEEN USING
BURMA-SHAVE

HE TRIED
TO CROSS
AS FAST TRAIN NEARED
DEATH DIDN'T DRAFT
    HIM
HE VOLUNTEERED
BURMA-SHAVE

MY JOB IS
KEEPING FACES CLEAN
AND NOBODY KNOWS
DE STUBBLE
I'VE SEEN
BURMA-SHAVE

HER CHARIOT
RACED 80 PER
THEY HAULED AWAY
WHAT HAD
BEN HUR
BURMA-SHAVE

(Burma-Shave Lotion Jingles, 1950)

SHE WILL
FLOOD YOUR FACE
WITH KISSES
'CAUSE YOU SMELL
SO DARN DELICIOUS
BURMA-SHAVE LOTION

IT HAS A TINGLE
AND A TANG
THAT STARTS
THE DAY OFF
WITH A BANG
BURMA-SHAVE LOTION

USE BURMA-SHAVE
IN TUBE
OR JAR
THEN FOLLOW UP
WITH OUR NEW STAR
BURMA-SHAVE LOTION

BRACING AS
AN OCEAN BREEZE
FOR AFTER SHAVING
IT'S SURE
TO PLEASE
BURMA-SHAVE LOTION

FOR EARLY
MORNING
PEP AND BOUNCE
A BRAND NEW PRODUCT
WE ANNOUNCE
BURMA-SHAVE LOTION

THE LADIES
TAKE ONE WHIFF
AND PURR—
IT'S NO WONDER
MEN PREFER
BURMA-SHAVE LOTION

HIS FACE
WAS SMOOTH
AND COOL AS ICE
AND OH! LOUISE!
HE SMELLED SO NICE
BURMA-SHAVE LOTION

1951

(Middle West and East)

I'D HEARD
IT PRAISED
BY DRUG STORE CLERKS
I TRIED THE STUFF
HOT DOG! IT WORKS
BURMA-SHAVE

SOAP
MAY DO
FOR LADS WITH FUZZ
BUT SIR, YOU AIN'T
THE KID YOU WUZ
BURMA-SHAVE

TRAIN WRECKS FEW
REASON CLEAR
FIREMAN
NEVER HUGS
ENGINEER
BURMA-SHAVE

SHE EYED
HIS BEARD
AND SAID NO DICE
THE WEDDING'S OFF—
I'LL *COOK* THE RICE
BURMA-SHAVE

ALTHO INSURED
REMEMBER, KIDDO
THEY DON'T PAY YOU
THEY PAY
YOUR WIDOW
BURMA-SHAVE

TRAIN APPROACHING
WHISTLE SQUEALING
PAUSE!
AVOID THAT
RUNDOWN FEELING!
BURMA-SHAVE

MY CHEEK
SAYS SHE
FEELS SMOOTH AS SATIN
HA! HA! SAYS HE
THAT'S MINE YOU'RE
PATTIN'
BURMA-SHAVE

UNLESS
YOUR FACE
IS STINGER FREE
YOU'D BETTER LET
YOUR HONEY BE
BURMA-SHAVE

110

ANOTHER
RED SKIN
BIT THE DUST
WHEN PA TRIED
WHAT THESE SIGNS
    DISCUSSED
BURMA-SHAVE

THE BAND
FOR WHICH
THE GRAND STAND
    ROOTS
IS NOT MADE UP
SUBSTI-TOOTS!
BURMA-SHAVE

CAUTIOUS RIDER
TO HER
RECKLESS DEAR
LET'S HAVE LESS BULL
AND LOTS MORE STEER
BURMA-SHAVE

SPRING
HAS SPRUNG
THE GRASS HAS RIZ
WHERE LAST YEAR'S
CARELESS DRIVERS IS
BURMA-SHAVE

BIG BLUE TUBE
IT'S A HONEY
BEST SQUEEZE PLAY
FOR LOVE
OR MONEY
BURMA-SHAVE

PROPER
DISTANCE
TO HIM WAS BUNK
THEY PULLED HIM OUT
OF SOME GUY'S TRUNK
BURMA-SHAVE

SUBSTITUTES
CAN DO
MORE HARM
THAN CITY FELLERS
ON A FARM
BURMA-SHAVE

PAT'S BRISTLES
SCRATCHED
BRIDGET'S NOSE
THAT'S WHEN
HER WILD IRISH ROSE
BURMA-SHAVE

THE HOBO
LETS HIS
WHISKERS SPROUT
IT'S TRAINS—NOT GIRLS
THAT HE TAKES OUT
BURMA-SHAVE

A BEARD
THAT'S ROUGH
AND OVERGROWN
IS BETTER THAN
A CHAPERONE
BURMA-SHAVE

DRINKING DRIVERS
DON'T YOU KNOW
GREAT BANGS
FROM LITTLE
BINGES GROW?
BURMA-SHAVE

I KNOW
HE'S A WOLF
SAID RIDING HOOD
BUT GRANDMA DEAR,
HE SMELLS SO GOOD
BURMA-SHAVE

(West Coast and South)

THE WIFE
WHO KEEPS ON
BEING KISSED
ALWAYS HEADS
HER SHOPPING LIST
BURMA-SHAVE

IS HE
LONESOME
OR JUST BLIND—
THIS GUY WHO DRIVES
SO CLOSE BEHIND?
BURMA-SHAVE

PEDRO
WALKED
BACK HOME BY GOLLY
HIS BRISTLY CHIN
WAS HOT-TO-MOLLY
BURMA-SHAVE

MISSIN'
KISSIN'?
PERHAPS YOUR THRUSH
CAN'T GET THRU
THE UNDERBRUSH—TRY
BURMA-SHAVE

CLANCY'S
WHISKERS
TICKLE NANCY
NANCY LOWERED THE
    BOOM
ON CLANCY!
BURMA-SHAVE

A CHIN
WHERE BARBED WIRE
BRISTLES STAND
IS BOUND TO BE
A NO MA'AMS LAND
BURMA-SHAVE

LEAVES
FACE SOFT
AS WOMAN'S TOUCH
YET DOESN'T COST YOU
NEAR AS MUCH
BURMA-SHAVE

WE CAN'T
PROVIDE YOU
WITH A DATE
BUT WE DO SUPPLY
THE BEST DARN BAIT
BURMA-SHAVE

THE WOLF
IS SHAVED
SO NEAT AND TRIM
RED RIDING HOOD
IS CHASING HIM
BURMA-SHAVE

RELIEF
FOR FACES
CHAPPED AND SORE
KEEPS 'EM COMIN'
BACK FOR MORE
BURMA-SHAVE

HIS
TOMATO
WAS THE MUSHY TYPE
UNTIL HIS BEARD
GREW OVER-RIPE
BURMA-SHAVE

HEAVEN'S
LATEST
NEOPHYTE
SIGNALLED LEFT
THEN TURNED RIGHT
BURMA-SHAVE

BETTER TRY
LESS SPEED PER MILE
THAT CAR
MAY HAVE TO
LAST A WHILE
BURMA-SHAVE

TO STEAL
A KISS
HE HAD THE KNACK
BUT LACKED THE CHEEK
TO GET ONE BACK
BURMA-SHAVE

WE'VE MADE
GRANDPA
LOOK SO TRIM
THE LOCAL
DRAFT BOARD'S AFTER
    HIM
BURMA-SHAVE

"NO, NO,"
SHE SAID
TO HER BRISTLY BEAU
"I'D RATHER
EAT THE MISTLETOE"
BURMA-SHAVE

HIS ROSE
IS WED
HIS VIOLET BLEW
BUT HIS SUGAR IS SWEET
SINCE HE TOOK THIS CUE
BURMA-SHAVE

WHY IS IT
WHEN YOU
TRY TO PASS
THE GUY IN FRONT
GOES TWICE AS FAST?
BURMA-SHAVE

SHE PUT
A BULLET
THRU HIS HAT
BUT HE'S HAD
CLOSER SHAVES THAN
    THAT
BURMA-SHAVE

5-STAR
GENERALS
PRIVATES 1ST CLASS
SHOW EQUAL RANK
IN THE LOOKING-GLASS
BURMA-SHAVE

1953

(Middle West and East)

WHEN YOU LAY
THOSE FEW CENTS DOWN
YOU'VE BOUGHT
THE SMOOTHEST
SHAVE IN TOWN
BURMA-SHAVE

SUBSTITUTES
ARE LIKE A GIRDLE
THEY FIND SOME JOBS
THEY JUST
CAN'T HURDLE
BURMA-SHAVE

GUT RASIERT? ("IF YOU
    WANT A GOOD
    SHAVE?"—GERMAN)
————(CHINESE)
LA MEJOR AFEITADA
    ("THE BEST SHAVE"—
    SPANISH)
THE BEST SHAVE
IN ANY LANGUAGE
BURMA-SHAVE

WE'RE WIDELY READ
AND OFTEN QUOTED
BUT IT'S SHAVES
NOT SIGNS
FOR WHICH WE'RE NOTED
BURMA-SHAVE

MEN WHO
HAVE TO
TRAVEL LIGHT
FIND THE 35¢ TUBE
JUST RIGHT
BURMA-SHAVE

IT GAVE
MC DONALD
THAT NEEDED CHARM
HELLO HOLLYWOOD
GOOD-BY FARM
BURMA-SHAVE

A SHAVE
THAT'S REAL
NO CUTS TO HEAL
A SOOTHING
VELVET AFTER-FEEL
BURMA-SHAVE

AROUND
THE CURVE
LICKETY-SPLIT
IT'S A BEAUTIFUL CAR
WASN'T IT?
BURMA-SHAVE

OUR FORTUNE
IS YOUR
SHAVEN FACE
IT'S OUR BEST
ADVERTISING SPACE
BURMA-SHAVE

IF CRUSOE'D
KEPT HIS CHIN
MORE TIDY
HE MIGHT HAVE FOUND
A LADY FRIDAY
BURMA-SHAVE

FEEL YOUR FACE
AS YOU RIDE BY
NOW DON'T
YOU THINK
IT'S TIME TO TRY
BURMA-SHAVE

IF ANYTHING
WILL PLEASE
YOUR JILL
A LITTLE JACK
FOR THIS JAR WILL
BURMA-SHAVE

THAT BAREFOOT
CHAP
WITH CHEEKS OF TAN
WON'T LET 'EM CHAP
WHEN HE'S A MAN
BURMA-SHAVE

IF HARMONY
IS WHAT
YOU CRAVE
THEN GET
A TUBA
BURMA-SHAVE

THE BEARDED DEVIL
IS FORCED
TO DWELL
IN THE ONLY PLACE
WHERE THEY DON'T SELL
BURMA-SHAVE

THIS CREAM
MAKES THE
GARDENER'S DAUGHTER
PLANT HER TU-LIPS
WHERE SHE OUGHTER
BURMA-SHAVE

TOUGHEST
WHISKERS
IN THE TOWN
WE HOLD 'EM UP
YOU MOW 'EM DOWN
BURMA-SHAVE

NO MATTER
THE PRICE
NO MATTER HOW NEW
THE BEST SAFETY DEVICE
IN YOUR CAR IS YOU
BURMA-SHAVE

THESE SIGNS
ARE NOT
FOR LAUGHS ALONE
THE FACE THEY SAVE
MAY BE YOUR OWN
BURMA-SHAVE

HE ASKED
HIS KITTEN
TO PET AND PURR
SHE EYED HIS PUSS
AND SCREAMED "WHAT
    FUR!"
BURMA-SHAVE

THE HERO
WAS BRAVE AND STRONG
AND WILLIN'
SHE FELT HIS CHIN—
THEN WED THE VILLAIN
BURMA-SHAVE

THE SAFEST RULE
NO IFS OR BUTS
JUST DRIVE
LIKE EVERY ONE ELSE
IS NUTS!
BURMA-SHAVE

1955

DINAH DOESN'T
TREAT HIM RIGHT
BUT IF HE'D
SHAVE
DYNA-MITE!
BURMA-SHAVE

THO STIFF
THE BEARD
THAT NATURE GAVE
IT SHAVES
LIKE DOWN WITH
BURMA-SHAVE

TO CHANGE THAT
SHAVING JOB
TO JOY
YOU GOTTA USE
THE REAL MC COY
BURMA-SHAVE

HIS CROP OF
WHISKERS
NEEDED REAPING
THAT'S WHAT KEPT
HIS LENA LEAPING
BURMA-SHAVE

115

THE BLACKENED FOREST
SMOULDERS YET
BECAUSE
HE FLIPPED
A CIGARET
BURMA-SHAVE

JAR SO BIG
COST SO SMALL
COOLEST
SMOOTHEST
SHAVE OF ALL
BURMA-SHAVE

SLOW DOWN, PA
SAKES ALIVE
MA MISSED SIGNS
FOUR
AND FIVE
BURMA-SHAVE

GRANDPA KNOWS
IT AIN'T TOO LATE
HE'S GONE
TO GIT
SOME WIDDER BAIT
BURMA-SHAVE

FREE—FREE
A TRIP
TO MARS
FOR 900
EMPTY JARS
BURMA-SHAVE

A CHRISTMAS HUG
A BIRTHDAY KISS
AWAITS
THE WOMAN
WHO GIVES THIS
BURMA-SHAVE

THE BIG BLUE TUBE'S
JUST LIKE LOUISE
YOU GET
A THRILL
FROM EVERY SQUEEZE
BURMA-SHAVE

THE MONKEY TOOK
ONE LOOK AT JIM
AND THREW THE
    PEANUTS
BACK AT HIM
HE NEEDED
BURMA-SHAVE

SUBSTITUTES
CAN LET YOU DOWN
QUICKER
THAN A
STRAPLESS GOWN
BURMA-SHAVE

FOR SHAVING COMFORT
WITHOUT
A STING
THAT BIG BLUE TUBE
HAS EVERYTHING
BURMA-SHAVE

6 MILLION HOUSEWIVES
CAN'T BE WRONG
WHO KEEP
THEIR HUSBANDS
RIGHT ALONG IN
BURMA-SHAVE

TRY A TUBE
ITS COOLING
POWER
REFRESHES LIKE
AN APRIL SHOWER
BURMA-SHAVE

ONE SHAVE LASTS
ALL DAY THROUGH
FACE FEELS
COOL AND
SMOOTHER TOO
BURMA-SHAVE

TAKE
YOUR
TIME
NOT
YOUR LIFE
BURMA-SHAVE

WITHIN THIS VALE
OF TOIL
AND SIN
YOUR HEAD GROWS BALD
BUT NOT YOUR CHIN
BURMA-SHAVE

CATTLE CROSSING
MEANS GO SLOW
THAT OLD BULL
IS SOME
COW'S BEAU
BURMA-SHAVE

DOES YOUR HUSBAND
MISBEHAVE
GRUNT AND GRUMBLE
RANT AND RAVE
SHOOT THE BRUTE SOME
BURMA-SHAVE

1959

THE DRAFTEE
TRIED A TUBE
AND PURRED
WELL WHADDYA KNOW
I'VE BEEN DEFURRED
BURMA-SHAVE

MEN
WITH WHISKERS
'NEATH THEIR NOSES
OUGHTA HAVE TO KISS
LIKE ESKIMOSES
BURMA-SHAVE

THIS COOLING SHAVE
WILL NEVER FAIL
TO STAMP
ITS USER
FIRST CLASS MALE
BURMA-SHAVE

SAID FARMER BROWN
WHO'S BALD
ON TOP
WISH I COULD
ROTATE THE CROP
BURMA-SHAVE

DRINKING DRIVERS—
NOTHING WORSE
THEY PUT
THE QUART
BEFORE THE HEARSE
BURMA-SHAVE

DON'T
TRY PASSING
ON A SLOPE
UNLESS YOU HAVE
A PERISCOPE
BURMA-SHAVE

117

PASSING CARS
WHEN YOU CAN'T SEE
MAY GET YOU
A GLIMPSE
OF ETERNITY
BURMA-SHAVE

USE THIS CREAM
A DAY
OR TWO
THEN DON'T CALL HER—
SHE'LL CALL YOU
BURMA-SHAVE

DON'T LEAVE SAFETY
TO MERE CHANCE
THAT'S WHY
BELTS ARE
SOLD WITH PANTS
BURMA-SHAVE

THE POOREST GUY
IN THE
HUMAN RACE
CAN HAVE A
MILLION DOLLAR FACE
BURMA-SHAVE

AT A QUIZ
PA AIN'T
NO WHIZ
BUT HE KNOWS HOW
TO KEEP MA HIS
BURMA-SHAVE

IF DAISIES
ARE YOUR
FAVORITE FLOWER
KEEP PUSHIN' UP THOSE
MILES-PER-HOUR
BURMA-SHAVE

MANY A FOREST
USED TO STAND
WHERE A
LIGHTED MATCH
GOT OUT OF HAND
BURMA-SHAVE

HE LIT A MATCH
TO CHECK GAS TANK
THAT'S WHY
THEY CALL HIM
SKINLESS FRANK
BURMA-SHAVE

BABY YOUR SKIN
KEEP IT FITTER
OR "BABY"
WILL GET
ANOTHER SITTER
BURMA-SHAVE

THE ONE WHO
DRIVES WHEN
HE'S BEEN DRINKING
DEPENDS ON YOU
TO DO HIS THINKING
BURMA-SHAVE

1960

THIS CREAM
IS LIKE
A PARACHUTE
THERE ISN'T
ANY SUBSTITUTE
BURMA-SHAVE

TEMPTED TO TRY IT?
FOLLOW YOUR HUNCH
BE "TOP BANANA"
NOT ONE
OF THE BUNCH
BURMA-SHAVE

BRISTLES SCRATCHED
HIS COOKIE'S MAP
THAT'S WHAT
MADE POOR
GINGER SNAP
BURMA-SHAVE

WE'VE MADE GRANDPA
LOOK SO YOUTHFUL
HIS PENSION BOARD
THINKS
HE'S UNTRUTHFUL
BURMA-SHAVE

USE OUR CREAM
AND WE BETCHA
GIRLS WON'T WAIT
THEY'LL COME
AND GETCHA
BURMA-SHAVE

HENRY THE EIGHTH
SURE HAD
TROUBLE
SHORT TERM WIVES
LONG TERM STUBBLE
BURMA-SHAVE

ANGELS
WHO GUARD YOU
WHEN YOU DRIVE
USUALLY
RETIRE AT 65
BURMA-SHAVE

FOREST FIRES
START FROM SCRATCH
SO THINK BEFORE
YOU TOSS
THAT MATCH
BURMA-SHAVE

DIM YOUR LIGHTS
BEHIND A CAR
LET FOLKS SEE
HOW BRIGHT
YOU ARE
BURMA-SHAVE

THIRTY DAYS
HATH SEPTEMBER
APRIL
JUNE AND THE
SPEED OFFENDER
BURMA-SHAVE

OTHERS CLAIM
THEIR PRODUCT GOOD
BUT OURS
DOES WHAT
YOU THINK IT SHOULD
BURMA-SHAVE

BEN
MET ANNA
MADE A HIT
NEGLECTED BEARD
BEN-ANNA SPLIT
BURMA-SHAVE

DROWSY?
JUST REMEMBER, PARD
THAT MARBLE SLAB
IS DOGGONE
HARD
BURMA-SHAVE

STATISTICS PROVE
NEAR AND FAR
THAT FOLKS WHO
DRIVE LIKE CRAZY
—ARE!
BURMA-SHAVE

DEAR LOVER BOY,
YOUR PHOTO CAME
BUT YOUR DOGGONE
 BEARD
WON'T FIT
THE FRAME
BURMA-SHAVE

THIS WILL NEVER
COME TO PASS
A BACK-SEAT
DRIVER
OUT OF GAS
BURMA-SHAVE

1963

DON'T LOSE
YOUR HEAD
TO GAIN A MINUTE
YOU NEED YOUR HEAD
YOUR BRAINS ARE IN IT
BURMA-SHAVE

FILM PROTECTS
YOUR NECK
AND CHIN
SO YOUR RAZOR
WON'T DIG IN
BURMA-SHAVE

IF A GIFT
YOU MUST CHOOSE
GIVE HIM ONE
HE'LL LIKE
TO USE
BURMA-SHAVE

A SHAVE
THAT'S REAL
NO CUTS TO HEAL
A SOOTHING
VELVET AFTER-FEEL
BURMA-SHAVE

PEDRO
WALKED
BACK HOME, BY GOLLY
HIS BRISTLY CHIN
WAS HOT-TO-MOLLY
BURMA-SHAVE

IF HUGGING
ON HIGHWAYS
IS YOUR SPORT
TRADE IN YOUR CAR
FOR A DAVENPORT
BURMA-SHAVE

IF OUR ROAD SIGNS
CATCH YOUR EYE
SMILE
BUT DON'T FORGET
TO BUY
BURMA-SHAVE

IN CUPID'S LITTLE
BAG OF TRIX
HERE'S THE ONE
THAT CLIX
WITH CHIX
BURMA-SHAVE

WHEN THE STORK
DELIVERS A BOY
OUR WHOLE
DARN FACTORY
JUMPS FOR JOY
BURMA-SHAVE

A GUY
WHO WANTS
TO MIDDLE-AISLE IT
MUST NEVER SCRATCH
HIS LITTLE VIOLET
BURMA-SHAVE

EVERY DAY
WE DO
OUR PART
TO MAKE YOUR FACE
A WORK OF ART
BURMA-SHAVE

THRIFTY JARS FOR
STAY AT HOMES
HANDY TUBES
FOR HIM
WHO ROAMS
BURMA-SHAVE

WE DON'T
KNOW HOW
TO SPLIT AN ATOM
BUT AS TO WHISKERS
LET US AT 'EM
BURMA-SHAVE

IF YOU WANT
A HEARTY SQUEEZE
GET OUR
FEMALE
ANTI-FREEZE
BURMA-SHAVE

CAN'T SHAVE DAILY?
TENDER HIDE?
NOW BE HONEST
HAVE YOU
TRIED
BURMA-SHAVE

THE CHICK
HE WED
LET OUT A WHOOP
FELT HIS CHIN AND
FLEW THE COOP
BURMA-SHAVE

OUR FORTUNE
IS YOUR
SHAVEN FACE
IT'S OUR BEST
ADVERTISING SPACE
BURMA-SHAVE

*　　*　　*